2

JAMES FISK, JR.

THE LIFE
OF
JAMES FISK, JR.,

THE STORY OF HIS YOUTH AND MANHOOD, WITH FULL ACCOUNTS OF ALL THE SCHEMES AND ENTERPRISES IN WHICH HE WAS ENGAGED, INCLUDING THE

GREAT FRAUDS
OF
THE TAMMANY RING.

BIOGRAPHICAL SKETCHES OF RAILROAD MAGNATES AND GREAT FINANCIERS, WITH BRILLIANT PEN PICTURES IN THE

LIGHTS AND SHADOWS
OF
NEW YORK LIFE.

"JOSIE MANSFIELD" THE "SIREN."

How a beautiful woman captivated and ruined her victims. The Mansfield Mansion. The rejected and the accepted suitors.

EDWARD S. STOKES, THE ASSASSIN.

And an account of the Assassination.

BY WILLOUGHBY JONES.

PROFUSELY ILLUSTRATED.

SOLD BY SUBSCRIPTION ONLY.

UNION PUBLISHING COMPANY,
26 SOUTH SEVENTH STREET, PHILADELPHIA, PA.,
165 TWENTY-SECOND ST., CHICAGO, ILLS.,
176 W. FOURTH ST., CINCINNATI, O.
1872.

PREFACE.

James Fisk, Jr., is dead. The record of his life is closed. Judged by a worldly standard, whether he was a good man or a bad man, will appear by striking a balance of the acts of his life. That he did both good and bad none will question—and of whom can it be said that all his acts were good? If the good over-balances the bad, then the public verdict must be in his favor; otherwise, not.

Certainly, he was an extraordinary man. He accomplished more work, and made a greater stir in social and commercial circles in the short life he lived, than it is possible for most other men to do, though they live to twice his age. Thirty years ago he was a sprightly village boy; twelve years ago he was a country peddler; five years ago he was a banker in New York; a millionnaire in Wall street; and soon thereafter he became the master of a great railroad corporation; the owner of two lines of magnificent sound and coast steamers, and the terror of Wall street financiers—all this—and assassinated in the thirty-seventh year of his age. Here, then, is a problem worthy of study with a view to a correct solution. Let no man praise or condemn without due deliberation, and with all the facts before him.

To gain a proper insight into the character of this man, it will be necessary to understand the scope of the great enterprises he was engaged in, and also to know something of the men with whom he was associated in business. A sketch of the railroad and steamboat lines, of the theatrical establishments, and stock and gold speculations in which Fisk was interested, are, therefore, set forth, as well as brief biographies of the noted characters involved in those operations, together with the men who aided, and those who confronted him in his most daring feats in financial and corporation achievements.

All of the most striking and characteristic episodes in this versatile life were indigenous to New York; they could not have been enacted elsewhere. They were the natural products of metropolitan social life and business tricks. It is, therefore, necessary to exhibit to the reader some of the scenes and incidents of New York life, drawing both the "lights and shadows" of the pictures of that real life, which is ever more varied, and stranger even than fiction. This includes names great in finance, great in corporation management, great in politics, great in fraud, great in robbery, great in crime of the darkest hue; all of these were made to dance attendance to the presence of this man of marvelous power, whose life they moulded, magnified and destroyed.

NEW YORK, *January* 16, 1872.

ILLUSTRATIONS.

CONTENTS.

CHAPTER IV.

"PRINCE ERIE."

CHAPTER V.

ADMIRAL OF THE SOUND FLEET.

CHAPTER VI.

FISK AS A MILITARY MAN—COL. FISK.

CHAPTER VII.

THE GOLD RING.

CHAPTER VIII.

WHAT FISK SAID OF THE GOLD CONSPIRACY.

CHAPTER IX.

REPORT OF THE COMMITTEE OF CONGRESS.

CHAPTER X.

TAMMANY FRAUDS—MILLIONS STOLEN.

CHAPTER XI.

FISK'S ASSOCIATES.

CHAPTER XII.

NEW YORK LIFE—PEN SKETCHES.

CHAPTER XIII.

HELEN JOSEPHINE MANSFIELD.

CHAPTER XIV.

THE ASSASSINATION.

CHAPTER XV.

THE LAST OF FISK.

CHAPTER XVI.

CHARACTERISTIC INCIDENTS

CHAPTER XVII.

EDWARD S. STOKES.

CHAPTER XVIII.

WHAT FOLLOWED.

FISK'S HOTEL, BRATTLEBORO.

THE LIFE OF JAMES FISK, Jr.

CHAPTER I.

HIS YOUTH AND EDUCATION.

Unparalleled Achievements—Matchless Exploits—The Youth of the Actor—A Green Mountain Boy—A Country Peddler—Enterprising and Honest in Dealing—Did an Extensive Business, and Bore a Good Name.

"The evil that men do lives after them;
The good is oft interred with their bones."

On Sunday January 7th, 1872, in the City of New York, closed the life of a man whose exploits are unequalled. James Fisk, Jr., came to New York in the end of the year 1864, a young man and a stranger; he went into Wall Street without experience in, or knowledge of the dark ways and vain tricks of that indescribable intermixture of all-manner-of-men, that constitute the "Gold Board" and "Stock Exchange." He grappled at close quarters and in hot conflict with men and with combinations of men, who controlled unmeasured capital, and who had, during many years, ruled the money market of the Metropolis almost at will; in the mightiest contests on that financial field, this

2

New England youth overmatched the greatest and all of them. In the short period of three years, he was master of the situation. He owned great lines of steamers; he controlled one of the principal railroads, connecting the Metropolis with the West; he ruled Wall Street with imperious sway; he dictated the decrees of the courts of New York, so far, that, at his bidding, men were restrained by judicial writs from doing what he wished to have left undone, or were compelled to do what he wished to have done; at his command men were arrested and imprisoned; "Railroad Rings" and "Monied Princes," who, before his advent, were great men in New York, dwindled into nothingness beneath the exploits of this matchless adventurer.

Here is an exhibit of power, of personal force, deep insight, boldness of execution, fearlessness of action, such as the world rarely witnesses. The man, who, amidst such surroundings, in the presence of such competitors and in the face of such opposition as are presented in New York, accomplished the results that make the name of Fisk historic, must have possessed extraordinary endowments. His life was like the sweep of a fiery meteor, or a great comet, appearing suddenly in the sphere of the terrestrial atmosphere, plunging with terrific velocity and dazzling brilliancy across the horizon, whirling into its blazing train broken fortunes, raving financiers, reckless speculators, corporations, magnates and public officers, municipal, state and national, civil and military, judges, priests and presidents.

THE VILLAGE SCHOOL.

Whence came this man? What were his attendants? What his education? By what manner of early training was he prepared for such a struggle?

James Fisk was born in Burlington, Vermont, a town of Revolutionary fame. His father was a peddler, traveling through the Green Mountain Country, selling all manner of notions, from a silk dress to a darning needle. Soon after the birth of James, the family moved to Brattleboro, and here, in the midst of one of the most picturesque portions of the Green Mountain State, the child grew and was educated. The village school supplied the learning necessary to prepare the lad for the battle of life, that he was destined to fight.

James was a bright boy at school, a general favorite in the village, with so much humor in his nature as to make his presence indispensable in the jovial evening parties at the Fisk Hotel of Brattleboro'. During a short time he was employed as a waiter-boy at the hotel, but that was not the sort of life he was destined to lead. A wider and more varied sphere awaited him. He was to act a more conspicuous part than that which falls to a country tavern keeper. His father was a man of note; plain, unpretending, successful in business, and favorably known throughout the southern counties of Vermont.

At a very early period in his life, James persuaded his father to permit him to accompany him in his journeying through the country as a peddler. In these tours the boy was not an idle or passive companion; he closely noted the operations of his father, witnessed his efforts to dispose of his goods, as he drove his wagon from house to house, and from village to village, and thus early gained an insight into the business. After having made a few trips of this sort, which were as so many lessons in the school of traffic, he asked and obtained permission of his father to make short trips alone. In these first efforts, the junior peddler was very successful, and soon convinced the father that he was a very useful assistant. The growing success of the young man finally led to a partnership between father and son. The business increased, and the profits soon enhanced so rapidly, that James inspirated by the extent and profitableness of their transactions, was anxious to launch out in more extended efforts. He proposed to increase the number of wagons, and to employ men to drive them, and thus organize the business into a system of wholesale and retail dry good and notion trade. To this the father objected. The son then proposed to buy out his father's interest in the co-partnership, and conduct the business himself, in his own way. Terms were at once agreed upon. The firm of Fisk & Son disappeared, and the name of James Fisk, Jr., in gaudy and showy letters, was painted on the panels of the wagons.

Several new and more elaborately constructed wagons were now made to order. The best and most spirited horses were procured, brilliantly mounted harnesses were provided, men were em-

BEGINNING BUSINESS.

A DRY GOODS CLERK.

ployed, and business was organized on a scale of grandeur that astonished the plain people of Brattleboro, who had known James only as the son of the father, an unassuming, quiet sort of man.

When all these preparations were complete, a larger stock of goods, purchased from the house of Jordan, Marsh, & Co., of Boston, arrived at Brattleboro. The wagons and gaily caparisoned teams were drawn up at the warehouse to receive supplies. Two very imposing establishments, larger and more conspicuous than the rest, were commanded by father and son—the former now an employee of the latter. James Fisk had already marked out a map of the routes the several wagons were to take; the distances they should proceed during the first week, and the place of rendezvous, at which all should meet on Saturday. Each employee was required to give, at the end of every week an account of the business done, goods sold, and goods on hand, together with a requisition for new goods required. By this plan of organized labor the sales were largely increased, and Fisk became a merchant of no mean standing. He always drove fine horses, in a dashing style, and at a high rate of speed, giving an air of dash and boldness to his surroundings, that made his appearance in any village of his native State, an event long to be remembered by the young people, and a topic for conversation with the ambitious boys of the Green Mountain region.

Notwithstanding his dash, enterprise, and prosperity, Fisk always bore a fair name in his native town; among his neighbors, his character was that of a sharp, but honest dealer. He might drive close bargains, but was prompt in meeting his engagements. During the whole of his eventful life, the home of his childhood, and the scenes of his early life never lost that delightful charm, which men so frequently throw around the places of their nativity, and he was always a most welcome visitor at Brattleboro.

CHAPTER II.

FISK AS A BOSTON CLERK AND MERCHANT.

His Advent in Boston—Becomes a Clerk in a Large Dry Goods House and Fails—Demands a New Trial and Succeeds—Is admitted to a Partnership in the Great Firm—Government Contracts—Profitable Operations—Bold Enterprises—Amasses Wealth—Attempts to set up for Himself and Fails.

THE extensive trade built up rapidly in Vermont by Mr. Fisk, the large orders for goods and his occasional visits to the house of the Boston firm, from whom he purchased his goods, brought the country customer and the city merchant into close and agreeable contact with each other. Finally, the firm of Jordan, Marsh & Co. invited Mr. Fisk to a clerkship in its house. The offer was accepted; the business in Vermont was wound up rapidly and satisfactory, and the country peddler was merged in the city clerk. Fisk soon discovered that the narrow limits of the dry goods house oppressed him. He had roamed over Southern Vermont with a freedom and dash that made life ever fresh and varied. In the country he was a great man—a proprietor—a power—a man of note. In the city he was an obscure clerk—a servant—unknown without standing in society. The change of situation was keenly felt, and produced a marked effect on

Fisk. The proprietors also discovered that they had spoiled a good peddler and made a poor clerk. Mr. Jordan, finally, after a trial of a few months, suggested to Fisk that he had better go back to peddling. Against this the young man flatly protested, and demanded a further trial, with a change of duties. The metal had not been thoroughly tested, but it was not the nature of Fisk to acknowledge failure. A new arrangement was agreed upon; Fisk was permitted to devote more time to outside work and less to sales from the counter.

The war of the rebellion was at this time in progress; government was almost daily awarding large contracts to manufacturers, merchants and politicians, for blankets, tents, clothing in cotton and woollen, boots, shoes, ammunition, groceries and other supplies for the army and navy. Here was a new field opened that gave full scope to the enterprise of the restless and ambitious salesman. Through the influence of a Boston lady and New England Senator he secured a large and profitable contract for supplying underclothing to the army. The acknowledged respectability of the house he represented, ensured the satisfactory fulfilment of any contract that should be awarded. It was, therefore, comparatively easy to draw to the firm a very large and profitable share of the trade with the government.

Fisk was so eminently successful in this work that the business of the house was rapidly increased, and the profits before counted by hundreds, were

A WAITER BOY.

THE SHOWMAN.

now returned by tens of thousands of dollars. This fairly earned for Mr. Fisk an interest in the business, and he was accordingly admitted a member of the great firm of Jordan Marsh & Co.

The new position brought new duties and additional enterprise. Mr. Fisk, now again was a man of note; a "Green Mountain Boy" only a few years ago; a lad in a country tavern; a rollicking peddler; an indifferent clerk; junior partner of one of New England's greatest mercantile houses.

He regarded these successive steps, acts of his own, what he was he had earned, this reflection stimulated him to renewed efforts in the hope of achieving still more. He had already observed that the materials required to fill the contracts he had secured, were purchased from the manufacturing establishments in Boston and other New England towns. The manufacturers were extending their facilities and gave unmistakable signs of unusual prosperity. Fisk concluded that his firm might to advantage use their large surplus capital in manufacturing operations, and thus secure double profits—namely, those of the manufacturer and those of the dealer. He, therefore, proposed to Mr. Jordan that they engage in the manufacture of certain staple articles. The experiment was at first entered upon in a limited extent, but rapidly expanded until several of the largest establishments in the East were owned and managed by this enterprising firm.

The vigilance of Fisk was the marvel of his associates. He anticipated with unerring certainty the fluctuations of the markets, and the new supplies that would be needed, and thus frequently achieved wonders by being ready at the precise day in advance of all competitors with some new articles of merchandise, and with a needed stock of what was in immediate demand. The confidence of the firm in the young member was unbounded; he would telegraph instructions from any part of the country and they were implicitly obeyed. In this manner he at one time telegraphed from New York, that the firm should send an agent to purchase a factory which had the monopoly of an article that was coming into the market. This was his first attempt to make a corner, and proved to be entirely successful, giving his house the control of a very profitable market.

James Fisk was not only a far-seeing, bold operator, in mercantile and manufacturing operations, but his quick mind seemed able to grasp instantly all the conditions, and the entire situation in any new complication or event that might arise.

In September, 1862, the news of the great battle of Antietam was telegraphed to Boston. The people were in a state of unbounded excitement. The battle closed on Wednesday, but it was not until Saturday that full newspaper accounts of the engagement and report of the terrible destruction of life were published. On Sunday morning Fisk sought the senior member of his firm, and proposed to him the project of converting the churches for that day into hospital supply depots, and the congregations into Samaritan bands. This grand idea was instantly acted upon, and thus within a few hours the Christian people of Boston were performing their sacrifices unto God by deeds of charity and works of love. Ladies and gentlemen, girls and boys, everybody were scraping lint, tearing bandages, collecting jellies, fruits, wines and other things useful to the wounded, sick and dying patriots lying in the fields and houses in and around Sharpsburg. Tremont Temple was made the grand central depot, to which all the stores were sent to be packed and shipped. During the entire day Fisk was ubiquitous and indefatigable. It is not surprising, therefore, when he says as the cars laden with these supplies collected at his suggestion, moved out on the road, that he gave utterance to his feelings of just pride at the achievements of the city, in which he had already become a respectable and influential citizen.

More recently, a similar evidence was given of the generous impulses of this man's heart. When the news of the conflagration of Chicago reached New York, and the extent of the privations, sufferings and destitution of a large portion of the population of the destroyed city become known, Fisk appeared in Broadway with his "four-in-hand," and called on all the people to contribute articles of domestic use of every nature for the suffering people of Chicago. The appeals were responded to with unmeasured generosity, and very soon the Erie Railway depot, of which Fisk was at the time master, presented the appearance of a general market and warehousing establishment; car load after car load of goods were shipped over Fisk's road without charge; and thus among the first to administer relief to the terrified and impoverished citizens of the burned city was this erratic, matchless Green Mountain Boy who, amidst the stir and glare of city life, the dash and selfishness of Wall street operations, kept glowing brightly in his heart the generous impulses inherited and inhaled from the surroundings and pure air of his childhood home.

After a short and brilliant career as a member of the house of Jordan, Marsh & Co., Mr. Fisk was able to withdraw with a capital of nearly one hundred thousand dollars. He opened a dry good house of his own, but having laid in his stock at a time when fabrics of every class were falling in price, he very soon discovered that by the gradnal sinking of the market, not only his reasonable profits but his original capital would be melted away, and that by this process he would inevitably be reduced to poverty. He, therefore, towards the latter part of the year 1864, resolved to close out his business and go to New York, hoping there to find a more extensive field for the exercise of his peculiar talents as an operator in outside speculations. The war was drawing to a close and the control of government contracts had settled into permanent channels, so that there was nothing to be hoped for from that source.

During the war Fisk had engaged in the purchase

of cotton in the Confederate States, and by a system of agencies that extended into all of the cotton States, he developed a very profitable trade for the benefit of himself and those with whom he was engaged. This was but another illustration of the quickness and keenness of the foresight of this man. As soon as it was announced by President Lincoln, that it would be the policy of his administration to deprive the Southern Confederacy of as much cotton as possible, whether by capture or purchase, Fisk instantly saw, that here was an opportunity for a grand and profitable speculation. Accordingly he procured the necessary permits for a corps of agents to pass the lines of the army, and then despatched his men to the coast of the cotton States, to the Gulf of Mexico, and to the military posts on the Mississippi river, wherever cotton could be delivered from the Confederate lines. This was a very lucrative trade; it also gave full scope to the adventurous and reckless enterprise of this man of peculiar genius. His efforts were rewarded by gains that should have satisfied even a prince.

Before leaving Boston, Fisk had married an estimable young lady of Springfield, Massachusetts, and lived in good style, moving in respectable society. Mrs. Fisk did not accompany her husband to New York, but continued her residence in Boston, and thus it was, that during the first year of Fisk's operations in New York, he maintained his citizenship in Massachusetts. He supported his family in fine and luxuriant style, and settled the

Boston homestead on his wife, so that no mishap to him would deprive her of a home. In the summer seasons Mrs. Fisk occupied a villa at Newport, and supported a fine carriage and equipage that attracted almost as much attention as her husband's grand establishments at Long Branch.

JAMES FISK, JR., AS A PEDDLER.

CHAPTER III.

FISK IN NEW YORK.

James Fisk goes to New York—Gravitates to Wall street—He seeks adventures—Finds what he was hunting for—He "is broke" —Resolves on revenge and gets it—Invests in a patent—Makes a raise—Meets Daniel Drew—Makes another raise—Appears in Wall street—Becomes a pupil to Drew—Outdoes his instructor—Is a man of wealth and power.

NEAR the end of the year 1864, James Fisk, Jr., opened an office as Broker, on Broad street, in New York. He went into stock operations in Wall street with the boldness that characterized all his movements, and with a recklessness that must speedily make or lose fortunes. Some of his ventures were successful, more of them were disastrous. Within a few months after he had entered the arena of the Brokers' Board, he had lost all the capital he had brought from Boston, and he found himself without means to maintain himself in business. "Wall street has ruined me and Wall street shall pay for it," was the defiant conclusion which he reached, after a careful and serious survey of his situation. He closed his office and returned to Boston. On his way thither, he met a passenger on the train who had, like himself, failed and was returning home disheartened and sad. The stranger was the owner of a patent right which he knew to be very valuable, but which no one else wanted to purchase. Fisk examined the contrivance, which was an improvement in machinery used in cotton and woollen factories; he induced the owner to accompany him to Boston where Fisk found a purchaser for the patent, reserving an interest for himself. From this operation he gained a new start; he realized a considerable sum of money, with which he resolved to return to New York.

Fisk carried with him on this second trip something that proved to be vastly more valuable to him than all the money he had ever possessed before. This was a letter of introduction to Daniel Drew, then a noted financier in Wall street, the owner of lines of steamboats, and the magnate of the Erie Railway Company. The venerable New-Yorker was favorably impressed with the manners and appearance of the New England youth. He commissioned him to negotiate the sale of the Bristol Line of Steamers. The prompt and satisfactory manner in which Fisk executed this trust, strengthened him in the confidence of Drew, and won for him a very valuable friend. Moreover, he secured by way of commission, a very considerable sum of money. He formed a partnership under the name of Fisk & Belden, brokers. This firm dealt largely in the stocks of the Erie Railway Company, of which Drew was a director and treasurer. The senior member of the firm being the especial friend of Erie magnate, of course, knew the secrets of the "Ring," and was thus enabled to buy and sell stocks with a reasonable certainty of making large margins. Fisk proved himself to be a very apt pupil in Drew's school; and being young, impulsive, bold and reckless, frequently far exceeded the instructions of the master, in such a manner as to reap the larger part of the gains in the great "Corner" operations in Erie. His success was so great that he rapidly accumulated a fortune and drew to himself a number of very powerful associates. In October, 1867, he was elected a member of the Board of Directors of the Erie Railway Company. At the same election Jay Gould, a broker on Broad street, and a financier of some note, also came into the Erie Board. This was the result of a compromise between the Drew and Vanderbilt factions. Drew and Vanderbilt had been waging fierce war upon each other for years. The former held Erie, and the latter controlled the New York Central, the Hudson River and the Harlem. A compromise was finally made. Drew put Fisk into the board of Erie directors, and Vanderbilt placed his friend Gould in, as a fair offset. The peace thus concluded was but short-lived. The old warriors were uneasy out of service; both soon resumed their weapons and rushed into battle more fiercely than ever—Drew pushing Erie stocks down, and Vanderbilt driving them up, and both struggling for the control of the directorship.

Fisk and Gould could see no profit to themselves in such a fight unless they struck hands and gathered up the spoils, while their chiefs joined in battle.

This they accordingly did; and, therefore, while Drew and Vanderbilt threw Wall street, and indeed the markets of the world, into excitement, over the rapid and inexplicable fluctuations in Erie stocks, Fisk and Gould so managed their investments as to win millions of dollars from these great operators, and from the smaller brokers who ventured into the field. Drew won from Vanderbilt, Vanderbilt won from Drew—both lost, and Fisk and Gould won.

The fiercest contest that ever ensued over Erie stocks, began in the month of February, 1868. Drew was then treasurer of the Erie Company, and held 58,000 shares of stock as collateral securities for a temporary loan. Vanderbilt began the assault by suing out of Judge Barnard's Court an injunction to restrain Drew from using the stock remaining in his possession as collateral. The Legislature of New York had made it unlawful for railroad companies to issue new stock without proper notice and authority regularly obtained. Vanderbilt, therefore, felt that he could count the Erie stock afloat, and arrange to make a "corner" in it. On the 19th of February, a second order from Barnard was served on Drew, suspending him from the treasury of Erie and also from the Board. This was a bold movement, and to a man less fertile in resources than Drew, would have been disastrous. But the magnate of Erie had prepared himself for this contest. He had induced his Board to issue bonds to the amount of $10,000,000, and these the law permitted him to convert into stock, which he very quietly did, and then complacently awaited developments. "Go a head, Mr. Barnard; Go a head, Mr. Vanderbilt; your injunctions don't alarm me in the least said Mr. Drew."

True, 58,000 shares had been locked up, but 100,000 new shares had been issued. Of the new stock, Drew held 50,000, and Fisk 50,000. Vanderbilt was in blissful ignorance of the existence of this stock; he was prepared to purchase all the old stock, but he had not provided money to buy new stock as rapidly as his crafty old competitor chose to give it out; nevertheless, it was plainly this that he must do, if he would gain his object. On the last day of February, Erie was quoted at 68; Drew gave orders to his brokers to sell his 50,000 shares. Vanderbilt's brokers were buying all that was offered, and they accordingly snatched up this new batch, but the price almost instantly dropped to 65, and then rallied and rose to 73. A fierce battle was now raging between the "bulls" and "bears" of Wall street, which continued during several days. Drew, knowing that Fisk held 50,000 shares of new stock, sold "short," being sure that the price must fall; but Vanderbilt bravely drove up the price until the 10th of March, when it stood at 79. On that day, Drew became alarmed, and ordered his brokers to buy to cover his shorts. Under this new pressure, both Drew and Vanderbilt now buying, the price went up to 83. This was Fisk's opportunity. He immediately threw his

50,000 shares on the market, got the highest price, and then sent it down to 71. The appearance of this new stock, in the name of James Fisk, Jr., created a storm of excitement that shook the money centers of New York with fierce convulsions; $10,000,000 worth of stock had been poured into the market, and Vanderbilt alone sustained the entire weight of the shock. This was a fearful load, but to waiver, or to show the slightest symptoms of "shaking," would have invoked instantaneous and total ruin. When, therefore, the contest ended, Fisk alone was victorious without wounds. As between Vanderbilt and Drew, it was a drawn battle, in which both combatants were scarred with many cuts and bruises, though Drew was able to bear away the spoils.

Of course, the injunctions of Judge Barnard had been disregarded. The wrathful judge, therefore resolved on vengeance dire. On the morning of the 11th, an army of the sheriff's deputies, with numerous warrants, ran to and fro through the streets of New York, in search of the Erie Directors. These gentlemen having learned of the warlike spirit of "His Honor," had, at the suggestion of the versatile, ingenious Fisk, transferred themselves and the treasury box of Erie to Taylor's Hotel, in Jersey City, beyond the jurisdiction of the offended Judge. From Jersey City, Fisk dictated such legislation as was needful to relieve himself and his associates from embarrassment, to legalize their unlawful acts, and put it out of the power of

Vanderbilt to molest them. This accomplished, the parties agreed to treat. A settlement was made, and the spoils of war fairly divided; some took stock, some took bonds, and others, money. Fisk and Gould received as their share the whole establishment of the Erie Railway—road, rolling stock, equipments, officers—everything. From the date of this settlement until the day of his death. Fisk was master of the great corporation, and held it in defiance of various and powerful efforts to wrest it from his grasp. He was ever thereafter justly titled "Prince Erie."

CHAPTER IV.

"PRINCE ERIE."

Fisk as a railway director—The Erie Railway under new management—New combinations—Exeunt Drew and Eldridge—Enter Tweed and Sweeney—A batch of law suits—Fisk on the witness stand—Testimony extraordinary—Amusing account of "tricks that are vain"—Hands joined all around—"Log Rolling" at Albany—The classification bill—Erie captured and bagged—Frauds—New York Society—How young men are ruined.

THE general settlement between the contending parties for the possession of Erie, and the division of spoils, took place early in the spring of 1869, but the terms of the peace were not made known to the public, until the middle of the summer. Erie had been stripped of every thing, even to good name. It was poor and in disrepute, when it came into the possession of Fisk and Gould. Eldridge and Drew, the men who were the only experienced railroad managers in the board of directors, retired and left the whole conduct of the road in the hands of the young adventurers, who were now to be tested in a new field of enterprise. Fisk had already displayed great versatility of character, and had proven himself equal to any and every emergency. He did not feel the slightest embarrassment in his new position, but resolved to make new combinations and to restore his road to public confidence. The struggle with Drew and Vanderbilt had taught Fisk, that there was nothing

STOCK EXCHANGE, N. Y.

so much to be depended upon in a crisis as self reliance. In the critical moment he had escaped from the wrath of Vanderbilt and the offended honor of Judge Barnard, by fleeing into New Jersey, and while in exile in the Jerseys, he had escaped from the conspiracy of Drew, by seizing the private funds of that gentleman and holding them as a pledge for the safe delivery of the Erie treasury. This done, he negotiated with the then all powerful William M. Tweed, for needful legislation at Albany, to confirm his acts, and to give the semblance of law to the rather questionable transactions, whereby he had gained possession of the management of the great broad gauge road connecting the Hudson river and Lake Erie.

Fisk had demonstrated that he could control Wall street at will; he had learned all the tricks of the cliques; he had improved on the operations of the most skilful manipulators, and had patented his improvements. He, therefore, felt entirely secure at that end of the line. The free use of injunctions by Vanderbilt, to facilitate his stock operations and to circumvent his rival Drew, and the invoking of counter injunctions to neutralize the first instalment, had taught Fisk that a "friend at court" was a very convenient instrument for either attack or defence. He, therefore, very naturally concluded, that to control this new power would be immensely to his advantage.

Now, at this time, William M. Tweed and Peter B. Sweeney, were masters of New York City, and owners of the legislative ring that ruled with imperious sway at Albany; by a union of forces and fortunes, the combined power would be irresistible. Fisk and Gould, therefore, took unto themselves Tweed and Sweeney—Erie and Tammany Hall were united. New York City in all its municipal affairs, its finances, its legislation, its improvements, its expenditures, its offices, executive and judiciary, was made subject to the power of this combination. At the nod of Tweed, or at the command of Fisk, laws were made and unmade—millions of revenue were levied and expended. As these men desired, so the laws were construed by the courts; whom these men condemned to punishment, they were punished by the courts; whom these men shielded, the arm of the law would not restrain. No such power, so absolute in its sway has elsewhere manifested itself on this continent. Before it, the legislative, the judiciary and the executive departments of the city and State bowed in unresisting submission.

Governor, mayor, judge and legislator fell down before the golden image these men had set up; but the people would not fall down nor worship before this shrine. This alliance of Tammany and Erie held unlimited sway until the people rose in their might and crushed it, ground it into dust and scattered its powdered fragments before the storm of popular indignation in the year 1871.

As to Erie, Gould was made president and treasurer, and Fisk was made controller; these two together, with Tweed and Lane, constituted the executive committee. The only care of these men was to perpetuate their own power in the Erie company. With all the machinery in their control this was not a very difficult feat. They so managed the sale and transfer of stocks as to secure the registry of a large quantity in their own names, and then closed the books so as to make any further transfers impossible. Thus they re-elected themselves on other people's stock at the annual meeting.

After the re-election had been secured, the Erie managers organized a gigantic scheme to lock up the currency in New York, so as to produce a tightness in the money market and a depression in all stocks. The Secretary of the United States Treasury was contracting the currency at the time and thus unintentionly aided the Wall street speculators. The "ring" had the absolute control of fourteen million dollars in currency and suddenly withdrew it from circulation. All stocks immediately tumbled 10, 20, even 50 per cent., carrying bankruptcy and ruin into many a prosperous house. The Erie managers manufactured new stock and sold it without regard to price, and locked up the money received fôr it. The crisis of this outrageous conspiracy came in the first week of November, 1868, and was then crushed by Secretary McCulloch, who re-issued fifty millions of currency to break the lock.

The agents of the foreign stockholders held a meeting in New York and determined to apply to the courts for relief from the management of Fisk and Gould. It was agreed that a suit should be brought in the name of Mr. August Belmont, asking for the appointment of a receiver for the Erie Company, upon the plea that the affairs of the company were managed to the serious injury of the stockholders.

Fisk and Gould obtained information of the purposes of their enemies, and instantly devised means to defeat them. They went early in the morning to the residence of the notorious Judge Barnard with a petition, asking for the appointment of a receiver. Barnard, who a short time previous had been so prolific in injunctions against Fisk and his associates, was now the most supple of all instruments in their hands. He unhesitatingly granted the request of the petitioners, and appointed Jay Gould, receiver, with James Fisk, Jr., as his surety. This was all accomplished before the hour for opening the courts. When the courts opened, Mr. Belmont and his associates appeared before Judge Sunderland with their petition for the appointment of a receiver, but before their proceedings had advanced to judgment, they learned with indescribable astonishment, that the futile Barnard had already disposed of the case and that Fisk and Gould were masters of the situation. This is one of the many examples of the manner in which "justice" is dispensed in New York. The very fountains of justice have become so corrupt, that the foul stream carries disease, rottenness and pollution down its entire course. Money, money, is all powerful in that great city. Money dictates legislation; money interprets laws; money buys decrees from the courts. A bold man, with unlimited means, may violate law with perfect impunity. Money will buy punishment for the innocent and escape for the guilty. This is the normal condition of New York society. It has been thus for many years and is so now.

James Fisk, Jr., did not corrupt the courts of New York, he found them reeking with corruption. He found them on the streets, offering decrees and writs to the highest bidder. These decrees he first saw knocked down to his enemies and used against him, whereupon he resolved to outbid his competitors and turn their own batteries upon his enemy. For him to resolve was to do. He bought up as many courts as he required for his purpose and then kept them so as to have them ready for use whenever needed. He was, therefore, at a moment's notice, by personal application and by telegraph, able to obtain a decree authorizing himself and his friends to do what they wished, or an injunction to restrain his enemies from doing what they wished to do.

Several attempts were made to break the power of the "Erie Ring," but without success. Fisk used his power both to make money for himself and friends in schemes, that, for boldness and amounts involved, were perfectly appalling. He would make millions of dollars at a single operation, and throw the whole financial world into a fever of excitement, yet to him the spectacle of broken fortunes and ruined prosperity were matters of amusement.

Having gained control of courts and using Wall street as a play ground, Fisk found leisure towards the end of the year 1869 to annoy his rivals and punish enemies. He began suits against a number of the leading men in New York. He brought suit against

Belmont on a charge of conspiring to injure the Erie railway, laying damages at a million dollars. He sued Vanderbilt for the recovery of over three million dolars paid him at the time of the general settlement, alleging that settlement to have been illegal. The venerable Drew was also made the subject of one of "Prince Erie's" suits.

In the Vanderbilt suit, Fisk was put on the witness stand and gave his testimony in a characteristically humorous strain. The trial, of course, was held in Judge Barnard's court, and Fisk testified as follows:—

I remember an interview with Commodore Vanderbilt in the summer of 1868. I don't remember just when the first interview was. It was after I returned from Jersey. I was absent in Jersey for a lapse of time (laughter), and on my return I made the Commodore a call. (Laughter.) He said several of the directors were trying to make a trade with him and he would like to know who was the best man to trade with. I told him if the trade was a good one, he had better trade with me. (Laughter.) He said old man Drew was no better than a batter pudding (great laughter); Eldridge was completely demoralized, and there was no head or tail to our concern. (Laughter.) I said I thought so, too. (Great laughter.) He said he had got his bloodhounds on us and would pursue us till we took his stock off his hands—he'd be d—d if he'd keep it. I said I'd be d—d if we'd take it back (sensation), that we would sell him stock as long as he'd stand up and take it. (Great laughter.) Upon this he mellowed down (laughter), and said we must get together and arrange this matter. He said when we were in Jersey, Drew used to slip over and see him whenever he could get out from under our eyes; that he had had a good deal of talk with him and wanted to know if a trade made with Drew and Eldridge could be slipped through our board, saying that if it could, we should all be landed in the haven of peace and harmony. (Looking very determined.) I told him I would not submit to a robbery of the road under any circumstances, and that I was dumbfounded that our directors—whom I had supposed respectable men—(great laughter) would have anything to do with such proceedings.

Counsel!—Is that all that was said?

Mr. Fisk—I presume not. We had half an hour's conversation, and I think I could say more than that in half an hour. (Laughter.)

Counsel—Can you give anything more that was said?

Mr. Fisk—I don't remember what more was said. I remember the Commodore put on his other shoe. (Laughter.) I remember that shoe on account of the buckle. (Laughter.) You see, there were four buckles on that shoe. I hadn't ever seen any of that kind before, and I remember it passed through my mind that if such men wore that kind of shoe, I must get me a pair. (Great laughter.) This passed through my mind, but I didn't speak of it to the Commodore. I was very civil to him. (Laughter.)

Counsel—Where was Gould all this time?

Mr. Fisk—He was in the front room, I suppose. I

left him there and found him there, but I don't know where he may have been in the meantime. (Laughter.) The next interview was at the house of Mr. Pierrepoint. Gould and I had an appointment with Eldridge at the Fifth Avenue Hotel, and as we did not find him there, we went out to see if we could find him.

Counsel—Can you give the date of that meeting? A. No, sir.

Q. Can you give the week? A. No, sir.

Q. Can you give the month? A. No, sir.

Q. Can you give the year? A. No, sir. Not without reference.

Q. What reference do you want? A. Well, I shall have to refer back to the various events of my life to see just where that day comes in, and the almighty robbery committed by this man Vanderbilt against the Erie railway was the most impressive event in my life. (Laughter.) The meeting at Pierrepoint's was a week, or ten days after the first interview with Vanderbilt. Gould and I went there about nine o'clock. We stepped into the hall together. We asked if Mr. Pierrepoint was in. The servant said he would see. When the servant went into the drawing-room I was very careful to keep on a line with the door, so I could see in. (Laughter.) Presently Mr. Pierrepoint stepped into the hall, resembling a man who wasn't in *much*. (Laughter.) I asked him if our president was there. After some thoughtfulness on his part, he said he thought he was. (Laughter.) During this time I had moved along towards the drawing-room door, Mr. Pierrepoint having neglected to invite us in. (Laughter.)

Q. Where was Gould? A. Oh, he was just behind me; he's always right behind at such times (laughter), and while he entertained Pierrepoint I opened the door and stepped in (laughter), and found most of our directors there. I stepped up to Mr. Eldridge and told him we had been to the Fifth Avenue Hotel and did not find him. He said he knew he was not there. (Laughter.) I asked what was going on, and everybody seemed to wait for some one else to answer. (Laughter.) Being better acquainted with Drew than any of the rest of them, though perhaps having less confidence in him (laughter), I asked him what under heaven was up. He said they were arranging the suits. I told him they ought to adopt a very different manner of doing it than being there in the night—that no settlement could be made without requiring the money of the corporation. He begun to picture his miseries to me, told me how he had suffered during his pilgrimage, saying he was worn and thrown away from his family, and wanted to settle matters up; that he had done everything he could, and saw no other way out either for himself or the company. I told him I guessed he was more particular about himself than the company, and he said, well, he was (laughter)! that he was an old man and wanted to get out of the fight and his troubles; that they were much older in such affairs than we were—I was very glad to hear him say that (laughter)—and that it was no uncommon thing for great corporations to make arrangements of this sort. I told him if that was the case I thought our state prisons ought to be enlarged. (Laughter.) Then Eldridge he took hold of me. He talked about his great exertions, what he had done and consummated; that there was only two dissenting voices in the board—Gould and myself—and that if we came into the matter to-morrow the company would be all right, as he had got the Commodore and Work and Schell to settle on a price. I told him I couldn't see it; I had fought that position for seven months night and day, and for seven weeks in Jersey I had hardly taken off my clothes, fighting to keep the money of the company from being robbed; and I could see no reason why we should not fight it on still. He said he didn't want to go into it, but had tried to do the best he could with Gould and myself and could do nothing, and now an arrangement had been made with Vanderbilt, and it was all right and must go through that night. I said I did not believe it was legal; these lawyers were all on one side, and I wanted to see my lawyer. He said that was of no use. (Laughter.) Then Mr. Pierrepoint argued with me. He said he did not think there was any one present who was not going to derive benefit from it. Rapallo was writing at a table. Schell was buzzing around (laughter), interested in getting his share of the plunder. Work was sitting on a sofa. I had nothing to say to him (laughter), as we were not on very good terms. Gould and I had a conversation together, and not till twelve o'clock at night did we give our consent. I told him I did not believe the proceedings were legal; that we had no lawyers; that the lawyers there were sold to Eldridge—hook, line and sinker. (Laughter.) Gould said Eldridge had paid Evarts $10,000 for an opinion that it was all right. and Eaton had been paid $15,000 for an opinion, and said it was legal. I told him I thought it a queer way of classifying opinions. (Laughter.) Gould consented first. He said he had made up his mind to do so, as the best way to get out of the matter. I told him I would consent if he did. Drew came to me with tears in his eyes and asked me to consent, and I consented. Then there was some paper drawn up and passed around for us to sign. I don't know what it contained. I didn't read it. I don't think I noticed a word of it. I don't know the contents, and have always been glad I didn't. (Laughter.) I have thought of it a thousand times. I don't know what other documents I signed—signed everything that was put before me. (Laughter.) After the devil once got hold of me I kept on signing. (Laughter.) Didn't read any of them, and have no idea what they were. Don't know how many I signed—kept no account after the first. I went with the robbers then and have been ever since. (Laughter.) After signing all the papers I took my hat and left at once in disgust. (Laughter.) I don't know whether we sat down or not. I know we didn't have anything to eat. (Laughter.)

Counsel—Didn't you have a glass of wine or something of that sort?

Mr. Fisk—I don't remember.

Counsel—Wouldn't that have made an impression upon you? (Laughter.)

Mr. Fisk—No, sir; I never drink! (Laughter.) I think I left at once as soon as I had done signing. As we went out I said to Gould we had sold our souls to the devil. (Laughter.) He agreed to that, and said he thought so too. (Laughter.) I remember Mr. White, the cashier, coming in with the check book under his arm, and as he came in I said to him that he was bearing in the balance of the remains of our corporation to put into Vanderbilt's tomb. (Laughter.)

The next interview with Vanderbilt was several days after.

Counsel—Was Gould with you?

Mr. Fisk—Yes, sir! We never parted during that war. (Laughter.) We went to his office one morning and found his man Friday in the front room. (Laughter.) Don't know his name. It was the same man I had seen a hundred times before when I had been there with Drew. We found the Commodore in the back room. I asked him how he was getting on. He said, "First rate" (laughter); that he had got the thing all arranged, and the only question now was, whether it could be slipped through our board. I told him that, after what I had seen the other night, I thought anything could be slipped through. (Laughter.) He said he would have to manage it carefully. I told him I didn't think so—that they would be careful to go it blind. (Laughter.) He said the trade had been consummated at Pierrepoint's house. I said I had no doubt of it. He said it ought not to have been carried out; that Schell had got the lion's share, and that some of the lawyers on the other side might have to go hungry.

RELIEF TO CHICAGO.

(Laughter.) He asked if we were conversant with the rest of the trade. I said I had no doubt the whole thing had been cooked in such a manner that it could be put through. He spoke about putting Banker and Stewart into our board, and said it would help both him and us to carry our stock, as people would say we had amalgamated, and Vanderbilt's men coming into the Erie board would strengthen the market. That was admitted; but it worked different from what we expected. (Laughter.) I next saw him a day or two before the prosecution was closed up. Gould thought the Commodore's losses had not been so large as represented, and asked to see his broker's account. The Commodore said he never showed anything and we must take his word. He reiterated his losses and said they were so large because when they had got him to give his order to sustain the market, the skunks had run and sold out on him. (Laughter.) As he was coming away he said, "Boys, you are young, and if you carry out this settlement there will be peace and harmony between the roads."

Previous to commencing this suit I made a tender of 50,000 shares of Erie stock to Vanderbilt. I went up to his house in company with T. G. Shearman. I received the certificates of shares from Gould and put them into a black satchel. (Laughter.) It was a bad stormy day, so we got into a carriage and I held the satchel tightly between my legs (laughter), knowing they were valuable (laughter). I told Shearman not much reliance could be placed on him if we were attacked, he was such a little fellow. (Laughter, in which

Mr. Shearman joined.) We concurred in the opinion that it was dangerous property to travel with—(laughter)—might blow up. (Laughter.) We rang the bell and went in. The gentleman came down and I said "Good morning, Commodore. I have come to tender you 50,000 shares of Erie stock and demand back the securities and money." He said he had had no transactions with the Erie Railway Company (laughter), and would have to consult his counsel. I told him I also demanded a million of dollars paid him for losses he purported to have sustained. He said he had nothing to do with it (laughter), and I bade him good morning. (Laughter.)

I became director in the Erie Railway on the 13th of October, 1867.

Counsel—You remember that date?

Mr. Fisk—I do well! It forms an episode in my life.

Counsel—What fixes it in your mind so well?

Mr. Fisk—I had no gray hairs then.

Counsel—You have gray hairs now?

Mr. Fisk—Plenty of them. And I saw more robbery during the next year than I had ever dreamed of as possible.

Counsel—You saw it, did you?

Mr. Fisk—I didn't see it but I knew it was going on. I am now a director of the Erie Railway and also comptroller. My duty, as comptroller, is to audit all the bills; as director, to manage the affairs of the corporation—*honestly.* (Laughter.)

I would like to make an apology to the court. This

is the first time I have been on the stand and I may overstep some of the rules. (Laughter.) If I do, it is wholly ignorance. It is new business to me, and if I don't keep within the rules, I ask my counsel to guide me, for I don't know when I may be imposed upon. (Laughter.)

Counsel—Your lawyer will look out for you.

Mr. Fisk—Oh, I'll look out for myself. (Laughter.) Don't give yourself any trouble about that.

Counsel—You seem to be a very frank and outspoken witness. (Laughter.)

Mr. Fisk—Well, I'm not much accustomed to you fellows. (Laughter.) I was never on the stand but once before.

Counsel—When was that?

Mr. Fisk—That was when I was a boy, up in the country—in a cow case. (Great laughter.)

The opening of the session of the Legislature at Albany, in January, 1869, gave Fisk employment in a new field, and he therefore dropped all the suits, so fiercely begun in the city against his old associates. Moreover, he now needed the assistance of those men he had lately been fighting. He, therefore, threw away his weapons of war and displayed the olive branch. Mr. Vanderbilt needed legislation in aid of his railroad schemes, and the Erie managers required similar service from the law-making power of the State. Both Vanderbilt and Fisk saw the propriety of joining forces in their raid on the Legislature. This, therefore, was accordingly done. Vanderbilt procured the passage of a bill legalizing his illegal stock dividends on the capital of the New York Central Railroad Company. Erie accomplished the enactment of the notorious classification bill, whereby the members of the Erie board were so divided that only one-fifth of them would be chosen annually. This virtually placed the Erie board in the hands of Gould, Fisk, Tweed and company for at least eight years. It was the boldest movement yet made to grasp uncontrollable power. The bill was engineered through the Legislature by Mr. Tweed, who was the leader of the Tammany ring, and all-powerful in New York City.

At the next annual election when the majority of the stock was controlled by Gould, Fisk and Tweed, these matchless managers elected a board composed entirely of their own friends, and thus established themselves finally in the possession of the Erie directorship.

Numerous efforts were made by the stockholders to break the power of this combination, but all failed totally. The injunctions of Judge Barnard were always at hand when required to forbid interference with the affairs of Erie. Millions of stock were issued and sold; millions of dollars were earned annually, only a very small portion of which was ever accounted for to the stockholders. Tammany and Erie kept their own counsel, and divided their gains among their own managers. What Tammany stole from the tax payers of New York City, and what the Erie directors withheld from the stockholders, was employed to control political nominations, to manipulate election returns, and to corrupt the Legislature and the courts. In this way immense fortunes were made by political managers in incredibly short periods of time, an artificial society of rich fools and rogues sprung up, whose members live in gaudily furnished houses and drive through the streets and in the park in flashing equipages that glitter in coarse vulgarity. Ignorance and base crime find every toleration beneath this superficial gloss of fraud-begotten wealth.

Into the whirlpool of this circumambient pollution, into these circles of thieves, into this vulgar society, young men, ambitious to rise, plunge heedlessly, eager for glittering prizes, which are won at the sacrifice of honor, of virtue and honesty.

The letter of introduction to Daniel Drew, which Fisk carried to New York, put him immediately into the very midst of these surroundings. From first to last his life in New York was unnatural, an inflated, a magnified life. It was like a raging conflagration, that roars and flashes, and leaps, and glares; that chars and blackens, and consumes all before it; that goes out and is forgotten. Flame, embers—ashes.

CHAPTER V.

ADMIRAL OF THE SOUND FLEET.

Fisk as admiral—The Sound steamers—The Narragansett line—The twin steamers, Providence and Bristol—The outfit of Fisk's boats—Superb Saloons—Costly furniture—Rich decorations—Bands of music—Distinguished travellers entertained—President Grant going to the Peace Jubilee—Preparing for the gold corner—The Plymouth Rock—Long Branch—The ferry boats "James Fisk, Jr., and "Jay Gould."

ONE of the most delightful routes between New York and Boston, is by way of the Long Island Sound steamers to Bristol, and thence by railroad to the capital of New England. In the summer of 1869, a new corporation was formed under the name of the Narragansett Steamship Company, and of this James Fisk, Jr., was chosen president. Two steamboats, the Providence and the Bristol, were fitted up and furnished in the most luxuriant style; furniture, upholstery and ornaments were of the richest and most elegant selection. The saloons and staterooms were complete in all their appointments, and the dining room was equal to that of a first-class city hotel. A band of music accompanied each boat and gave a first-class musical entertainment to the passengers. For a time these steamers were the chief pride of "Prince Erie." He procured for himself the full uniform of an admiral of the navy, and appeared in the glitter of gold lace and gilt buttons at the company's

THE STEAMER "BRISTOL."

pier, and gave general directions to the officers regarding the reception of passengers and freight. Frequently he continued on board the vessels during their trips up the Sound, and always on such occasions made his presence known and felt to all on board, by the magnificence of his entertainments. After his appearance in uniform he was named "Admiral Fisk," and was gazed upon by passengers as a prodigy, as one of the curiosities of life. Every officer and man employed on the vessels was required to appear in appropriate uniform, wearing a badge to indicate his position. The discipline was perfect, and the attention to shippers and travellers was all that could be desired.

Fisk's line of steamers at once became deservedly popular, and were patronized by the travelling public to an extent far beyond what had been attained by any other line.

Fisk was always delighted with the opportunity to entertain the great men of the country. When General McClellan was relieved from duty as commander of the Army of the Potomac, and was feasted and loaded with presents by his admirers, among the people of New York and New England, James Fisk, Jr., was one of the most conspicuous of all fawning worshippers of the deposed commander of the Army of the Potomac. "Little Mack" was precisely such a man as Fisk could lionize with all the zeal of the reckless impetuosity of his nature; and McClellan would be greatly pleased at the fussy attention that a man like Fisk would bestow upon him. For a time, therefore, while McClellan was "the rage," Fisk was in his glory, and when the furore subsided, he was ready for a new sensation, which he was at no time long in seeking.

The possession of a line of steamers plying on the Sound, in a route between the metropolis of America and the heart of New England, afforded numerous opportunities for entertaining distinguished and notorious men. No opportunity of the sort was ever allowed to pass unimproved by the Admiral in command of the fleet.

The "Peace Jubilee" was celebrated in Boston. All the world was going thither, and whoever went or returned and did not take passage in "Fisk's Sound Steamers" lost much that was worth enjoying in the way of travel.

Among those least likely to overlook the pleasures of such a route as this, was General U. S. Grant, President of the United States. Upon the arrival of the President in New York City, he was taken in charge by Admiral Fisk and conveyed to the steamer, and conducted into one of the grand saloons, where he was introduced to Mr. Jay Gould and others of Fisk's associates, who entertained in a most sumptuous manner, and instructed the Chief Magistrate of the nation in the art of finance, with a view to convincing him of the advantage it would be to the farmers of the West to keep gold at a high premium during the time the products of the farms were being sent to market in the fall of the year. To cap the climax of this affair, Fisk, in full uniform, accompanied President Grant to the Coliseum, where the jubilee was held, and from the very audacity of the act, attracted more attention from the gazing multitude than was bestowed upon the President himself. Fisk, however, was not working for empty honors. He saw from the beginning, that he could, by Ciceroning the President from New York to Boston and back, gain immense advantage in aid of his contemplated "Gold Corner." He even had the boldness to suppose that he might obtain from the President a pledge to discontinue the sales of gold in August and September. Whether this could be done or not, Fisk resolved to attempt it, and if he failed, then to play bluff on the strength of a paraded intimacy with the President and his views. That is, if he could not obtain such a pledge as he wanted, he could intimate that "it is all right." This insinuation, made at the critical moment, gave immense strength to the "Corner," but when, a few hours later, it was stated so positively that the Government officers were with the conspirators, that declaration invoked instantaneous and irretrievable ruin. This, the account of the operations of the "Gold Ring," in another chapter, will fully set forth.

In 1870 the "Plymouth Rock," by far the most elegantly finished and furnished steamboat on New York waters, was launched for the Long Branch trade. This vessel was the great sensation of the season, the pride of Admiral Fisk, and the object of admiration to all who went on board. There never was anything like it in the way of steamboat or ship. It surpassed in size and accommodations all previous efforts, and it will be unequalled until some new genius appears more lavish and versatile than Fisk.

If to these steamers be added the ferry boats, plying between the Erie depot in Pavonia and Twenty-third street, "James Fisk, Jr.," and "Jay Gould," the list of vessels in the Admiral's fleet will be complete. These ferry boats, of course, were far superior in finish to any other ferry boats in the country, for whatever belonged to Fisk or was controlled by him must necessarily outshine all else of its kind. To this general rule, the ferry boats were in no sense exceptions.

CHAPTER VI.

FISK AS A MILITARY MAN—COL. FISK.

The Albany and Susquehanna Railroad War—A battle of words—A battle of injunctions—A battle of shellalahs, stones, oaths and pistols—Fisk in Albany—Scenes that are rare—Fisk Arrested—Erie defeated—The corrupt courts of New York—The villany of New York judges—Writs, decrees and judgments bought and sold in Wall street—The downfall of rascality—Fisk is chosen Colonel of the Ninth Regiment—Great sensation—The condition of the Regiment—How Col. Fisk brought it out—Dress parades—"Camp Gould," Long Branch—Trip to Boston—The alarm of the City Fathers—Fisk not allowed to say his prayers on Boston Commons on Sunday—He worships in the theatre—The Orangemen's parade—The Riot—The gallant Ninth in action—The mishap to the Colonel—Killed, wounded and missing.

THE Albany and Susquehanna Railroad, connecting the Hudson at Albany with the Susquehanna at Binghamton, was completed in January, 1869. The building of the road was the result of private enterprise, and the line was intended to secure merely a local purpose, by giving an outlet to the products of the rich section of the State through which it passed. It was barely completed, however, when Fisk discovered that by gaining possession of this line he would be able to compete with Vanderbilt for the trade between New England and the West. That is, if the Erie Railway could deliver and receive freight at Albany, it would come directly in competition with the New York Central. Seeing this, Fisk resolved to get the prize, by treaty, by strategy, or by force.

The managers of the new road could not be persuaded to sell out. Gould and Fisk then began to scheme for the capture of the road, by the purchase of stock and the election of a board of directors, at the next annual election, that would be favorable to their purpose. The stock was controlled by a few men, who were opposed to the Erie party, but, nevertheless, Fisk contrived by paying far more than its value, to get a considerable quantity of it. There were numerous sums held by the towns along the line of the road, and the struggle to gain possession of these was sharp and varied. The stock was in reality worth only about 20 cents on the dollar, but the town officers were prohibited by law from selling any portion of it for less than its par value. Fisk entered into an arrangement with some of these town officers, whereby the stock was to be voted for his party, with the understanding that, after the election, he would purchase it at par. When this stock was presented at the office of the company for transfer, the secretary refused to make the transfer, unless evidences of actual sale were produced. This of course was virtually a defeat of the Erie scheme; there was no evidence of actual sale in existence, for the very good reason that there had been no actual sale of the stock in question.

This action of the secretary brought on a war of "Injunctions." Fisk had frequently felt the force of the strong arm of the law descending upon his head with all the power of judicial decrees. But he had now become proprietor of one of those anomalous establishments in New York, called a "Court of Justice." In this he had manufactured to order writs and decrees at the shortest notice, suited to any case. Over one of these establishments George G. Barnard presided. He was so thoroughly convinced of the propriety of yielding swift and implicit obedience to his master, Fisk, that he never questioned the power of his machinery to produce any article of legal document that "Prince Erie" should order, either by messenger, letter, or telegraphic dispatch. There is not the slightest doubt in the mind of any one, familiar with the organization of this admiral institution, that if Fisk had been in Paris, in 1871, he could have saved that City from invasion, by simply telegraphing by cable, to "His Honor" Judge Barnard for an injunction forbidding Van Moltke to open his batteries on the French capitol. Had "Prince Erie" demanded such an injunction, "His Honor" would certainly have issued it. Precisely how the arrival of "Prince Erie Admiral Colonel Fisk" at the Prussian Headquarters, armed with one of Barnard's formidable writs, would have affected Kaiser William, the Crown Prince, and the old hero, Von Moltke, cannot well be described. The situation would have been new, and therefore embarrassing. The wily minister, Count Bismark, would have been more familiar with the New York mode of warfare, and might have somewhat interfered with the execution of the writ. Of course he would have been forthwith indicted for contempt of "His Honor's" court, a warrant would have been telegraphed under the sea, and, unless he had fled the realm, as "Prince Erie" once did to New Jersey, he would have been arrested. Fortunately for the fate of nations, both Fisk and Barnard were too much engaged with their little "business operations" in New York to care for Chasseurs and Uhlans, for Emperor or Kaiser.

In August, 1869, the crisis in the Albany and Susquehanna Railroad was approached. "Prince Erie" ordered out an injunction from Barnard's court, forbidding Mr. Joseph H. Ramsey, president of the new railroad company, from doing sundry and several things that interfered with the Erie party in their efforts to capture his road. Mr. Ramsey, it seems, was a match for Fisk. He confronted him instantly, armed with like weapons. He procured from Judge Parker, at Owego, an injunction forbidding certain towns from transferring stock. Next day Erie had this injunction of the Owego Judge revoked and an opposite order issued, commanding the transfer to be made. Then followed another order removing Ramsey from the presidency, and forbidding him from acting as an officer of the road.

The office of the company was in Albany, and Mr. Ramsey stoutly refused to obey the order of the court, and the police force was called out to preserve the peace. During the night, the books were removed by the Ramsey party, so as to make the transfer of stock impossible. Just as the Erie party were about taking possession of the office on the following morning, August 6th, an injuction was served on them, forbidding them from acting as officers of the company. Thus the corporation was left without officers, one set having been removed by a New York injunction, and the other set by an Albany injunction, issued out of Judge Peckham's court.

This novel situation gave rise to a sharp skirmish for the possession of the unoccupied ground. Fisk telegraphed to New York for one of Barnard's orders, appointing him receiver of the company. The order came, as Fisk knew it would come, for he had ordered his judge to send it, and Fisk's servants, from coachman to court officers, had learned to obey promptly the commands of their master. The order arrived at Albany at midnight. Fisk retired, certain of complete victory on the morrow.

On the morning of the seventh, "Prince Erie" proceeded to offices of the Albany and Susquehanna Company, armed with his appointment as receiver, by Judge Barnard, and proposed to take possession at once, and wind up the affairs of the company. Mr. Van Vaulkenburg was in charge of the office, and to this gentleman Fisk announced his purposes. It appears, the Ramsey party were likewise men of resources; they had procured an order in advance of Barnard's, appointing Hon. Robert H. Pruyn, receiver, and of this fact Mr. Fisk was now informed by Van Vaulkenberg. Fisk attempted to dispossess the gentleman in charge, which attempt resulted in "Prince Erie" being very inelegantly thrust down stairs, and, thereafter, marched away to the police station. After this unexpected rout, Fisk telegraphed to Barnard for more orders. In due time an injunction came to hand, forbidding "all persons whatsoever" from interfering with Receiver Fisk. While attempting to enforce this new order, Fisk was again arrested, and that ended the battle for the week.

Fisk then went to New York and returned on Sunday night with his satchel filled with injunctions, "writs of assistance," warrants for the arrest of offenders, and such other court helps as "His Honor" conceived to be useful to him in his efforts to steal a railroad. When the Erie party arrived in Albany, they found that the Ramsey men had again out-generaled them. They had procured a new supply of injunctions, restraining everybody from doing anything that would in any manner interfere with Receiver Pruyn in the discharge of his duties. A train had been sent from Albany, down the road, to warn sheriffs and other officers of the existence of these orders.

Fisk, learning this, immediately telegraphed to the officers and employees of the Erie Company at Binghamton, directing them to start a train up the road to resist the progress of the train from Albany. The opposing parties met near Bainbridge station, about thirty miles from Binghamton, when the Erie train was run off the track and captured. The Albany train proceeded onward till it reached the tunnel, fifteen miles from Binghamton. There it was confronted by another of Fisk's trains, with about eight hundred men, who had come out to resist, by force, the advance of the Ramsey men, whose number was about four hundred.

The trains were run against each other near the tunnel, and a battle ensued, in which stones and clubs were very freely used, and occasional pistol shots were fired. Several of the men were wounded. Several bridges were burned, the track was torn up and cars destroyed. Finally the Forty-fourth Regiment of State troops, which had been ordered out by Gov. Hoffman, arrived on the ground and dispersed the rioters.

While this disgraceful and dastardly outrage was enacting at Binghamton, Fisk again attempted to gain possession of the offices at Albany on an order from his tool, Judge Barnard, and was again arrested for conspiring to disturb the peace. The affair had now reached a point at which it became necessary for the State authorities to interfere, and, therefore, Gov. Hoffman declared the district of the State through which the road passed to be in a state of insurrection, took possession of the line, placed over it two officers of his staff to run it as a military road, until the courts could decide into whose hands it should be delivered. This disposed of the question of possession. The war of injunctions was, however, kept up during a full month, when the annual election occurred, which resulted in the opening of two separate polls in the interest of the contending parties. Two sets of directors were chosen, which only added to the complication. Three months later the case came up for trial before Judge Smith, at Rochester, ending in a verdict for the Ramsey party; the Erie party were utterly defeated. For once, therefore, Fisk met more than his match, and was compelled to acknowledge himself outgeneraled.

The most humiliating feature of this disgraceful struggle is that, which exhibits the vile nature of the New York courts. There are few places in the United States where such conduct would be tolerated. The most sacred interests of the people are entrusted to the protection of the judiciary; fraud in the administration of justice is the worst evil that can befall a commonwealth, and a corrupt judge is the vilest of all public officers, yet for years the inhabitants of New York tamely submitted to the decrees of courts, whose presiding judges bartered and sold their writs and verdicts with an effrontery, that from its very boldness challenged the admiration of the people, who were plundered and oppressed by these mercenary scoundrels. The day of reckoning, however, came, and with it came also the doom of the felon upon the heads of the miscreant offenders.

Colonel of the Ninth Regiment.

The opening of the year 1870, brought a new episode in the life of Fisk. He had been successful as a corporation manager and as a bold financier, but he longed for diversion from the severe routine of business. Diversion without display was distateful to him. But he was never long in finding what he sought for. After a little manœuvering on his part, he was elected Colonel of the "Ninth Regiment National Guard, State of New York." This regiment possessed a noble war record, but it was poor, and its ranks were thin. It needed a colonel, money and excitement to "bring it up." In Fisk these three elements were united. The announcement of his election created a great flutter in the aristocratic military circles of New York; the unfavorable criticisms served only to spurr the Colonel to a determination to make the Ninth the model regiment in the State. At the muster to receive the new colonel, less than three hundred men were present. Fisk met the men and made known his determination to build up the organization. He offered a prize of $500 for the company, that would show the greatest number of recruits in a given time. Under this stimulant recruiting went forward rapidly, and in a few months the ranks of the regiment were full.

On the 20th of August Colonel Fisk took his regiment to Long Branch, where he established "Camp Gould." Ten days were spent in camp, most of the time being devoted to exercises in the manual. A grand military ball was given at the largest hotel at "the Branch," and other entertainments were provided at the expense of the generous hearted Colonel. On occasions of dress-parade the sojourners at this fashionable resort would visit the camp to witness the exercises of the regiment. The men became very warmly attached to their commanding officer; each regarded him as a personal friend. When the regiment returned to New York and marched up Broadway and down Twenty-third street, to the Grand Opera House, it attracted marked attention from the citizens who crowded these thoroughfares to greet the "boys in blue."

In the summer of 1871, Colonel Fisk terribly shocked the propriety of the city fathers of Boston, by announcing that he would, on the 17th of June, visit that city with his regiment. If it had been reported that a regiment of Stonewall Jackson's rebel troops were about to invade the sacred precincts of the "Hub," the staid Puritans would scarcely have been more sorely perplexed. Fisk wrote to the Mayor of Boston that he was coming. The Mayor laid the letter before the "Board of Aldermen." The lawmakers were alarmed; they did not know what to do about it, so they "laid the letter on the table." The newspapers ridiculed the whole affair, and thought Fisk had better not come. But over and above all this was Fisk's published declaration, that he was going, and of course he went, having first obtained the consent of the Governor of the Commonwealth to enter the State. At the appointed time, the New Yorkers entered Boston, were received by the military and obtained a hearty welcome from the people. The Colonel had asked permission to hold religious services on the Commons on Sunday, but was denied that privilege by the Mayor and Aldermen. Precisely on what ground the refusal was based has not been made public. Why a man, or a regiment of men, should be denied the privilege of saying prayers on Boston Commons on the Sabbath day, is a secret locked in the hearts of the lawmakers and Chief Magistrate of the most pious city on the continent. If Fisk and his men were the vilest of sinners, they had great need to pray, both on Boston Commons and elsewhere, and if on that occasion the Lord had

AT LONG BRANCH.

been pleased to cast the devils out of them, there is no public ground for the inference, that the said devils, suddenly cast out, would have entered into the Board of Aldermen to dwell there. At least no intimation was given that any such fear of possible results influenced the action of the Board, or provoked the refusal. As "Prince Erie" failed to state what sort of prayers he and his regiment proposed to say on Boston Commons, it is barely possible, that the pious men whose duty it is to defend the good name of the fathers, who landed on Plymouth Rock, had grave doubts as to the orthodoxy of the "religious services" that the Colonel of the "Ninth" might "hold." That "the Commons" should not be profaned, was of the utmost importance; that Fisk should say his prayers was of little moment to the city fathers. To Colonel Fisk, however, the matter was reversed, he had promised his men that they should "hold religious services in Boston on Sunday," and "hold" them they would. Being denied the "Commons" and the grounds about Bunker Hill Monument, the regiment went to one of the theatres, and there were led in the services by the Chaplain of the regiment. At the close of the services, Fisk addressed the audience, thanking the people for the hospitalities that had been extended to his command and publicly apologized for a failure to have honored the Mayor of the city with a proper salute, when the regiment passed him on the Common on Saturday, saying, his presence had not been detected until it was too late to give the order to the men.

Soon after the return of the regiment from this excursion to the East, it was called out in actual and severe service, to resist the rioters who attempted to break up the Orangemen's parade on the 12th of July. The duty performed on that day was most trying, and, among all the regiments, the Ninth suffered the severest loss. Throughout the excitement, the officers and men behaved with commendable gallantry, though it is said the Colonel was considerably demoralized by the assault of the mob on the head of his column.

The Parade of the Orangemen—The Riots.

In the summer of 1871, the societies of "Orangemen," in New York, made preparations for their annual parade, to take place on the 12th of July. The "Orangemen" are an association of Protestant Irishmen, who celebrate the struggle of their ancestors with their ancient enemies at the battle of Aughrim. The Catholic Irish in New York resolved to prohibit, or to break up the parade, and applied to the city authorities to have the celebration forbidden. Now, the city government was in the hands of the Tammany "ring," and Tammany was dependent chiefly on the Irish Catholic vote for its political power. Nothing, therefore, that the voters would ask could be with safety denied. Accordingly, the superintendent of police was instructed by the Tammany sachems to issue an order forbidding the Orangemen to parade.

This cowardly surrender to the mob was denounced in unmeasured terms by the entire respectable newspaper press of New York, and indeed of the whole country. The right, peaceably to assemble, is accorded to all sorts and conditions of men. Catholic societies parade in the streets of New York on St. Patrick's day; German societies parade in honor of foreign princes, and to celebrate the victories of their countrymen; Americans parade on national holidays; why, therefore, should Orangemen be denied the privileges accorded to all others? The mob, the low Irish Catholic mob, uncontrolled by priest or leader, but impelled by blind, superstitious bigotry, threatened to raise a riot if the Orangemen appeared on the streets. It was the plain duty of the city authorities to say to the mob, "If you disturb the peace of the city you will be punished—instantly, severely, surely punished. The law must be obeyed; the rights of all classes will be defended. If the Catholic societies parade the streets, they will be protected; and if Protestant societies parade in the streets, they, also, shall be protected by all the power, both civil and military, of the city and State." But no, the cowardly authorities made no such reply. They made a disgraceful surrender to the mob. The storm of indignation invoked by the surrender, that came swiftly and suddenly from all the people, struck terror to the hearts of the miscreant rulers. The magnates of Tammany quailed, trembled and repented. This offensive order had been issued only after the route of the parade had been announced; but such was the force of the popular rebuke on Tuesday, that before midnight the order was revoked. The parade was to take place on the following day, Wednesday, July 12th. On the morning of that day, the following proclamation was published in all the newspapers:

A Proclamation.

Having been only this day apprised, while at the Capitol, of the actual condition of things here with reference to proposed processions to-morrow, and having, in the belief that my presence was needed, repaired hither immediately, I do make this proclamation.

The order heretofore issued by the police authorities in reference to said processions having been duly revoked, I hereby give notice that any and all bodies of men desiring to assemble and march in peaceable procession in this city to-morrow, the 12th inst., will be permitted to do so. They will be protected to the fullest extent possible by the military and police authorities. A military and police escort will be furnished to any body of men desiring it, on application to me at my headquarters (which will be at Police Headquarters in this city) at any time during the day. I warn all persons to abstain from interference with any such assemblage or procession except by authority from me; and I give notice that all the powers at my command, civil and military, will be used to preserve the public peace, and to put down, at all hazards, every attempt at disturbance; and I call upon all citizens, of every race and religion, to unite with me and the local authorities in this determination to preserve the peace and honor of the city and State.

Dated at New York, this eleventh day of July, A. D. 1871.

JOHN T. HOFFMAN.

By the Governor:

JOHN D. VAN BUREN, *Private Secretary.*

The excitement on Wednesday morning when the Governor's proclamation appeared was intense. The rioters were sullen and defiant, while order-loving citizens congratulated one another that the city was not to be tamely surrendered to a mob. Men who had little sympathy with Orangeism, and even felt that the proposed celebration was in itself unwise, seeing that it was to be made a test of liberty as opposed to lawlessness, were anxious that it should not be abandoned.

The cowardice of Tammany and the hesitation and incompetency of the officials with which it afflicts New York, brought terrible but natural fruits of shame and of sorrow to the city. The more than weak, the pusillanimous surrender of Mayor Hall to the mob, of course, only encouraged it to more desperate resolution, for it was a thing to have been conquered by defiance; concession only gave it strength and courage to act. But after this fatal error had been partially remedied at the indignant demand of outraged public sentiment, mismanagement almost as stupid led to results as painful though not so momentous as those threatened by the surrender would have been. These disastrous, humiliating consequences of weakness and ignorance form a frightful narrative of carnage.

Threatening demonstrations of the rioters, early on Wednesday morning, revealed that the outraged cry of the people had not cured them as completely as it frightened Tammany. Sullen groups gathered on the street corners in threatened districts or in the localities where the Irish reside in greatest numbers. Among these groups women were most conspicuous by the vehemence with which they denounced Orangemen, police, and soldiers alike; and children of both sexes gathered about them, ignorant alike of their own danger and the desperate resolution of those about them. The men generally were gruff and silent, evidently angry that their opportunities for pillage had been wrested from them by the enforced action of the men, whom they had made Mayor and Governor. Separate gangs of ruffians, six or eight in number, moved from street to street, eager alike for fight or pillage. At the several rendezvous of the Hibernians many bore rifles without effort at concealment, regardless of the policemen on their beats, who made no attempt to disarm them. In the upper part of the city the rioters begun to move southward at an early hour, compelling all workmen on their routes to desist and join with them. In one or two instances, movements were made against the houses of men who had protected the Orangemen during the riots of last year, but as the rioters were without leadership they gradually dispersed before carrying their threats into execution. Attacks were made by the rioters on one or two armories where arms were known to be stored, but the resistance of a few determined policemen cowed the mob. The rioters were vicious and fierce enough for any purpose, but it was plain that they were without the organization they had boasted. Still their demonstrations were so threatening before ten o'clock, that the police were compelled to seize Hibernia Hall, and Gen. Shaler called for a regiment of troops from

Brooklyn, where, as in Jersey City, all had been comparatively quiet.

While the mob was without direction, divided counsels almost wholly destroyed the effectiveness of the troops and police. There does not appear to have been perfect consonance of action between the superintendent of police and the commander of the militia, and to this fact will eventually be traced many of the blunders which have aided to make the riot most serious in its consequences. Both police and troops were eager to do their full duty; there was no sympathy in the ranks with rioters.

About noon the fact became known that the Orangemen had resolved to parade, starting from their lodge room in Eighth avenue and Twenty-ninth street, and thither the rioters from all points in the city began to concentrate. Many marched in large bodies through the principal streets, undispersed. A large police force had previously been sent there, and these kept the rioters at a distance. Later in the day five regiments of troops marched to the same point, and by two o'clock the entire brigade and a large body of police had formed in Eighth avenue, hemmed in at all the cross streets by an angry mob.

Soon after the Orangemen made their apperance in the street, preparatory to taking their places in the line of march, the mob in Twenty-ninth street began hooting, and the police at once put them to flight. Subsequently, Twenty-eighth street was cleared in the same way, the police acting with great spirit. But the rioters soon returned to the places from which they had been driven, and prepared to renew their hooting, or to indulge in more violent demonstrations. A few shots were fired from houses in the avenue, before the procession moved, the police in one instance returning the fire by a single shot, but nothing really serious occurred until the head of the line had reached Twenty-third street and the Orangemen were opposite Twenty-fourth street. Here they were fired upon from a tenement house on the corner of Twenty-fourth street. But not more than half a dozen shots were discharged in all, and none of them apparently took effect on troops or policemen. The 84th Regiment, however, immediately and excitedly discharged their weapons at the house and at the crowd in the avenue and along the street. They had previously loaded with ball cartridge in the open street, as if to intimidate the rioters, and the effect of their fire was murderous. At the same time the 9th and 6th Regiments in the rear of the Orangemen also began firing indiscriminately, sweeping Twenty-fifth, Twenty-sixth, Twenty-seventh and Twenty-eighth streets, the extreme rear of the 9th firing a few shots up Eighth avenue into the platoon of policemen who were stationed at Twenty-ninth street. The troops of the 6th, 9th and 84th Regiments were for a moment completely demoralized and broken; their firing was as wild as it was uncalled for, and wholly without order. They soon recovered from their momentary panic, however, and reforming, marched on again leaving a hundred or more dead and wounded men, women and children behind them. The side streets from Twenty-fifth street to Twenty-eighth streets were instantly cleared of all but those unable to fly, the rioters abandoning their friends without compunction. They abandoned also the conflict.

No further attempt was made to obstruct the march of the Orangemen and their escort. The riot was suppressed by this single volley, and the most desperate and drunken of the mob could not be induced to resume the fight. It was a terrible remedy to apply, for ten innocent persons (if indeed idlers on such occasion can be called wholly guiltless) suffered for every rioter shot; but it was terribly effective. The mob sought safety in Seventh and Ninth avenues, and not one of the cowardly scoundrels returned to aid their wounded friends.

Almost the first shot that was fired by the mob at Twenty-sixth street, struck Henry C. Page, business manager of Fisk's Opera House, and a private in Company K, 9th Regiment, killing him instantly. Colonel Fisk ran to save him from falling, and received a blow with an iron implement above the ankle, which disabled him. He was taken away in a carriage by Jay Gould, and was attended by the 9th Regiment Surgeon, Dr. Pollock. The locality of the house to which Fisk was taken was kept a secret, as the mob threatened to take the life of any of the members of the 9th Regiment whom they could catch, and especially that of Colonel Fisk.

As the gray of the evening settled down upon the scene of the day's bloodshed, a strange wild picture, from the roughest mould of humanity, was presented. Crowds of excited men stood upon the corners, thronged the crossings, blocked up the sidewalks, gazed up at the shattered windows, or contemplated the effects of the firing as seen in the bullet-holes in the doors and shutters on the ground floors. A large number of hats belonging to the slain were collected on the south east corner of Twenty-fifth street and Eighth avenue, and at these, all bespattered more or less with blood and brains, a large crowd gazed as if fascinated.

The progress of the street cars was in many cases greatly impeded, and the presence of a large body of police was necessary to keep even the semblance of order. No attempt was made to disperse any of the crowds upon the corners, and the air was heavy with the pent-up thunder of a riot which threatened at any moment to break out anew. Wild-looking and bareheaded women were in the midst of the throng, cursing when the men blasphemed and swearing vengeance as their companions did. The stores which had been closed during the afternoon were not opened. The streets were gloomy and dismal in the extreme. The shutters of some of the stores on the east side of Eighth avenue were literally riddled with balls. At No. 316 there were ten bullets in the doors and shutters. The adjoining stores were almost as badly pierced.

The total number of deaths resulting from the riot was forty-eight. The number of wounded was one hundred and thirty four. The funerals of the soldiers, who were slain by the mob were conducted with all the solemn ceremony of military usage. The number of killed in the regiments was four, and but few were wounded. The casualties were chiefly among the rioters and the idle spectators who thronged the streets.

The blood of the victims, numbering nearly two hundred men, women and children, rests upon the heads of the Tammany rules. A. Oakey Hall, Mayor of the City of New York, surrendered to the mob, forced his creature at the Police Headquarters to make proclamation of the fact, and so invited Wednesday's work. John T. Hoffman, Governor of New York, made public no effort to spare the city from mob rule until the morning of the riot. The guilt of Mayor Hall is undeniable, and not denied. That of Governor Hoffman is equally clear, unless he can convince the people, whose trust he seems to have betrayed, that he acted with all the vigor he could command, the moment he knew the danger. Write on the tombstone of Wednesday's victims, "Murdered by the criminal management of Mayor A. Oakey Hall." Make rigid inquisition of blood before admitting that the name of Governor John T. Hoffman shall not be added to the inscription.

The lesson of the riot is thus written down by one of the ablest and wisest of living journalists.*

"The telegraph has borne over land and sea the tidings of last Wednesday's riot and its bloody results. The thoughtless will infer that New York is subject to the sway of its worse elements, when in

*Horace Greeley of the *New York Tribune.*

7

truth the very contrary was demonstrated. That we *have* such elements in unusual abundance and proportion—the drainage of European jails, fugitives from the quest of European sheriffs and police—is undoubted. There are not less than 50,000 denizens of our city who live by crime only—who have no idea of living otherwise. Probably twice that number live by pandering to lewdness, intoxication, and other forms of degrading sensuality; and from this to outright felony the transition is easy and frequent. Together with their habitual dupes and victims through the slavery of perverted appetite, these classes are very strong in this community; and they furnish material for a riot as naturally as boys run to a fire. But numerous as they are, the dangerous classes form but a small fraction of our city's vast population, of whom at least three-fourths, including nearly all who live by useful industry, are instinctively on the side of law and order, and ready to prove it by their acts. The bloody riot of Wednesday showed this, and demonstrated in addition these cheering truths:

I. There is no need that a riot should ever be endured or permitted. To prevent it, it is only requisite that the official guardians of the public peace shall never pander or truckle to the mob spirit, but make it always and everywhere clear that they will in no case fail to regard and treat a rioter as their deadly foe, whom they have no wish to conciliate, but stand ready to extinguish if they must. Palavering a mob, whether before or during a riot, is cowardice in the face of the enemy and treason to a high trust. The only language in which men in authority should address rioters runs thus: "You scoundrels! drop your "missiles and weapons this instant, and disperse, or "you shall be peppered with volleys of musketry "forthwith, and plowed by grape and canister so soon "as we can hurry up the big guns!" Tenderness toward such villains is cruelty to law-abiding people.

II. Authority will always be respected so long as it is respectable. Gov. Randolph had just such elements of disorder to deal with as our rulers; yet the Orangemen paraded wherever they chose in New Jersey, and no one was hurt or frightened. Irish Catholics are a mighty host in Jersey City, Newark, Paterson, New Brunswick, &c., yet the Orangemen were not molested wherever and however they saw fit to honor the triumph of William over James. It would have been just the same here had our rulers been Randolphs.

III. Of all the calamities that enfeeble and destroy a State, divided vacillating counsels are the most swiftly ruinous. The Hall-Kelso veto of the Orangemen's parade was atrocious; but that alone would not have bred a riot, because the Orangemen would have bowed to it, protesting against the outrage, and given up their parade. We should have had the triumph of usurpation to deplore, but no butchery. But when the Mayor proclaimed one day that the Orangemen should not parade, and the Governor on the next proclaimed that they *should* if they chose, and he would see that they were protected in so doing—this later manifesto appearing on the very morning of the Orange anniversary—a riot was inevitable. Either the Mayor or the Governor, had he alone spoken, would have been obeyed; since they both demonstrated, and in exactly opposite directions, they could not be.

IV. Given a nucleus, a rallying-point, the forces of law and order must always immensely preponderate over those of their natural antagonists. Here was a riot instigated and impelled by traditional devotion to Roman Catholicism; yet the Roman Catholic Archbishop and clergy promptly and vigorously denounced and reprobated it. We are confident that a large majority of the Catholics of our city heeded the counsels and obeyed the injunctions of their chief pastor, deeming them sound and wise. The police and military of our city are largely composed of Roman Catholics, who obeyed the call of duty as cheerfully and thoroughly as any Protestant. There was no flinching any where at any point below the Mayor's office. And, whenever it was understood by the rioters that the militia would fire, and that each cartridge included a ball, the riot was over.

V. Politics will not mislead our people very far. So far as we could see or learn, Oakey Hall's surrender in advance to the rioters was as promptly and as vehemently denounced by American Democrats as by Republicans.

VI. Men called out to face an angry mob as militia must not be expected nor asked to illustrate the principle of non-resistance; for they will not. It is possible that veteran regulars, led by officers they both loved and feared, might for a time be subjected to a shower of brick-bats, paving-stones, pistol-shots, &c., from a riotous mob immensely outnumbering them; but militia will do nothing of the sort. When dangerous missiles are rained upon their heads from crowded streets and house-tops, they will shoot, orders or no orders; and, if you object to this, you must manage to get on without them. If called out to preserve the public peace at peril of their lives, they will stand nothing stronger than a shower of dead cats. Whenever the heads of a dozen of them have been laid open, they will object to the performance going on without their being allowed to participate: if permission for this is not accorded, they will take it.

VII. Finally, there must *be* no more riots. Let it be understood that the first shot fired at police or militia, acting in the line of their duty, will be answered by bullets, the next by grape, and riots will henceforth be as rare here as at St. Petersburg.

THE FLIGHT OF FISK.

JIM FISK arose from dreams of wrath,
  In purple-dyed sublimity,*
And took his usual morning bath
  With soap and equanimity.

Then, girding him for cruel war,
  He buckled round his puny form
His bright, expensive cimetar,
  And donned his first-class uniform.

* Mrs. Browning.

He was to lead the Ninth without
Or horse or light artillery,
And Mayor Hall had called him out
For "qualities an*cill*ary."

But as the Ninth moved forward, then
He did not lead the column, for
He'd been compelled to leave his men—
That's what they looked so solemn for.

'Twas not another Erie vote,
Appointment of a lover, nor--
He'd gone to stop his Jersey boat
By order of the Governor.

But hearing now through rolling drums
Their voice, he joins them speedily,
Reflecting deeply as he comes
Upon the Riot Tweed-ily.

No *sabre de mon pere* he wore,
No coat, which was improperer ;
Thermometer at 94—
He'd left them at the Opera.

No matter now, the line was dressed
Just opposite the Armory,
While close upon the soldiers pressed
Of rioters a " swarmery."

These bore a scowling aspect, which
No London rough or navvy knew ;
And now Fisk saw three thosand *sich*
Come rushing down the avenue.

A moment, and the row broke out,
The rumpus and the rioting,
Sticks, bricks, and bullets flew about,
Ah nervous folk disquieting.

Without his hat, without his sword,
He rushed into the thick of it,
Till, in a moment, he was floored,
And very, very sick of it.

His comrades coming to his aid,
And finding him quite quakery,
His manly person straight conveyed
To a convenient bakery.

But such determined strength of mind,
Such resolution still is his.
Though crippled, he ne'er looked behind—
His case was like Achilles's.

And taking up his foot, he ran—
What stanch, unyielding will he had!—
More rapidly than any man
That's mentioned in the Iliad.

His comrades' voices rent the air—
"For ankle smashed what speed it is!"
They shouted, "*Ce n'est pas la guerre,*
Mais c'est superbe, indeed it is!"

Oh, where was then his coach-and-four?
Why should he not have sent for it?
He saw instead an open door,
And instantly he went for it.

On through the hall into the yard
He sped with strange temerity ;
But here a fence his progress barred,
And checked his high celerity.

An empty barrel stood at hand
(There seems no kind of doubt of it),
With which our hero quickly planned
A way of getting out of it.

For still resolved to hurry hence,
He with one hand the barrel held,
And leaping on it, jumped the fence
In manner quite unparalleled.

Fence after fence, yet unappalled,
He leaped them rather quieter,
And through a basement window crawled
To come upon a rioter.

A dressing he received from Pat,
But this was not inimical—
Old coat, old pantaloons, old hat,
Which made him pantomimical.

A New Departure now he ruled—
How blest to make a ride of it ;
A passing cab contained Jay Gould !
And so he got inside of it.

Thence to the Hoffman House they drove ;
But as the mob still harried him,
To Sandy Hook, our downy cove,
A steamer quickly carried him.

At last, supported by his friend,
  His wits beclouded, waxy, dense,
Long Branch he reached, the happy end
  Of all his morning accidents.

And now t'will be the final sum
  Of all incomprehensibles,
If Fighting Fisk should not become
  Field-Marshal of the Fencibles.

Who struck the blow that laid Fisk low
  Remains a hidden mystery;
His name, bedad, a Mac or O,*
  Will ne'er be writ in history.

But happily this thing is plain:
  To keep whatever pledge he meant,
He did not seek to strike the Braine
  Of that intrepid regiment.

* Not Maquereau.

Harper's Weekly.

CHAPTER VII.

THE GOLD RING.

The Great "Corner in Gold"—How Fisk made "Wall Street Pay."

IN the summer of 1869, a number of Wall street brokers combined for the purpose of speculating in gold. Specie was selling at 131 and it was believed by forming a "corner" in gold, it could be driven up at least 20 or 30 cents higher. Jay Gould was the originator and leader of the combination. Efforts were made to convince President Grant, that a rise in gold would be beneficial to the country during the fall of the year, while the grain and produce was going to market. These efforts were not entirely successful. Nevertheless, certain circumstances indicated that treasury officers expected a rise in gold, and therefore the operators inferred, that the Government would not sell large sums of gold, merely to break down the price.

Gould and his associates bought gold freely in August and during the first three weeks in September, driving the price to 137. The Government made its usual sales in August and September, and the price fell back to 131; this alarmed part of the clique, and upon a sudden rise they sold out, deserting Gould in the hour of trial. This was the 22d day of September. During that day gold had risen from 137 in the morning to 141 at the hour for closing. It was in this rise that Gould's weak associates deserted him, leaving the brunt of the battle to be borne on his own shoulders. At the close of business on Wednesday, Gould called on his friend, James Fisk, Jr., to help him through. An arrangement was agreed upon, and on Thursday morning "Prince Erie" stepped into the "Gold room," a terror to the crowd of bears that occupied the floor. The appearance of Fisk was an unmistakable indication of sharp work and broken fortunes; nevertheless his opposers resolved to present a bold front, and did so during the entire day. The whole financial interests of the city were in a state of excitement, the centre being in the Gold Room, where from half-past eight in the morning until nearly dark, the bulls and bears bellowed and roared with marvellous vigor of lung. First the bears gained a slight advantage, at one time crushing the price down from one forty-two and a half, to one forty-one in a twinkling; but before they had time to glory in their victory the bulls rallied in force, and in a second the indicator turned upward. Every rise was greeted with groans and yells, and cheers, and cries of exultant delight. Around the fountain in the Gold Room, where the brokers do their buying and selling—sometimes "doing" each other as well—the scene recalled the stirring times of the war, when a rise or fall of ten per cent. was not unusual.

The voices of the contending parties could be heard plainly in Broadway.

Opposite the Gold Room, near the Bank Exchange,

on New street, a multitude of outsiders gathered early in the morning—an hour before the opening of the Board—and renewed the old-time sport of betting on the indicator. One man, when the Gold Room indicator marked one hundred and forty-one and three-quarters per cent. premium, wagered twenty dollars that it would show forty-two within three minutes. "Taken," said another, and out came watches, and the gamblers watched the indicator with profound interest, as though they had two millions at stake instead of twenty dollars. During the whole day, this betting was kept up and large amounts changed hands. One bet of twenty to fifty dollars that during the day the indicator would make a "clean jump" of one-half per cent. premium, was eagerly taken.

It was a significant fact that more than two-thirds of the brokers arrived at the Gold Room before 8.30 A. M., and before nine gold was sold in large amounts and at figures considerably in advance of the quotations of Wednesday night.

The brokers were exhausted by heavy dealings, and the market, though continuing active, closed depressed and uninviting. Early in the day gold opened at one hundred and forty-one and five-eighths per cent. premium, but quickly dropped one-half per cent., when, under the influence of the well-authenticated rumors that the Secretary of the Treasury would anticipate the payment of the November interest, a large short interest was created, the amounts offered being taken by the bulls. About eleven o'clock the appearance of a prominent bull

CHARITY TO ALL.

operator in the room was the signal for an upward movement, and the price suddenly rose from one hundred and forty-one and three-eighths to one hundred and forty-two and one-quarter per cent. premium. From this point, the bears having been temporarily demoralized, a further rapid rise was effected, with little opposition, until the quotation reached one hundred and forty-four per cent. premium, when the bears rallied in force and a desperate struggle ensued.

In less time than required to record these changes, the price fluctuated between one hundred and forty-four and one-quarter and one hundred and forty-two and seven-eighths per cent. premium, finally ranging at one hundred and forty-three and one-half and one hundred and forty-three and one-quarter per cent. premium. The bulls, having proved themselves sufficiently powerful to control the market, quietly rested on their laurels, awaiting a further attack, but keeping the price steady at the advanced quotations.

The tactics adopted by the bull cliques are somewhat novel in the history of gold speculations. They keep cash gold abundant, and the rates for carrying easy, thus courting a larger short interest, which, as fast as put out, they are quick to take advantage of.

At noon the bears made another attempt to break the market by refusing to buy of or sell to the bulls; and while this was continued, the anomaly was presented of offerings of gold to any but the bull clique at one hundred and forty-two and one-half, while the bulls were bidding one hundred and forty-three per cent. premium at the same time. This last effort of the bears proving ineffectual, they quietly withdrew from the contest, though watching for a favorable opportunity to renew the attack.

On the following day a terrific hurricane swept over Wall street. Broad street, New street, and Exchange place were strewn with wrecks. Every gold and stock broker wore a pallid face. Moneyed men rushed about the streets as if insane. The gold excitement during the war and the fearful bank panic of 1857 were thrown into the shade. The dealings in gold absorbed everybody's attention, and stocks were comparatively of no account.

The bulls in gold had gained courage. The gold clique were satisfied that they stood upon a firm foundation, and resolved to make a determined onset. A Washington telegram announcing that Secretary Boutwell had refused to sell his surplus gold in order to relieve the stringency of the money market, had been backed up by private despatches to the same effect. It was positively averred that the distinguished bankers who had urged the Secretary to this course had been met with a flat refusal. The thing seemed to be settled. The bull clique, who held all the available gold, at once decided that the market should be forced to the highest point. The sales at the Fifth Avenue Hotel on the previous evening had given them renewed confidence. They felt satisfied that their net was too strong to be broken.

"We have it in our power to put gold up to two hundred, and we mean to do it," said one of the leading operators of the ring early in the morning. They attempted it and failed disastrously through Secretary Boutwell's announcement of his intention to buy in four millions of bonds. The bulls deny that this was the cause of their overthrow, but the fact is self-evident. They had blown up their bubble to its utmost extent, and on the mere announcement of Secretary Boutwell's intention it burst like a clap of thunder.

Before 9 A. M., both Broad and New streets were filled with outside operators. They seemed to snuff the approaching battle in the very air. Their white hats, with mourning bands, shook with excitement, and they flourished their little books in the air as if confident of winning a fortune in no time. Every man had his own little rumor, and industriously circulated it among his friends. "Gold! gold!"—this was all the talk. The indicator in front of the Gold Room, which resembles a time-board at a race-course, looked at the crowd in dumb silence, but it was to announce the death knell of many an ardent fortune-seeker before the close of the day.

At 9 A. M. the bidding began on the street. Gold was offered at one hundred and forty-five, and was snapped up on the instant. Down it went to one hundred and forty-four and a half in a twinkling, and was back to one hundred and forty-five within a half minute. The street became intensely excited. Men grew nervous. Up went the precious metal to one hundred and forty-six and one-eighth at a single jump. Then one hundred and forty-seven, and close on the heels of these figures one hundred and forty-eight. A spasmodic yell arose from the crowd at this result.

Men began to shriek and shout and flourish their little books more violently than ever. The bears on the street made a tremendous rally, and back gold went to one hundred and forty-seven. Another rush of the bears, and one hundred and forty-six and a half was reached. Confusion ensued. Everybody seemed to bid and offer at the same time, and one hundred and forty-nine grew out of the smoke. In a second one hundred and fifty and one hundred and fifty and a half was reached.

During these outside operations the members of the Gold Board dashed up the Broad and New street stairs and disappeared. It was but twenty steps to the lower gallery. Imagine a little fountain in the centre of the Hippotheatron. The centre of the fountain is a bronze Cupid, with a dolphin in its arms. From the head of Cupid arises a tiny silver stream, which falls in jets into the basin below. Fancy an iron railing ninety feet in circumference about this basin; then a space of some twenty feet between the walls and the fountain; and you have a rough idea of the Gold Room. On one side there are two galleries—the lower for the errand boys, and the upper for the spectators. Beyond the fountain, with his back toward New street, stood the Secretary, recording the sales which he caught by his ear. Near him is the telegraph operator. Wires run from his machine to nearly five hundred broker's offices, who are thus instantly informed of the state of the market, and are enabled to make their bids undisturbed by the furious excitement which rules in the Gold Room on momentous occasions.

BLACK FRIDAY.

At 10 A. M., on Friday, the Board opened, the Vice-President in the chair. Usually the heavy gold operators remain in their offices and base their bids, which they send by messengers, upon the reports received by their office telegraphs. But the magnitude of yesterday's fight drew most of the moguls into the amphitheatre, and they entered upon the combat with the ferocity of gladiators. The fight opened at 10 A. M., with gold at one hundred and fifty. The bull clique seemed unusually quiet. A quarter of an hour passed, and one hundred and fifty was still the ruling figure. The Secretary seemed in no wise overrun with business, and the telegraph operator worked his machine and conversed glibly with the bystanders. At ten and a half the situation was about the same, the market still standing at one hundred and fifty. The bears were cautious, and evidently suspicious that this skirmishing was preliminary to a bitter fight.

It was not until eleven o'clock that this comparative monotony was broken; one hundred and fifty and one-eighth was bid. The bears began to wince.

"Hell's to pay now!" shrieked a gray-haired man apparently burning over with agony. A hundred fists were shaken at each other over the little fountain, and an infernal series of yells filled the room. To an outsider it was impossible to distinguish either a bid or an offer. The bulls had now begun their grand charge. They swept the bears before them like chaff. From one hundred and fifty and an eighth the metal suddenly jumped to one hundred and fifty-five and a quarter. This was unprecedented. Men began to rave and shriek like mad dogs. They rushed about the little fountain in paroxysms of fury. The special wonder was that in the anxiety of the bears to sell and of the bulls to buy, so little regard was paid to the last reported quotation. Price on both sides seemed "no object." Men within a few feet of one another differed widely in prices, and there were a dozen different quotations for the metal in as many parts of the room. The bears gathered in a group, and snapped and snarled in turn. The bulls shouted with joy. Within fifteen minutes the premium was forced up to one hundred and sixty-two and a half. The bears sold very readily to their own clique at one hundred and thirty-five, when the market rate was one hundred and sixty. They refused to sell to the bulls at any price. Much of this traffic among the bears might have been "washes," or fictitious sales, reported at figures below the market, and to keep down the price; and much also of smaller lots than the big speculative blocks which the bulls were after.

Thus stood matters when Albert Speyer, a leader among the bulls, threw among the raving mob the tempting offer of one hundred and sixty. Such a marvellous bid coming from a dealer known to be fully responsible, startled the whole Room, and for a few moments no response was made. But before the thunderstruck auditors could regain their equipoise, James Brown, an equally well known broker and agent, offered to supply Mr. Speyer's wants with one, two, three, four, and up to five millions. The latter amount was promptly accepted. The prompt acceptance of this bid, while the bears were selling to their own crowd at one hundred and thirty-five, gave the bulls renewed confidence.

During the two minutes preceding this bid the market price had stood at one hundred and sixty-two and a half, one hundred and sixty-two, one hundred and sixty-one, and one hundred and sixty and a half. Mr. Speyer's bid was accepted under great excitement. The bears, though dismayed, were not panic-striken. Even in the face of Mr. Speyer's bid the premium dropped to one hundred and fifty-nine, but quickly rallied to one hundred and sixty. Again it touched one hundred and fifty-nine, and a third time touched one hundred and sixty.

This wavering is easily explained. A prominent bull, while within his office watching the telegrams from the Gold Room, received a private despatch from an employé of the Treasury Department in Washington, informing him that Secretary Boutwell would positively sell four million dollars. The rumor reached the Gold Room just as Messrs. Hallgarten & Co., in view of Mr. Brown's success in placing so large an amount at so inviting a price on the market, had offered a million at the same price. Some of this was taken up by other parties, but before the whole was absorbed the terrible rumor was circulated throughout the room. This instantly paralyzed the bulls to such an extent that the price fell to one hundred and fifty-five, and then to one hundred and fifty. The next bid was one hundred and forty-eight, then one hundred and forty-four, and finally one hundred and forty. Then dismay seized the members present, for the decline meant nothing less than the ruin of all concerned in the ring.

The bulls had gone into the fight fully prepared to take from ten million dollars to twenty million dollars. They had not taken seven million dollars when they heard of Secretary Boutwell's action. The rapidity of the movements and the magnetic influence of the Gold Room was too much for them. Their heads became giddy, and in a twinkling they lost control of the market. The Secretary's four million dollars threat was but a flea-bite, but they were fearful that his movement was a preconcerted one, and that twenty million dollars would be thrown upon them, if necessary, to crush the market. It was not until the rate grounded at one hundred and forty that they rallied. It was nearly noon. Gold again began to mount the stairs. It sprang from one hundred and forty to one hundred and fifty at a single jump. The bears acted as if a flash of lightning had passed through the room. Bedlam again broke loose. The room was filled with shrieks and curses. In another jump the metal struck one hundred and sixty.

Again came the Washington rumor, and this time, it was said, direct from the Special Treasury Agent in this city. It was asserted that President Grant had ordered Secretary Boutwell to sell the gold, and that he would order him to sell fifty million dollars if necessary. Away went the market in another grand crash, and never recovered until it touched one hundred and thirty-three. The battle was ended and the bulls were ruined.

CHAPTER VIII.

WHAT FISK SAID OF THE GOLD CONSPIRACY.

The investigation before the Committee of Congress—Fisk's testimony.

THE audacity and boldness of the great gold conspiracy, whose operations are recorded in the preceding chapter, created a profound sensation throughout the world. The efforts of the conspirators to involve government officers in the combination, induced Congress to appoint a committee to investigate the whole affair and report to the House of Representatives.

The examination of Fisk and Gould occupied six hours. Fisk was examined first and Gould afterwards. Much to Gould's chagrin, he was not permitted to be present when his confederate was examined, and Fisk was served in the same way. Members of the Committee describe the examination of Fisk as theatrical and ludicrous in the extreme. He talked with great rapidity and illustrated his utterances with grotesque actions, and interlarded them with copious interjections and profanity, and several times the Committee were convulsed with laughter. After his examination was over, Mr. Fisk stated that he testified in substance as follows before the Committee:

"In the first place, when I got down stairs, (alluding to the position of the Committee room in the basement of the Capitol,) I called for the reading of their authority, my object being to see precisely what they were gunning after. It seems the resolution of that Committee is that they shall inquire what led to the fluctuations in gold between September 21st and 29th, &c. Well, then, General Garfield said, 'Now you had better go ahead and stàte to the Committee your version of the matter as you understand it, and then when you are done we will ask you what questions we please. What you will have to do is to go into a history of the transaction." Mr. Fisk then proceeded to rattle off, at the rate off about one hundred and sixty words per minute, the following statement, which he said he had told the Committee:

"Well, in the first place, in order to get at the matter clearly, Mr. Gould, together with what little help I render him, is the manager of the Erie Railroad, a large corporation employing seventeen thousand or eighteen thousand men, and earning seventeen million dollars or eighteen million dollars per annum, most of which earning depends more or less upon the state of the country, of course. If the country is stagnant, so are all the crops at the West. We being one of the trunk lines, if the crops are held back, it materially decreases our receipts and paralyzes our business." (And here Mr. Fisk, as if to impress this point particularly, said, with a turn in his chair and a toss of his head, "*Do you see?*" and then he continued:) "Now, in 1866, 1867, 1868, with gold running from one hundred and forty-one to one hundred and forty-six and one hundred and forty-seven, the United States had no trouble in shipping their crop of grain to Europe at a profit. The market they had to compete with was, of course, up the Mediterranean, and of and up the Black Sea." Jay Gould, who had gathered himself in the corner of a lounge, looking at Fisk with his sinister black eye, interrupted by way of correction and explanation, with the remark, "The Greek ports; they have cheap labor and water transportation against our high labor and railroad transportation."

Fisk—"Yes; therefore, when we come to the summer we look forward to see whether there is anything in the country, or the finances of the country, or the foreign competition, to indicate to us whether our crop is going abroad or not." (Here Fisk took a long breath, and, arranging himself more comfortably in his chair, went on.) "As early as the 15th day of June last, General Grant was going to Boston to the Jubilee, and was to travel over our line, in the big boats, by the way of Fall River. We made up our minds—Mr. Gould and myself—that we would go with him and see if we could not find out what his policy would be for the Fall. Gold was then one hundred and thirty-five, and we knew that if gold remained at that figure our crops would not be shipped. We left New York to go to Boston with the General, about nine o'clock. We first gave him a supper about eight o'clock, and the conversation, of course, turned upon the important topic of the finances."

Q.—"Who was at the supper?"

Fisk—"Mr. Gould, Mr. Marston and myself. (Mr. Fisk, apparently impatient at the interrogation, went on.) This was the first real interview we had with him, I mean where we could settle down and talk with him. The first thing I made up my mind to was that Grant was studying into the finances; and if he was studying into them, of course he would exert a certain amount of power to rule them his way. The first thing that cropped out with him was that he was on his march to specie payment and a lower price for gold. That was the first thing that struck us. We, of course, went into an argument to show him that if gold fell to twenty, with the enormous crop on hand, it would not be brought forward at all. There was nobody to consume it. The home consumption would not begin to eat it up. It struck across us like cold water. We went into an argument to convince him that something should be done to get off this crop at a high price; that it was his policy to sell gold at a high price for the foreign market. I remember one remark he made particularly, and that was, after he had been talking an hour and a half: 'It was well, gentlemen. The bubble might as well be pricked at one time as another,' as much as to say," said Fisk, "If we are to have a crush it might as well be at one time as another." (Here Fisk laughed very heartily.) "Now," said he, with a peculiarly cunning smile, and a comical expression, "our idea of crashes is to have it all milk and honey with us, and let the other fellows stand it. Let the next man have all the trouble. But Grant did not seem to receive it quite that way. (With a sigh.) We came back from Boston along in July. I went down to Long Branch. There was no opportunity to talk there. (Emphatically.) About this time Mr. Gould had become acquainted with Mr. Corbin, who married the President's sister. Mr. Gould could not disabuse his mind. He paid more attention to it than I did, although I am doing all the talking. He could not disabuse his mind that this policy was going to bring us all up with a round turn."

Q.—"That it would ruin you?"

Fisk—"Yes. To-day there is not a man who is making a dollar that is trading in anything. The idea was that he, Grant, might be induced to stop pursuing this theory if it was properly put to him, and that he would understand it. We went down to Long Branch, but did not have a talk there. We wrote to Boutwell that it seemed to be Grant's idea that he was travelling for pleasure. He did not care to devote much time to business, only some six months or so, and the other six months to floating around for pleasure. I should think it was along in July that he was going to Newport again. We were then running two lines to Boston, one by Fall River, not landing at Newport, and the other by Newport, landing there, leaving New York at 6.30 P. M. Grant was to come down to the boat at five o'clock. Mr. Gould, in the afternoon, went to work and wrote a letter to him, in which he explained to him that we had the facts on our table that there was already on the sea, from the Greek ports to London and Liverpool, three hundred vessels, and that the beginning of what we had told him five or six weeks previous, had begun to work. Gold was then selling at thirty-three and thirty-four. He, Gould, asked me to take the letter down to Grant, have a talk with him, and, if I saw fit, to say to him that if the government would not sell gold, we, for the sake of getting this transportation, of getting employment for our motive power, which would make a difference of several million dollars—that, if he thought it advisable to put the gold market up and start up trade here—we could ship this crop. I started down and had a long conversation with General Grant on my way to Newport, and at that time, when I left General Grant, we decided that we would go to Newport the next Sunday, and he would telegraph to Boutwell, and either have Boutwell at Newport, or have some letter which we could tell something about."

Q. "Have a conversation?"

Fisk—"Yes, have a conversation. Just about that time it got along to be the first part of August. Mr. Gould and I had become interested in building the Paterson and Newark Road, where we became acquainted with Mr. Catherwood, who married Corbin's daughter. Catherwood had been put forward some time before this time as Assistant Treasurer, but it seems he was a little too near the family."

Q. "Had you not been trying to get Catherwood appointed?

Fisk—"They, Gould and Corbin, had been trying to do it, but they *drapped* him, concluding that he was not the man, and substituted Butterfield. Gould had made up his mind that the policy of the government would be to stand still until the crop was removed. But I was not in the thing at the time. Butterfield was then, through Corbin's influence, carried into the Assistant Treasurership, and it seems then that Corbin had taken up the matter on this theory: That this crop should be taken off at a high price. And the old gentleman went still further—that there was a great deal of money in it. Now, if you know anything about Corbin, you know that, when he reaches up, he takes along the shelf; he does not leave anything on it; he takes everything. He came very near sinking us, (with grim humor.). Corbin then conceived the idea that he could run the Treasury, having got Butterfield in there. Mr. Butterfield felt under some obligations to Mr. Corbin. All decided that there was a great deal of money to be made. They all conceived that with our power of carrying, a great deal of money would be made. The whole tide of the country seemed to be setting against gold going up; but Mr. Gould, in his great anxiety to get himself into a position of getting traffic for his road, had several interviews with Mr. Corbin; Corbin had his interviews with General Grant; Gould, too, had his interviews with Grant, and Corbin felt very firm in the belief that he could regulate this whole matter. That was the beginning of this purchase of gold. I had expressed to them my views on the matter; but in the beginning of it I was left out, and they commenced buying gold —Mr. Gould, from his resources. In all they probably bought about two million dollars of gold."

Q. "Did you buy?"

Fisk—"Yes, some at thirty-seven. Mr. Corbin told me that Mrs. Grant had five hundred thousand dollars; that General Porter had five hundred thousand dollars, and that he had one million five hundred thousand dollars himself. This ran along about five weeks, until about the 15th of September. Gold about that time had kept settling until it got down to thirty-one, and Mr. Gould had got a pretty bag of it. I could see by the way that he was tearing up little pieces of paper—every man has his peculiarities, you know—(with a laugh, Gould smiles also) that he was pretty well up to the handle. He was all the time running to Corbin. He would slip in every morning and take a dose of Corbin, you know. (Fisk laughing and meaning to be very funny.) I came into the office one morning and he was telling what a great purchase this gold was. I said: 'Gould, if I had as much gold as you have got, and it stood at such a loss as I think it will stand, I should think you would invite all of your able-bodied friends in to help bear the yoke.' I had not said much about gold for some weeks to him. We had always speculated together. Although he seemed to have a very good thing, he did not want to let me in. It seems, although I did not know it until afterwards, that he had got in and did not care to talk about it. But I could see, instantly, that if we were going to do anything, we should all put our shoulders to the wheel. We were dropping off in our earnings, and I had made up my mind that gold was not to be put up. We all knew that there was only thirteen or fourteen millions of gold in New

York. We started that morning, through Heath & Co., to buy gold; and afterwards I said to Mr. Gould: 'Have you got any understanding with Corbin, or have you carried out any of those theories with Grant that we talked about last July?' 'Yes,' said he; 'there is no gold to come out of the Government.' We can put the gold up to forty-five, and I think we shall make money out of it, and we shall get our winter and fall transportation for our road. My idea is to go ahead. Upon that base I started in myself, without any understanding that I was to share in his loss or he in mine. I made up my mind, and got what I could carry. I found that I could get all I wanted. (Laughing.) Gold was then about thirty-six and a quarter. He (pointing to Gould) had gold enough to sink a ship. I guess that the day after I commenced I said to Mr. Gould: 'Now you give me a letter to Corbin, stating that I know all about this affair; that he has got the Treasury fixed; that Butterfield thought he could get the Treasury news first. I want to talk with him freely, so that we shall know exactly where we stand.' I got the letter, and talked with Corbin three hours. He told me that everything was all running nicely; that he had got this gold with Mr. Gould; that he had received a check for twenty-five thousand dollars, which he had forwarded to Washington; that everything looked bright, and he was confident we were doing a great national good, (laughing,) as well as assisting the road to its transportation; that he saw more money in the transaction than he had seen in all his life. He had all the arrangements that he had made down here at his tongue's end. So I started back to our office. We have some telegraph wires there, and I thought I would be sure and get a good jag of it. This took us up to about the Monday or Tuesday before the 'black Friday'—about September 21st. I found after I left Corbin's office that I felt very like getting back there again and talking to Corbin. I was nervous and shaky all the time. This way, you know," said Fisk, getting up and shaking his knees, "but Corbin, when I got to him, said, 'You need give yourself no uneasiness;' but I felt that when I was talking to him I was a great deal better and stronger than when I was away from him. I saw him two or three times, in which he reassured me, and gave me a great deal more confidence. I think it was that night that Mr. Gould came down from his house to the office, about eight o'clock, and said: 'I want your special man—the man whom you send upon the most intricate business you have. I want him to take a letter to-night from Mr. Corbin to General Grant, at Washington, Penn.' I called Chapin, and he said to Chapin, 'I want you to-morrow morning at half-past six, to be at Corbin's house. He will give you a letter to General Grant, directed to Washington, Penn. I want you to take the train, to go by Pittsburg, and deliver this letter to Grant. See what he says. Go from there to the first telegraph station and telegraph me what the reply is; that is, if you can do it without communicating any secrets.' I was afraid he would sleep too long, and I said to my brother-in-law, 'Go to Mr. Chapin and see him aboard the train, so that when I come to the office in the morning, I may know that it is all right.' In the morning they were there. 'Old Hamlet Corbin' came down stairs at half-past six and delivered him a letter directed to General Grant. Chapin came out and got into a carriage, and drove to the Jersey Central Railroad. He travelled and never stopped until he delivered that letter to General Grant at Washington, Penn. When he arrived at the house in Washington, it was very early in the morning, about seven o'clock. He rang them up, and sent his card, 'William O. Chapin, from Mr. Corbin.' He then went into the parlor and very soon the General came down, opened and read the letter clear through and went out, evidently as if to show it to Mrs. Grant or some one else. He was gone about fifteen minutes, and when he came back said to Mr. Chapin 'All right,' and bid him good morning. Mr. Chapin drove to the next station, and we received a despatch, viz.: 'Delivered—all right.' That was all the despatch said. He wended his way back. It took us up to Thursday morning. I was around to see Corbin. He said that everything was A No. 1; that this letter had settled everything beyond a doubt; that the interests involved to the nation and otherwise had rendered everything safe. On Thursday afternoon I had been into Wall street. Mr. Gould and I drove to Belden's office and gave an order to Mr. Heath. When we arrived gold was thirty-six and five-eighths, and when we left the street that night gold was at forty-one. There was a great deal of excitement, and the evening papers had statements that the government was interested, and that there was a sharp, quick corner in gold, and that the government would not sell. During this time Boutwell had come on and the 'bears' got up a dinner for him—one of those self-admiration dinners. They told Boutwell that he was the greatest financier on the face of the earth, and if he would only tell them what he was going to do they would fish a big thing out of the sea. But Boutwell kept a very close mouth. He did not know where he stood, and therefore not knowing where his position was he thought he had better keep still. I do not think that they got anything out of Mr. Boutwell. But now it seems that after this dinner there was a sort of flurry in the ranks, some not liking his declaration that in case he was cornered he would not sell. The other party stood it out, and at about four in the afternoon of Thursday, they started into cover and put the gold up to forty-one, together with what little help we gave them. Mr. Belden, who was then of the firm of William Belden—who had a brother-in-law of mine in partnership with him, and with whom we had more or less business—had seen so much for the last week, made up his mind that we had so much gold on hand that we exactly knew our position, or else we should not be caught in such a position as we were then in. He said to me on the evening before Friday: 'Now, if you have got all this gold and you want any assistance you had better let me come in and help.' Said I, 'If you want to come in we will give you a hand in.' 'I have not got time now,' he replied. I told him we could go to the

GOLD DEALERS ON BLACK FRIDAY.

back office at Heath's in the morning. 'I will bring my broker in there, and you can give me a letter'—which he did, that letter was signed by William Belden and I understood that it gave me full unlimited authority to make purchases and sales of gold, during the day, to any extent I should deem advisable, and to report all such sales as early as possible, with the understanding that the profits arising from the operations under such order were to belong entirely to Belden; and, of course, that he would bear the loss, if any should result, from the transactions for the day.

"On Friday morning Mr. Belden brought in one Speyers, introduced us, and said to me, 'Mr. Fisk, Mr. Speyers will execute any orders of mine, any orders that you may give him,' and, turning to Speyers, said: 'When you have executed these orders you will report to me.' Gold was then one hundred and forty-three, and I said to Speyers the quicker he was there the quicker he would get some of it, as it was then a little scarce. Speyers, being one of those Roman Saxonians that belong to the 'chosen band,' snuffed the breeze, and started off to fill Belden's orders. I told Speyers I did not limit him—'now go ahead and buy your gold.' By the time Speyers had got out there gold was sixty. Speyers did not see why, if gold would go twenty or thirty in two or three minutes, it could not go to three hundred in half an hour, and so he commenced the assault on them at one hundred and sixty. Judging from what he told me he got a pretty good lead on it at that. [Laughing.] During this time

I did not know how it was going. That morning there had been an article in the *Times* in which the Administration was charged with being in league with us in putting up gold. Gould and I read it coming down town in our carriage, and we made up our minds that that article would be telegraphed to Grant and Boutwell. I looked right at it, and it made me feel weak in the knees. After you read you would study on it. We made up our minds that if it was laid on Boutwell's desk and on the table of the President, who had never speculated before this time, that they would be almighty weak; and, as I heard some ten or twenty minutes afterward, Mr. Boutwell went over to the Executive Mansion, and when he got back there was a thunder-clap struck us in the shape of a Sub-Treasury order to sell four millions of gold. I would rather take forty millions of the short gold than four of the real stuff. Speyers was meanwhile going it at sixty when the market caved right in. He, Speyers, following what he thought was the right track, kept at one hundred and sixty. I saw him next without either coat or collar. He came right through the rooms saying: 'Mine Got! mine Got! the whole thing is gone up! Mine Got! I have got sixty millions at one hundred and sixty, and it is now one hundred and forty-one!' [Fisk fairly convulsed.] In that time I had got a little disorganized, so that I was not so much interested; and I said to him, 'If you don't know anything better than to be out there buying gold at one hundred and sixty, you had better be out of it.' Speyers started, and by that time it was thirty-three. But Speyers' voice had failed, and he gave out. When we started home the thing got pretty hot. We thought we would go to a cooler clime. We started up town, and the first thing I saw on a bulletin board was, 'Queer pranks of the crazy brokers,' and so on. We did not know how it was, and of course when we got up town we knew still less. We did not know whether we were going to right or left. There never was any excitement like it. I got very bad by this time, and I said: 'I will step around and see this old villain Corbin, and see what he says about it.' I went into the house, and the old man came down. I will admit that I was pretty mad. When we got inside the door I said: 'This is a pretty piece of business you have set up to wipe us off the face of the earth.' He said he had only just heard it. I should think you might have heard it through the rumbling of the ground, I replied; after giving twenty-five thousand dollars, and drawing you a check for one hundred thousand dollars, and after you had positively assured us that your message to the President, which our messenger took, had fixed the business, to serve us in this way.' 'Well,' said he, 'my boy, how are you? How do you stand? It looks as though we were ruined, and we cannot tell anything—whether we have got it or somebody else has.' I asked him if there was anything in the thing, or if the whole performance was not of his own concoction. He stuck to his position that he had arranged everything not to sell. This was on Friday about five o'clock. I said to him, 'Now I shall be back about 7.30 o'clock, and something must be done.' Said he, 'If you think it is best to have all the gold withdrawn from the market, I will go to Washington at 7.30.' I went back and told him I should like to see Mrs. Corbin. I had several interviews with her before this. She came down, and she was precisely of the opinion of Mr. Corbin—that they had either got frightened at Washington, or that Boutwell had sold the gold without consulting the President. Mrs. Grant had written her a letter, in which she said she hoped this gold business would be over as soon as possible; that it made her husband as nervous as possible. I replied that we must get out of it as soon as possible, and that the best thing they could do would be to go to Washington and see what it all meant. Upon that they packed up on Saturday night, and telegraphed that they would breakfast at the Executive Mansion on Sunday morning, and he said that he would be back on Monday morning and let me know the whole story of the thing. Corbin went on his way, and I went mine, and (said Fisk, dramatically) that is about the beginning and the end of the gold panic on the 'black Friday of September 24th.'"

Fisk then added by way of postscript:

"The Committee seemed very anxious to obtain from me whether any government official was connected with the affair. They repeatedly put this question to me: 'Now, Mr. Fisk, will you state to the committee if any government officer was connected with you in the gold transactions in the city of New York?' 'Now,' said I, 'Mr. Chairman of the Committee, I beg to tell you that I have told you under oath here exactly in what connection I consider the government officers of this country figured with me in that gold transaction.' They were," said Fisk, "evidently trying to get out of me that no government officer was in it. Then they would make up their report that I said so. Every time they asked me the question I said, gentlemen, I have stated to you the precise position in which General Grant stood, which I have derived from Mr. and Mrs. Corbin, and that is all the information you can get. I said to the committee that I had a great desire that they should examine Mrs. Grant and Mrs. Corbin—that I demanded it."

CHAPTER IX.

REPORT OF THE COMMITTEE OF CONGRESS.

The operations of the gold ring—The full report of the committee on banking and currency—Feasting President Grant to learn his policy—A troublesome brother-in-law—The Pool—A pliant tool—A game of bluff—Men of show—Assault on the conspirators—Tremendous crash—Total rout.

IN the House of Representatives, March 1st, 1870, Mr. GARFIELD, Chairman of the Committee on Banking and Currency, made the following report:

The Committee on Banking and Currency, having been directed by a resolution of the House of Representatives, passed December 13th, 1869, "to investigate the causes that led to the unusual and extraordinary fluctuations of gold in the city of New York, from the 21st to the 27th of September, 1869," beg leave to submit the following report:

In obedience to the order of the House, the committee resolved to examine the following topics, in the order named:

First. The Gold Exchange and the Gold Exchange Bank; their history, the character of their ordinary operations, and their relations to the gold panic of September.

Second. The alleged conspiracy of September, to raise the price of gold; the persons engaged in it, and the instrumentalities made use of.

Third. Whether any officers of the national government were directly or indirectly engaged in the alleged conspiracy.

The peculiar character of the operations to be investigated, and the secrecy with which they were carried on, made it difficult for the committee to find the clue to many transactions, a knowledge of which was essential to a full understanding of the subject; and the large number of persons engaged in the movement, and the reluctance of many of them to disclose their own transactions, have protracted the investigation and swelled the volume of the testimony to an extent which the committee regret, but could not reasonably avoid.

In narrating the facts developed by the investigation, the committee have used the language of the witnesses themselves wherever it could conveniently be done, and have, in the main, followed the chronological order of events.

The history of the gold panic will itself include all the topics above named, and they need not, therefore, be treated separately. In order to exhibit the full history, it will be necessary to review briefly the movement of gold during the year previous to September last.

On the first of September, 1868, the price of gold was 145. During the autumn and winter it continued to decline, interrupted only by occasional fluctuations, till in March, 1869, it touched 130¼, (its lowest point for three years,) and continued near that rate until the middle of April, the earliest period to which the evidence taken by the committee refers. At that time, Mr. Jay Gould, President of the Erie Railroad

Company, bought seven millions of gold, and put up the price from 132 to 140. Other brokers followed his example, and by the 20th of May had put up the price to 144⅞, from which point, in spite of speculation, it continued to decline, and on the last day of July stood at 136.

The first indication of a concerted movement on the part of those who were prominent in the panic of September was an effort to secure the appointment of some person who should be subservient to their schemes, as Assistant Treasurer at New York, in place of Mr. H. H. Van Dyck, who resigned in the month of June. In this effort Mr. Gould and Mr. A. R. Corbin appear to have been closely and intimately connected. If the testimony of the witnesses is to be believed, Mr. Corbin suggested the name of his step-son-in-law, Robert B. Catherwood, and Mr. Gould joined in the suggestion. This led to an interview with Catherwood, the object of which is disclosed in his own testimony, as follows:

"I went the next day to have a conversation with Mr. Gould and Mr. Corbin, and I found that the remark was simply this: That the parties could operate in a legitimate way and make a great deal of money, and that all could be benefitted by it in a legitimate manner. I satisfied myself that I could not fill the bill."

And again:

"Mr. Gould, Mr. Corbin, myself, and some other associates, had an understanding that we would go into some operations, such as the purchase of gold, stocks, &c., and that we would share and share alike."

And, "I declined to go into this sub-treasury business."

On what grounds Mr. Catherwood declined to be a candidate does not appear.

The parties next turned their attention to General Butterfield, and, both before and after his appointment, claimed to be his supporters. Gould and Catherwood testify that Corbin claimed to have secured the appointment, though Corbin swears that he made no recommendation in the case. General Butterfield was appointed Assistant Treasurer, and entered upon the duties of that office on the first of July.

It is, however, proper to state that the committee have no evidence that Catherwood's name was ever proposed to the President or Secretary as a candidate for the position, nor that General Butterfield was in any way cognizant of the corrupt schemes which led the conspirators to desire his appointment, nor that their recommendation had any weight in securing it. In addition to these efforts, the conspirators resolved to discover, if possible, the purposes of the President and the Secretary of the Treasury in regard to sales of gold. The first attempt in this direction, as exhibited in the evidence, was made on the 15th of June, when the President was on board one of Messrs. Fisk and Gould's Fall River steamers, on his way to Boston. At nine o'clock in the evening supper was served on board, and the presence at the table of such men as Cyrus W. Field, with several leading citizens of New York and Boston, was sufficient to prevent any suspicion that this occasion was to be used for the benefit of private speculation; but the testimony of Fisk and

Gould indicates clearly the purpose they had in view. Mr. Fisk says:

"On our passage over to Boston with General Grant we endeavored to ascertain what his position in regard to finances was. We went down to supper about nine o'clock, intending while we were there to have this thing pretty thoroughly talked up, and, if possible, to relieve him from any idea of putting the price of gold down."

Mr. Gould's account is as follows:

"At this supper the question came up about the state of the country, the crops, prospects ahead, &c. The President was a listener; the other gentlemen were discussing; some were in favor of Boutwell's selling gold, and some opposed to it. After they had all interchanged views, some one asked the President what his view was. He remarked that he thought there was a certain amount of fictitiousness about the prosperity of the country, and that the bubble might as well be tapped in one way as another. We supposed, from that conversation, that the President was a contractionist. * * * His remark struck across us like a wet blanket."

It appears that these skilfully-contrived efforts elicited from the President only one remark, and this opened a gloomy prospect for the speculators; for Mr. Gould testifies that early next morning he was at the telegraph office, and found there one of his associates telegraphing to New York to sell out his stocks.

Upon their return to New York, Fisk and Gould determined to bring a great pressure upon the adminis-

tration, to prevent, if possible, a further decline in gold, which would seriously interfere with their purposes of speculation.

This was to be effected by facts and arguments presented in the name of the country and its business interests; and a financial theory was agreed upon, which, on its face, would appeal to the business interests of the country, and enlist in its support many patriotic citizens, but would, if adopted, incidentally enable the conspirators to make their speculation eminently successful. That theory was, that the business interests of the country required an advance in the price of gold; that in order to move the fall crops and secure the foreign market for our grain, it was necessary that gold should be put up to 145. According to Mr. Gould, this theory, for the benefit of American trade and commerce, was suggested by Mr. James McHenry, a prominent English financier, who furnished Mr. Gould the data with which to advocate it. This theory is exhibited very fully in the testimony of Mr. Gould and of Mr. Fisk.

The chosen instrument through whom these views were to be laid before the President was Mr. Corbin, who soon became a willing convert to the theory. The previous purchase and carrying of two millions of United States bonds by Mr. Gould for Corbin's profit may have aided in his conversion. Gould says:

"Mr. Corbin is a very shrewd old gentleman; much more far-seeing than the newspapers give him credit for. He saw at a glance the whole case, and said that he thought it was the true platform to stand on; that whatever the government could do legitimately and fairly to facilitate the exportation of breadstuffs, and procure good prices for the products of the West, they ought to do."

Having thus secured a concord of purpose to put up the price of gold for the public good, their next step was to press these views upon the President. Corbin also testifies as follows:

"I had been out of politics for a good many years, but still a remembrance remained with me; and I was now the more interested, as I had a natural desire for the success of the administration of the brother of my wife, especially during its first year. While at home Mr. Gould used to call at my house occasionally; and as I had heard that he was a Wall street operator I always improved the opportunity to talk with him. I took advantage of every occasion to impress upon him what I thought was a vital point, and that was, to let the farmers and mechanics and manufacturers have good prices for their productions."

Mr. Gould testifies:

"Corbin was anxious that I should see the President and communicate to him my view of the subject. Being connected in my railroad business with the matter of transportation, and knowing the views of those managing the other trunk lines, he thought that I knew the substance of the concentrated views of these people; and he was anxious that I should see the President and talk with him, and he made an appointment with me to do so. I went to Mr. Corbin's and was introduced to the President."

It appears from the testimony that in these interviews secured by Corbin, great care was taken to urge only the patriotic side of the question, and its relation to the great business interests of the country. Still, Mr. Corbin says that the President engaged in these conversations with reluctance, and the moment any allusion was made to the future policy of the government he became very reticent, and on one occasion reprimanded a servant for allowing Mr. Gould such ready access.

In pursuance of this system of espionage, Mr. Fisk, hearing that the President had gone to Newport, followed him. He says in his evidence:

"General Grant started to go to Newport. I then went down to see him. I had seen him before, but not feeling as thoroughly acquainted as I desired to for this purpose, I took a letter of introduction from Mr. Gould, in which it was written that there were three hundred sail of vessels on the Mediterranean from the Black Sea, with grain to supply the Liverpool market. Gold was then about 34; if it continued at that price we had very little chance of carrying forward the crop during the fall. I know that we felt very nervous about it. I talked with General Grant on the subject and endeavored as far as I could to convince him that his policy was one that would bring destruction on us all."

This visit of Mr. Fisk brought no comfort to him or his associates. On his return he found that Gould had joined with two brokers, W. S. Woodward and Arthur Kimber, and had bought a large amount of gold, but had not been able greatly to advance the price.

All their efforts had thus far failed to secure any promising prospect of a rise in gold, and Gould was still unable to induce Fisk to co-operate in his purchases.

A new scheme was started. If by any means they could make the people believe that the Treasury would not sell gold for a month or two, this belief would be almost as valuable to them as though it were true. They therefore sought by stratagem to make an impression to that effect on the public mind, through the press, and in this they came very near being successful.

On the 5th of August, the Hon. John Bigelow, editor of the New York Times, had an interview with the President, during which the financial condition and prospects of the country were discussed.

The statements in two editorial articles which appeared in the Times of August 6th and 7th were understood to represent the President's views, if they were not directly inspired by him.

On the 19th of August the President passed through New York, and immediately thereafter, the conspirators sought to use the columns of the Times for the publication of an article which should appear to be a semi-official declaration of the financial policy of the administration, but which should have the effect to raise the price of gold, and thus aid their speculation.

At the suggestion of Jay Gould, Mr. Corbin, on the 23d of August, had completed an article (the manuscript text of which, in his own handwriting, is in possession of the committee) in which it was declared to be the policy of the administration to advance the price of gold, and in which the transportation theory of Gould and Fisk was advocated. This article was headed "Grant's financial policy." It was agreed that it should be published as a leading editorial, for only in that form could the purpose of its authors be accomplished. Its publication was to be managed by Mr. Gould, and lest his personal application to the editor of the Times should carry with it a flavor of Wall street, he secured the services of Mr. James McHenry, a prominent English capitalist, and a personal friend of Mr. Bigelow, who called at the Times office and presented the article as the expression of a person in the intimate confidence of the President, and whose utterances were faithful pictures of the presidential mind. The article was put in type and double-leaded, for a leading editorial; but, on reading it over, suspicions were aroused, and the financial editor, Mr. Norvell, was sent for. He testifies:

"Not knowing where the article came from, yet, from whatever source it orignated, I suspected there might be, from the statements of the last paragraph, a sinister purpose to bull gold; so the double leads were taken out, the tail of the article stricken off, and the article, as it appears, published on the 25th. * * * * *

"The intention, I have no doubt, was that it should appear just as much semi-officially as the other article of the 6th of August, which Mr. Bigelow himself wrote after his interview with the President."

The article as it was written, and the amended article as published, appear in parallel columns in Mr. Norvell's testimony.

A comparison of the doctrines of the two will show how cunning was the fraud attempted.

Hoping still to make this article useful, Mr. Gould addressed a letter to the Secretary of the Treasury, August 30th, with the manifest purpose of drawing out a denial or admission that the article in the Times correctly reflected the intended financial policy of the administration for the next three or four months. This letter is made a part of Mr. Boutwell's testimony. The brief and formal reply of the Secretary gave Gould no clue to the purposes of the government.

About the 1st of September, and just before leaving New York, the President wrote a letter to Secretary Boutwell, who was then at his home in Massachusetts, in which the President spoke of the financial condition of the country, and suggested that it would not be wise to sell gold in such large amounts, to force down the price, while the crops were moving, as it might thus embarrass the West.

This letter was received by the Secretary on the 4th September, and though it gave no order, but left the whole subject to his discretion, yet he determined not to sell so large an amount during September as he had done in the preceding months, and telegraphed the Assistant Secretary at Washington not to sell any gold in addition to the amount required for the sinking fund.

Whether the conspirators obtained any knowledge

of this letter and telegram, the committee have been unable to determine; but on the 3d and 4th of September gold again commenced to rise rapidly, and on the 6th touched 137⅝.

All this time Gould continued to make large purchases. But, as Fisk well said, "the whole country was against them," and one after another of Gould's associates became alarmed. W. S. Woodward testifies, that he bought far more than he intended to, and that he got Gould to take all but four millions off his hands. Other brokers felt the same alarm. It was evident that the movement was wholly artificial. The confidence in United States bonds increased in Europe every day. The prospect for abundant crops was flattering.

In spite of many forced operations, the export of specie was unusually light. Gold came pouring in from all quarters, and even commenced to return from Europe. Jay Gould himself testifies:

"I did not want to buy so much gold. * * * I had to buy or else to back down and show the white feather. * * * I was forced into it by the bears selling out. They were bound to put it down. I got into the contest. And all these other fellows deserted me like rats from a ship. Kimber sold out and got short."

In Mr. Gould's efforts to force up the price of gold he seems to have left no means untried to open every avenue of information, and to buy or conciliate all possible influence and aid. He placed General Butterfield under obligation to him by a private loan, and by inviting him to join in buying a controlling share of the stock of the Tenth National Bank; and he swears, though General Butterfield denies it, that he bought and carried, during August and September, on the General's order, and for his profit, $1,500,000 of gold.

To secure the more earnest aid of Corbin, and his pretended knowledge of the views and purposes of the President, he bought, in two lots, and carried for Corbin, one and a half millions of gold. This is admitted by Corbin, and the memorandum of the purchase, dated September 2d, is a part of the evidence. On the 6th of September, Corbin received from Gould $25,000, the profits which had accrued in one week on the smaller of the two lots. These purchases were made by Gould without margins or security.

In addition to the influence thus obtained by purchase, he pretended that the President had become a convert to his theory of putting up the price of gold to aid the business of the country; and he had heard the President tell Corbin that he (the President) had countermanded Boutwell's order to sell gold during the month of September. Corbin swears that he never heard the President make such a statement, and Mr. Boutwell testifies that the President gave no order on the subject.

Such were the means employed by Gould to secure influence in his effort to depreciate the currency of the country.

With all the purchases he had made up to the middle of September, he had not been able to hold the price above 135 and 136. Deserted by Woodward and Kimber, and unsupported by his old associate, his situation grew desperate, and he once more invited Fisk to join him.

Fisk replied that the skies did not look bright; that the tendency of gold was downward; that everybody was opposed to an upward movement, and that if they should buy much the Treasury would sell.

It would appear that nothing but the scent of corruption could sharpen the appetite of Fisk for the game which his leader was pursuing. His own testimony on this point exhibits his singular depravity and the kind of influences which could move him to act in opposition to his own judgment.

He was told that Corbin had enlisted the interest of persons high in authority, that the President, Mrs. Grant, General Porter and General Butterfield were corruptly interested in the movement, and that the Secretary of the Treasury had been forbidden to sell gold. Though these declarations were wickedly false, as the evidence abundantly shows, yet the compounded villainy presented by Gould and Corbin was too tempting a bait for Fisk to resist. He joined the movement at once, and brought to its aid all the force of his magnetic and infectious enthusiasm. The malign influence which Cataline wielded over the reckless and abandoned youth of Rome finds a fitting parallel in the power which Fisk carried into Wall street, when, followed by the thugs of Erie and the debauchees of the Opera House, he swept into the gold-room and defied both the street and the Treasury. Indeed, the whole gold movement is not an unworthy copy of that great conspiracy to lay Rome in ashes and deluge its streets in blood, for the purpose of enriching those who were to apply the torch and wield the dagger.

With the great revenues of the Erie Railway Company at their command, and having converted the Tenth National Bank into a manufactory of certified checks to be used as cash at their pleasure, they terrified all opponents by the gigantic power of their combination, and amazed and dazzled the dissolute gamblers of Wall street by declaring that they had in league with them the chief officers of the national government. On this point, Mr. Hodgskin testifies:

"When they had purchased a large amount of this gold, probably thirty or forty millions, they began to circulate the rumor, or, at all events, the rumors began to be afloat—about the middle of September, as nearly as I can recollect—that the parties who, as the expression was, were manipulating the gold market, had in league with them pretty much everybody in authority in the United States, beginning with President Grant and ending with the doorkeepers of Congress. The President was reported as having a large interest, as well as every member of his cabinet, especially the Secretary of the Treasury; also, a large number of the members of Congress. There is no doubt but that these stories were set afloat by these men themselves, in order to frighten people into buying gold."

Possessed of these real and pretended powers, the conspirators soon had at their command an army of brokers, as corrupt as themselves, though less powerful and daring. They opened an account for the "pool," which they styled the national gold account, hoping thus to strengthen the pretence that officers of the national government were interested with them.

They gradually pushed the price of gold from 135½, where it stood on the morning of the 13th September, until on the evening of Wednesday, the 22d, they held it firm at 140½. Russell A. Hills, clerk for William Heath & Co., had bought seven millions for the clique. James Ellis, partner of the same firm, had bought for them $6,895,000 more, under orders to put up the price and hold it there.

Woodward testifies that he bought eighteen millions, of which ten millions were taken by Gould.

H. K. Enos testifies that he bought ten millions.

E. K. Willard testifies that he bought ten millions.

Chas. E. Quincy, of Heath and Co., testifies that he held over fourteen millions.

On the evening of Wednesday, the 22d, gold stood at 140½, and according to Fisk's testimony the conspirators held calls from fifty to sixty millions. Mr. Gould thinks it was not more than twenty-five millions, but his partner (Smith) testifies that they held from forty to fifty or fifty-five millions, in the purchase of which they had employed from fifty to sixty brokers. No better proof was needed that the natural tendency of gold was downward than the fact that it required these enormous purchases, with all the accompaniments of fraud, to hold it three cents higher than it had stood sixteen days before.

During the ten days in which these purchases were

made, the conspirators were disturbed by the movements of the Secretary of the Treasury.

About the 14th of September it became known in New York that within a few days Secretary Boutwell would pass through the city, and that he had accepted an invitation to dine at the Union League Club. It was noised about that the dinner was gotten up by parties short of gold, who expected to use the occasion to influence the Secretary in favor of increasing his sales of gold, and breaking up the supposed clique. Mr. Gould became alarmed at the confident manner in which the Secretary's intentions were spoken of, and solicitous as to what effect the bears and business men might have on the Secretary's policy.

He called on Corbin, and communicated his fears. The testimony shows that he distrusted Corbin's pretended influence. For nearly a fortnight he had called twice a day, and while studying the situation was narrowly watching Corbin's behavior. He knew that every cent of advance in the price of gold added $15,000 to Corbin's profit from the gold movement, and that this fact might explain Corbin's pretence of knowing the President's purposes, and of being able to influence them.

Corbin continued to assure Gould that there was no danger, and on the evening of the 17th of September it was agreed that the former should address a letter to the President, urging him not to interfere in the gold market by ordering or permitting sales from the Treasury. During that night Corbin wrote a long letter on the subject, which was not considered worth preserving, but was destroyed soon after it was received by the President. The testimony shows that the letter contained no reference to the private speculations of Corbin, but urged the President not to interfere in the fight then going on between the bulls and bears, nor to allow the Secretary of the Treasury to do so by any sales of gold. The letter also repeated the old arguments in regard to transportation of the crops. Its contents are exhibited in the testimony of both Corbin and Gould.

While Corbin was writing it, Gould called upon Fisk to furnish his most faithful servant to carry the letter. W. O. Chapin was designated as the messenger, and early on the following morning went to Mr. Corbin's house and received it, together with a note to General Porter. He was instructed to proceed with all possible haste, and telegraph Fisk as soon as the letter was delivered. He reached Pittsburg a little after midnight, and proceeding at once by carriage to Washington, Pennsylvania, thirty miles distant, delivered the letter to the President, and, after waiting some time, asked if there was any answer. The President told him there was no answer, and he hurried away to the nearest telegraph office and sent to Mr. Fisk this despatch: "Letters delivered all right," and then returned to New York.

Mr. Fisk appears to have interpreted the "all right" of the despatch as an answer to the doctrine of the Corbin letter, and says he proceeded in his enormous purchases upon that supposition. The relation of this letter to the whole transaction is sufficiently important to warrant a fuller statement in regard to it. The messenger Chapin, in his evidence before the committee, details with great minuteness, his part in this transaction. He says he delivered a letter addressed to General Porter in the parlor, and that a few minutes afterwards, as the President entered the porch of the house, he delivered the letter addressed to him. Chapin's testimony is as follows:

"Q. Were any words said either by the President or General Porter giving the least information as to what these letters contained?—A. No, sir; there was not.

Q. Were you informed before you left New York what the substance of the letters was?—A. No, sir; I was not. I had no knowledge of it in any way.

Q. Did you mean by your telegram to say that the President answered that the contents of the letter were all right?—A. No; I did not know anything about the contents of the letter. I meant to say that he had received the letters and read them; that they had been delivered all right.

Q. You did not, in your telegram, allude to the contents of the letters or the subject-matter of them?—A. No, nothing of the kind."

The account given of this transaction by General Porter is as follows:

"While we were stopping at Washington, Pennsylvania, the President and I were engaged one morning playing a game of croquet in the yard. I was told that there was a gentleman there who wanted to see me, and I sent him word to wait till we had finished the game. I then walked into the parlor, the President taking a seat in the porch, near the window A gentleman in the room handed me a letter, which I opened. It was to this effect:

"*New York*, (I forget the date.)

"The bearer has a letter which he desires to deliver to the President. Please afford him an opportunity of doing so. A. R. CORBIN."

"I called to the President, and he stepped into the parlor, and a letter was handed to him by this messenger. The President walked out, I think, on the stoop, reading it, and in a few minutes I walked out in another direction. The messenger was still sitting in the parlor alone. A few moments afterward the President returned, and this gentleman arose, hesitated a moment, and said: 'Any reply?' or 'Anything further?' The President said 'No answer;' and the messenger started off, got into a buggy, and drove away. I said to the President, 'Who is that man?' He said, 'I do not know. Why?' I said, 'I merely asked on account of the peculiarity of the letter of introduction which he brought to me; his name is not mentioned in it.' He said, 'Letter of introduction from whom?' I replied, 'from Mr. Corbin of New York.' He said, 'Is that messenger from New York?' I said, 'He appears to be.' He seemed quite surprised, and was silent for a few moments, and then, and in some subsequent conversation, he gave me the impression that he supposed this man was a messenger from the post office, who had merely brought the mail up. It had been customary for the postmaster himself, or one of his clerks, to bring the mail to the President, and deliver it in person.

Q. In what the President said to the messenger, did you understand that any reference was made to the contents of the letter?—A. No, sir.

Q. Is the letter which you received in existence?—A. It is not. It was an ordinary note, which I tore up a moment afterwards.

Q. Do you know whether the letter addressed to the President is in existence or not?—A. My understanding is that it is not. It was destroyed at the time.

Q. State what is the habit of the President in that respect; whether he is in the habit of destroying letters addressed to him or not.—A. He destroys a great many, all that are not of importance for the files.

Q. Do you keep his files?—A. Yes, sir.

Q. If that letter was in existence, would you have knowledge of it?—A. It would be in my custody in all probability."

This letter, which Corbin had led his co-conspirators to trust as their safeguard against interference from Mr. Boutwell, finally proved their ruin. Its effect was the very reverse of what they anticipated.

General Porter testifies:

"The letter would have been like hundreds of other letters received by the President, if it had not been for the fact that it was sent by a special messenger from New York to Washington, Pennsylvania, the messenger having to take a carriage and ride some twenty-eight miles from Pittsburg. This letter, sent in that way, urging a certain policy on the administration, taken in connection with some rumors that had got into the newspapers at that time as to Mr. Corbin's having become a great bull in gold, excited the President's suspicions and he believed that Mr. Corbin must have a pecuniary interest in those speculations; that he was not actuated simply by a desire to see a certain policy carried out for the benefit of the administration. Feeling in that way, he suggested to Mrs. Grant to say, in a letter she was writing to Mrs. Corbin, that rumors had reached her that Mr. Corbin was connected with speculators in New York, and that she hoped that if this was so he would disengage himself from them at once; that he (the President) was very much distressed at such rumors. She wrote a letter that evening, which I did not see. That, I think, was the night after the messenger arrived, and while we were still at Washington, Pennsylvania."

Both Mr. Gould and Mr. Corbin have testified in regard to this letter, and they state its contents substantially as given by General Porter.

It was received in New York on the evening of Wednesday, the 22d. Late that night Mr. Gould called at Corbin's house. Corbin disclosed the contents of the letter, and they sat down to consider its significance. Both have detailed at length in their evidence what transpired between them that night and the following morning.

This letter created the utmost alarm in the minds of both these conspirators. It showed Corbin that his duplicity was now strongly suspected, if not actually discovered, It showed Gould that he had been deceived by Corbin's representations, and that a blow from the Treasury might fall upon him at any hour.

The picture of these two men that night, as presented in the evidence, is a remarkable one. Shut up in the library, near midnight, Corbin was bending over the table and straining with dim eyes to decipher and read the contents of a letter, written in pencil, to his wife, while the great gold gambler, looking over his shoulder, caught with his sharper vision every word.

The envelope was examined, with its post-mark and date, and all the circumstances which lent significance to the document. In that interview Corbin had the advantage, for he had had time to mature a plan. He seems to have determined, by a new deception, to save his credit with the President, and at the same time reap the profit from his speculation with Mr. Gould. He represented to Gould the danger of allowing the President any reason to believe that he, Corbin, was engaged in speculation, and said he had prepared a letter to the President denying that he had any interest in the movement, direct or indirect, and said he must send the letter by the first mail, but that in order to send it it must be true. He proposed, therefore, to Gould that they should settle the purchase of a million and a half by Gould, paying to him the accrued profits, which as gold stood that night, would amount to over $100,000 in addition to the $25,000 he had already received.

Gould was unwilling either to refuse or accept the

proposition. Fearful, on the one hand, of losing his money, and on the other of incurring Corbin's hostility, he asked a delay until morning, and in the meantime enjoined and maintained secrecy in regard to the existence of the letter. The next morning they met again and concerning this interview their testimony disagrees Corbin says that Gould offered him $100,000 on account if he would remain in the pool, but swears that, by an heroic effort of virtue on his part, and urged by the entreaty of his wife, he declined the offer. Gould swears that Corbin insisted on receiving full payment and discharge. Corbin says that Gould gave him a look of deep distrust, exclaiming, "If the contents of Mrs. Grant's letter is known, I am a ruined man. Corbin promised secrecy, and the conference broke up.

Gould went from Corbin's house to the office of the Erie Railroad, still keeping Mrs. Grant's letter a secret from Fisk. Later in the day he disclosed only enough of the truth to make Fisk jointly responsible for whatever amount of money he should pay to Corbin. Of this transaction Mr. Fisk says:

"Mr. Gould says to me, 'Old Corbin feels troubled and nervous about some gold; he wants a hundred thousand dollars.' 'What do you think of it?' Said I, "If he wants that money to deal out to people, and it will help to strengthen our position in regard to this gold, we will give him one hundred or two hundred thousand.' 'Well,' said he, 'do as you please.' I went immediately and got a check for a hundred thousand dollars and gave it to Gould, who said he would give it to Corbin that night."

Mr. Gould testifies that the check was drawn but never paid to Corbin.

Mr. Fisk knew only of Corbin's nervousness, but Gould knew far more. He says that Corbin had deceived him in pretending to possess knowledge of the President's purposes, and of being in any way able to influence them. He saw the whole extent of the danger and the ruin which a Treasury sale would bring upon him. New victims were prepared and a new scheme devised to save himself.

Mr. Gould's plan appears to have been that Fisk and others should push on the work of buying and crowding up the price of gold, but that he himself would buy only enough to keep up appearances, while he was quietly and rapidly selling as large amounts as possible without exciting the suspicions of his associates. William Belden, a former partner of Fisk, became a ready tool for the accomplishment of this purpose. Bringing with him a crowd of fresh brokers, he went noisily into the street, proclaiming everywhere that gold was going up much higher, and gave unlimited orders to buy. That he might have the credit on which to base his purchases, he referred to Fisk and Smith, Gould, Martin & Co., as his principals and backers. Whether it was an afterthought to cover the retreat of the conspirators, or a device prepared in advance to enable them to repudiate their purchases, is a matter of doubt; but it appears in the evidence that Fisk held a letter from Belden, which gave him unlimited authority to purchase gold at Belden's risk, and to give any orders he chose to Belden's brokers. Belden swears he has no remembrance of this letter. Early Thursday morning Belden brought into his back office Mr. Albert Speyers and introduced him to Fisk, Gould, and Smith, telling him to take orders from Mr. Fisk, and made the undoubted impression on Speyer's mind that he was to act as broker of the whole party. Armed with this authority, and in common with many other brokers, Speyers proceeded to buy gold. His first order was "buy quickly two millions;" and a few minutes later, "continue to buy." When he hesitated he was told to go on and buy without fear. Mr. Stimson bought many millions under an order to put gold to forty-four. Many other brokers bought vast sums under similar orders. But while these tools and victims of the clique were buying, Gould himself was selling. He says of that days's business:

"My purchases were very light. I was a seller of gold that day. I purchased merely enough to make believe that I was a bull."

While Gould was quietly selling many millions, and Belden buying more millions than he knew of, Fisk spent half an hour in the gold-room, the scene of the greatest excitement, received the adulation of his satelites, and struck terror into the hearts of the bears by offering to bet any part of $50,000 that gold would sell at 200. After gloating awhile over the impending ruin which they had planned he withdrew to collect his forces for the next day's work.

Thursday afternoon gold closed at about 144, and the conspirators, flushed with apparent success, held a meeting that evening to lay plans for the next day's campaign. The operations of the gold-clearing house, which usually amount to seventy millions, had reached that day, two hundred and thirty-nine millions. The clique held calls for more than one hundred millions of gold, and as there were not more than fifteen millions of actual gold and gold certificates in New York, outside of the sub-treasury, they seemed to be masters of the situation. Every man that had bought or loaned gold owed it to them, and must buy it of them or settle at such ruinous rates as they might dictate. They had a full list of all who were short of gold, including more than two hundred and fifty prominent firms in New York, many of them leading bankers and merchants, whose legitimate business required large purchases of gold.

At that meeting it was proposed to publish this list next morning in all the city papers, stating the amount each firm was short, and how much gold the clique held, and informing the victims that if they did not settle at 160 before 3 o'clock a higher rate would be demanded.

So strongly did this shameless proposal commend itself to some of the conspirators that they sent for counsel to inquire whether there was any legal obstacle in the way. They were informed that such a course would constitute a conspiracy under the statutes of New York, and for this reason, or perhaps for fear of popular fury, the scheme was abandoned.

It was finally determined to put gold up still further and to continue the work of the previous day on a still larger scale. Early on Friday morning Fisk and Gould drove down to Wall street, reading on their way from the morning papers the unmistakable signs of the wrath in store for them. Nothing can more strikingly exhibit the artificial and unnatural character of speculation in gold than one of the answers of Mr. Fisk when asked why he feared any sale the Treasury could make, while the clique held calls for six times as much gold as there was in New York outside the sub-treasury, and much more than both the Treasury and the city could command, he answered, "Oh, our phantom gold can't stand the weight of the real stuff."

They made Heath's office their headquarters, and, with bullies standing as guards at the door and a crowd of runners at their elbows, issued the final orders for their grand assault upon the commercial community.

Belden was the man of straw, in whose name all purchases that day were to be made. Fisk was to give the orders to buy, so as to leave it to be inferred that they were for account of himself and Gould, otherwise brokers would not have executed the orders. Willard was to attend to the loans and to force the collection of all the money they could by way of margins from borrowers. Speyers, deceived and confiding, but utterly imprudent and injudicious, was to be the convenient tool to bid up the market in the gold-room.

Smith, Osborne, Dater, and Simpson, and other leading brokers of this clique, were to frighten the borrowers of gold into private settlements in their office, and Jay Gould, the guilty plotter of all these criminal proceedings, determined to betray his own associates, silent and imperturbable, by nods and whispers, directed all. He knew that day better than ever the value of silence, and as he testified to the committee:

"I had my own plans, and did not mean that anybody should say that I had opened my mouth that day, and I did not."

At nine o'clock Speyers received his first instructions. He testifies that he met Belden coming out of his office, who said:

"'Come with me to Heath's office.' He also said, 'This will be the last day of the gold-room. We have got over $110,000,000 of calls, (meaning that they had a right to call for $110,000,000 at a certain price,) and we have an immense amount of money and can buy all the gold the government dare to sell. You need not be afraid of any orders that are given you; you will be all right.' We had now reached Mr. Heath's office, (this was said on the way to Heath's office,) where I found Fisk and Gould and others. Fisk told me to buy all the gold I could get at 145, or under. *He spoke loud in the hearing of everybody.* The market price (that was before the board) was then 143¼. I then went to the gold-room and began to buy cautiously until it passed my limit of 145. Then, while I was standing there, a slip of paper was handed to me, on which was written, 'Put it to 150 at once,' signed, 'James Fisk, Jr.,' and addressed 'A. Speyers.' I continued to buy until I got it up to 150. I went back to Mr. Heath's office several times during my purchases, and reported to Messrs. Fisk and Gould, showing both of them what I had done. Fisk said, 'All right. Go back and take all what you can get at 150.'"

Again,

"I then went back to Mr. Fisk and told him what had happened, (viz., that gold had gone above 150.) He said he had heard of it, and he added: 'Go and bid gold up to 160. Take all you can get at 160. But you will be too late, for I have given orders to other brokers already to buy at 160." I then went back and bought gold until I got it up to 160. After I had bought a lot at 160, I reported again to Mr. Fisk, and he told me I should continue to buy at 160. Gold passed 160 and went up to 163½."

Before noon Speyers had purchased nearly sixty millions, and other brokers had so swelled the amount that Belden swears he has no means of knowing how much gold was bought in his name.

In the meantime Osborne, and Willard, and Smith were taking the borrowers of gold, one after another, into their private offices, and by working on their fears, and threatening them to advance the market to 200, frightened and bullied them into making private settlements at ruinous rates. At short intervals Willard, and Smith, and others, came into the office where Gould was sitting, and reported these settlements, and still Speyers was ordered to buy, buy, buy, and to not let the price go below 160.

One thing was, of course, essential to complete

success that day. The clique needed vast sums of money so as to be able to pay for the gold that parties who declined to place margins in their hands might return to them. For this Gould had made, as he thought, ample provision. He had some time before purchased a controlling interest in the Tenth National Bank, and used that institution as a convenience to certify the checks of his firm. To this bank he wrote a letter the day before the panic, guaranteeing them from loss through certifying the checks of William Heath & Co.

Russell A. Hills, clerk of Heath & Co., says:

"He told me that the Tenth National Bank had agreed to certify to an unlimited extent, day by day. A short time afterwards one of the officers of the bank came into the office of William Heath & Co., and said that it was impossible for the bank to certify, as there were three bank examiners in there to prevent it."

It is in evidence that on Thursday the bank certified checks to the amount of twenty-five millions, and on Friday, notwithstanding the presence of the examiners, certified fourteen millions more.

While this desperate work was going on in New York, its alarming and ruinous effects were reaching and paralyzing the business of the whole country and carrying terror and ruin to thousands. Business men everywhere, from Boston to San Francisco, read disaster in every new bulletin. The price of gold fluctuated so rapidly that the telegraphic indicators could not keep pace with its movement. The com-

UNITED STATES TREASURY BUILDING.

plicated mechanism of these indicators is moved by the electric current carried over telegraphic wires directly from the gold-room, and it is in evidence that in many instances these wires were melted or burned off in the efforts of operators to keep up with the news.

In the meantime two forces were preparing to strike the conspirators a blow. One was a movement led by James Brown, a Scotch banker of New York, and supported by many leading bankers and merchants. The situation of all those whose legitimate business required the purchase of gold was exceedingly critical, and the boldest of them, under the lead of Brown, joined the great crowd of speculative bears in desperate efforts to break down the conspiracy and put down the price of gold by heavy sales. The other was a movement at the national Capital.

The President returned from Pennsylvania to Washington on Thursday, the 23d, and that evening had a consultation with the Secretary of the Treasury concerning the condition of the gold market. The testimony of Mr. Boutwell shows that both the President and himself concurred in the opinion that they should, if possible, avoid any interference on the part of the government in a contest where both parties were struggling for private gain; but both agreed that if the price of gold should be forced still higher, so as to threaten a general financial panic, it would be their duty to interfere and protect the business interests of the country. The next morning the price advanced rapidly, and telegrams poured into Washington from all parts of the country, exhibiting the general alarm and urging the government to interfere and, if possible, prevent a financial crash. Soon after eleven o'clock the Secretary called at the Executive Mansion. Concerning that visit Mr. Boutwell says:

"He [the President] expressed the opinion, almost at the beginning of the conversation, that we ought to sell $5,000,000. I recollect expressing the opinion that we should sell $3,000,000, because that was the amount that I had in my mind when I left the office, and I thought it would be sufficient for the purpose. We had very little conversation beyond that. I returned almost immediately, without saying to him whether I would order the sale of $5,000,000, or of $3,000,000, or of any other sum, except that it was agreed that gold should be sold. Upon going back to my office, I came to the conclusion that I would advertise the sale of $4,000,000; and immediately upon my return to my office I dictated a dispatch, which was taken by Mr. Bartlett, my short-hand writer. The following is a copy:

"TREASURY DEPARTMENT, *September* 24, 1869.

"DANIEL BUTTERFIELD,

Assistant Treasurer U. S., New York:

"Sell four millions ($4,000,000) gold to-morrow, and buy four millions ($4,000,000) bonds.

"GEO. S. BOUTWELL,

"*Secretary Treasury.*

"Charge to Department.

"Sent 11.42 A. M."

The message was not in cipher, and there was no attempt to keep it secret. It was duplicated, and a copy sent over each of the rival lines. The one sent by the Western Union line was dated at the Treasury 11.42, Washington time, and reached General Butterfield 12.10, New York time. That sent over the Franklin line was dated at the Treasury 11.45, and was delivered to General Butterfield at 12.05 New York time. The actual time occupied in transmitting the dispatch from the Secretary to General Butterfield, including messenger travel at both ends of the line, was eight minutes, the same over each line; but in the branch office of the Western Union Company, at Washington, there was a delay of eight minutes before the operator could get control of the wire. The committee, after careful examination, found no evidence that any officers or employes of either company were unfaithful to their duty in regard to this dispatch. Its contents may have been heard in some of the telegraph offices in New York, by outside experts standing near the instruments, and thus the news may have been known in the gold-room in advance of its publication; but the evidence on that point is not conclusive. A few minutes before noon, when the excitement in the gold-room had risen to a tempest, James Brown offered to sell one million at 162; then another million at 161; and then five millions more at 160; and the market broke. About ten minutes afterwards the news came that the Treasury would sell, and the break was complete. Within the space of fifteen minutes the price fell from 160 to 133, and, in the language of one of the witnesses, half of Wall street was involved in ruin.

It was not without difficulty that the conspirators escaped from the fury of their victims and took refuge in their up-town stronghold—the office of the Erie Railroad Company.

During Thursday and Friday they had sold out, at high rates, a large part of the gold they had previously purchased, and had made many private settlements at rates ruinous to their victims. They at once repudiated all the purchases they had made through Belden, amounting to seventy millions, and it is evident that, either before or after the fact, they bought Belden's consent to this villainy.

The gold clearing-house, with its unlimited facilities for settling the accounts of gold gamblers, was suffocated under the crushing weight of its transactions, and its doors were closed.

Whatever may have been the final pecuniary results to the conspirators, it is evident that on that day Mr. Fisk, at least, supposed they had suffered enormous losses. He called on Corbin and overwhelmed him with threats and denunciations. In his evidence concerning this interview he says:

"I knew that somebody had run a saw right into us, and said I, 'This whole thing has turned out just as I told you it would, I considered the whole party a pack of cowards;' and I expected that when we came to clear our hands they would sock it right into us. I said to him, 'I don't know whether you have lied or not, and I don't know what ought to be done with you.'

He was on one side of the table weeping and wailing, and I was gnashing my teeth."

Gould seemed to have hope that Corbin might still be of some service, by going to Washington and representing to the President that the effects of the disaster on all parties might be mitigated by suspending the government's order to sell gold. Fisk joined in this proposal with but little hope, and said in regard to Corbin's going: "I thought that the further off he was the happier I should be." Two days before this Corbin had written to the President denying, in the most positive terms, that he had any interest, direct or indirect, in the gold movement, and ventured to go to Washington on Saturday night, and on Sunday attempted to talk with the President on the subject. According to his own testimony, and also that of General Porter, the President cut him short with the remark that that subject was closed up. Corbin pursued the attempt no further, and that night returned to New York. The fact that they received no dispatch on Sunday, and that the next morning further sales of government gold were ordered, showed Fisk and Gould that Corbin's mission had failed. He made no report, and the three conspirators never met again. Fisk says of this mission of Corbin's "Matters took such a turn that it was no use. It was, each man drag out his own corpse."

On Monday, the 27th, Fisk and Gould tried another method of saving what they could from the ruins of Friday. To answer the demand for settlement, made by scores of victims, they obtained from some of the courts of New York City, in a single day, twelve injunctions and judicial orders, which placed the gold-clearing house in the hands of a receiver; restrained its officers from making settlements, except on the order of the courts; restrained the officers of the Gold Exchange from enforcing against the conspirators their rules to compel settlements among its members. The committee do not consider it necessary to follow the history of the settlements further.

In reviewing the whole subject, the committee submit the following conclusions:

First. The Gold Exchange and the Gold Exchange Bank are creations of this country and this decade alone. All their operations are founded on the difference between the price of gold and of paper money. All the foreign trade of the country, and indeed all transactions where the commodity is purchased in one currency and sold in another, require a purchase, loan, or sale of gold to complete the transaction. To meet this legitimate necessity of business these institutions were organized, in 1862-63, but they soon became the instruments of reckless speculation. The prominent bankers and merchants who testified before the committee were nearly unanimous in the opinion that there was no sufficient reason for the existence of these institutions; that they were the source of measureless evils, and ought to be destroyed. The testimony of William E. Dodge, Sr., expresses the opinion of the committee and of many witnesses. He says in regard to the gold-room:

"My opinion is, that without that organization it

would have been utterly impossible to have got up that panic. In the open market no such excitement can occur. In the gold-room, gold—or, rather, the ownership of gold—changes hands at fictitious values; men of almost no capital buy and sell gold, which they do not, in reality, possess, merely for purposes of speculation. There is no legitimate business about it, and the commerce of the country is obliged to make settlements at the current rate of gold, according to the fictitious prices established by those gamblers. Unscrupulous and irresponsible men, without a hundred dollars in the world, either in gold or currency, buy and sell to the extent of millions at fictitious prices; and every merchant in the United States is at their mercy. The legitimate gold transactions are very large, but they bear no kind of proportion to the amount that changes hands in the gold-room, solely as a matter of speculation. On a return to specie payments, there would be no necessity for a gold-room or Gold Exchange Bank, in the regular course of commerce—not the least in the world; it might exist for a time as a mere gambling house, nothing else. Take the gold-room out of the way, and the commerce in gold will regulate itself. I look upon the whole thing as a gambling operation. Such transactions ought to be placed entirely outside the pale of commerce. The law ought to treat it as *gambling*, for that is what it is; gambling in the very life-blood of the nation, in the currency of the country, in which every person throughout the land is interested."

It is proper to add, that the testimony of Mr. Hodgskin gives the strongest points that have been presented in favor of these institutions.

Second. The gold conspiracy has already been so fully exhibited that but little more need be said. It is evident that the tendency of gold was downward, and that the movement of the conspirators was wholly artificial and unnatural, and that its effects were most disastrous to the legitimate business of the country. It dealt a heavy blow to our credit abroad by shaking the faith of foreign capitalists in the stability of our trade and the honesty of our people. At home its effects extended far beyond the circle of those who participated in it. One produced another, and hundreds of firms engaged in legitimate business were wholly ruined or seriously crippled. Importers of foreign goods were for many days at the mercy of the gamblers, and suffered heavy losses. For many weeks the business of the whole country was paralyzed—a vast volume of currency was drawn from the great channels of industry and held in the grasp of the conspirators. Hundreds of active, ambitious men were lured from the honest pursuit of wealth by the delusive vision of sudden fortune.

The effects of the panic are thus stated by Mr. George Opdyke:

"It produced an impression on the mercantile and financial mind, not only in this country but all over the world, that we here are a set of gamblers, and that it is not safe to enter into any contracts with us when it is possible for a small combination of speculators to monopolize one branch of our currency, the coin, which performs its functions now as it did before the suspension of specie payments, so far as our foreign trade is concerned.

The shock was so universal, not only in America but abroad, that our railroad aud other securities, which before that had been selling very freely on the continent, especially in Germany and Holland, have since found but little market abroad."

The foundations of business morality were rudely shaken, and the numerous defalcations that shortly followed are clearly traceable to the mad spirit engendered by speculation. But, however strongly we may condemn the conspirators themselves, we cannot lose sight of those causes which lie behind the actors and spring from our financial condition. The conspiracy and its baneful consequences must be set down as one of the items in the great bill of costs which the nation is paying for the support of its present financial machinery. For all purposes of internal trade gold is not money, but an article of merchandise; but for all purposes of foreign commerce it is our only currency,

So long as we have two standards of value recognized by law, which may be made to vary in respect to each other by artificial means, so long will speculation in the price of gold offer temptations too great to be resisted, and so long may capital continue to be diverted from enterprises which add to the national wealth, and be used in this reckless gambling which ruins the great majority of those who engage in it, and endangers the business of the whole country.

Not the least among the evils which grow out of the condition of our currency is the necessity which makes the national government a dealer in gold. Whether the surplus gold be hoarded or sold, it creates an artificial interference in the business of the country, and devolves upon the officers who manage it most delicate and difficult duties.

The committee find that the custom adopted by some of the national banks of certifying checks which do not represent cash deposits, and which if presented immediately cannot be paid, is a dangerous and pernicious practice, and that the use of such checks greatly aided the conspirators. It is in evidence that one bank, the Tenth National, certified thirty-nine millions of dollars checks in the course to two days, and with all its cash reserve was unable of make settlement, and only by large loans was saved from breaking.

Third. In regard to the relation of officers of the government to the gold movement, the committee find that the wicked and cunningly devised attempts of the conspirators to compromise the President of the United States or his family utterly failed.

Mr. Corbin, using the opportunities which his family relationship to the President afforded, and under that worst form of hypocrisy which puts on the guise of religion and patriotism, used all his arts to learn something from the private conversation of the President which could be made profitable to him and his co-conspirators. But with this and all the efforts of his associates, the testimony has not elicited a word or an act of the President inconsistent with that patriotism and integrity which befit the Chief Executive of the nation.

Even Mr. Gould, notwithstanding all his attempts to discover the purposes and influence the opinions of the President, testifies as follows:

"I am satisfied that the President has never had any connection, directly or indirectly, with any of these movements that have been made.

Nothing ever occurred in any of these interviews that did not impress me that the President was a very pure, high-minded man; that if he was satisfied what was the best thing, that was what he would do.

Question. By the Chairman: Was there anything said or intimated at any of these interviews to the President, or in the President's hearing, that would have led him to suppose any private purpose of speculation or gain was sought to be reached through these interviews, so far as you know?—Answer. No, sir."

The following letter to the Secretary of the Treasury exhibits both the wisdom of the President's opinions and the prudence of his conduct in reference to the gold movement:

NEW YORK CITY, *September* 12, 1869.

DEAR SIR:—I leave here for Western Pennsylvania to-morrow morning, and will not reach Washington before the middle or last of next week. Had I known before making my arrangements for starting that you would be in this city early this week, I would have remained to meet you. I am satisfied that on your arrival you will be met by the bulls and bears of Wall street, and probably by merchants, too, to induce you to sell gold, or pay the November interest in advance, on the one side, and to hold fast on the other. The fact is, a desperate struggle is now taking place and each party wants the government to help them out. I write this letter to advise you of what I think you may expect, to put you on your guard.

I think, from the lights before me, I would move on without change until the present struggle is over. If you want to write me this week, my address will be Washington, Pennsylvania. I would like to hear your experience with the factions, at all events, if they give you time to write. No doubt you will have a better chance to judge than I, for I have avoided general discussion on the subject.

Yours truly, U. S. GRANT.

Hon. GEORGE S. BOUTWELL,

Secretary of Treasury.

The message sent to Corbin, when his duplicity was first suspected, and the final order, which laid the strong hand of the government upon the conspirators and broke their power, are the most significant declarations that the President held and treated them as enemies of the credit and business of the country.

It is impossible to say whether the groundless and wicked charge that Mrs. Grant was interested in this speculation, originated with Fisk or with Corbin; and the charge is only made on the hearsay testimony of Mr. Fisk. He swears that Corbin told him that $500,000 of the gold that Gould was carrying for Corbin's account was for Mrs. Grant, and that the

$25,000 profit paid to Corbin by Gould had been forwarded to Mrs. Grant. This statement is denied by Corbin, and unsupported by Gould. The committee required Mr. Gould to produce the original check for $25,000, and required Corbin to show what use he made of it. The check was produced, and Corbin produced the account of the officers of the Bank of America, showing that immediately on the receipt of the check, Corbin paid it on a debt which he owed to the bank. Corbin swears that he never sent or promised to send any money to Mrs. Grant or to any of the President's family; and that he never proposed to give any of them any interest in this gold speculation. And Mr. Gould swears that he did not believe that any member of the President's family had any knowledge of this gold speculation.

The pretence of Mr. Fisk, that Horace Porter, private secretary of the President, was interested in this speculation is utterly groundless.

Fisk admitted that he knew nothing on the subject except what Gould and Corbin had told him. Corbin swears positively that he never proposed to Mr. Porter to take any interest in their speculation, and never told Fisk that Porter had any such interest.

Mr. Gould was asked if he knew of any officer of the government who was interested in the gold movement, and, during a long and searching examination, he not only gave no intimation that Mr. Porter was, in any way, connected with it, but his testimony makes such a conclusion impossible. Moreover, it is in evidence that Gould once proposed to buy gold for

Mr. Porter, and received from that worthy officer a prompt and merited rebuke.

In regard to General Butterfield, it appears from the evidence that, during his administration, the affairs of the sub-treasury were managed with vigor and intelligence, and all the public funds intrusted to his charge were faithfully accounted for.

It is not conclusively proved that he was interested with the conspirators in raising the price of gold; though on this point the testimony is conflicting. Mr. Gould swears positively that he bought two lots of gold for General Butterfield, amounting in all to $1,500,000, and on cross-examination details the conversation that occurred between them when the order was given. General Butterfield, under oath, denies this statement. He admits that Gould proposed to buy gold for him, but says he made no response either of assent or dissent.

Both Fisk and Gould swear that they received messages from Butterfield, and answers to messages which they sent him during the days of the panic, in reference to news from Washington, and this statement receives some support from the testimony of Robert P. Brown, a messenger of the sub-treasury. General Butterfield swears that he answered all inquiries sent to him, but sent no other messages to these men. But it is proved by the testimony that during the days of the panic two firms of brokers, not acting for the conspirators, sold gold on General Butterfield's order and for his profit, and that during his whole term of office he was dealing in United States bonds on his own account. Early in the week of the panic he sent for Joseph Seligman, a prominent broker, to come to the sub-treasury; told him he thought that the treasury would interfere, and that the price would come down, and gave him orders to sell. During the 22d, 23d, and 24th of September, while the panic was reaching its crisis, Seligman sold on this order $700,000, on which General Butterfield made a net profit of $35,000. Morton & Co. also bought bonds and sold gold for General Butterfield while he was in the sub-treasury; and other firms bought bonds for him.

The explanation of General Butterfield that the gold sold for him was not really speculation in gold, but an incident to dealing in bonds on a gold basis, does not, in the opinion of the committee, change the real nature of the transaction. And if it did, it is in evidence that his sale of gold through Seligman was made independently of the purchase of bonds, which had been bought before, and the profits on which were used as a margin for the sale of gold.

It does not appear from the testimony that General Butterfield disclosed the dispatches of the Secretary before making them public; but it is in evidence that during the last day of the panic he received important dispatches from the Secretary, and sent several to him, in which he exhibited the state of affairs in the gold market. Before the break in the market he sent the following dispatch:

FRANKLIN TELEGRAPH COMPANY,
September 24, 1869.

I am requested to represent to you condition of affairs here. Gold is 150. Much feeling and accusations of government complicity. The propositions of Weatherspoon, Duncan, Sherman & Co., and Seligman, if accepted, would relieve exchange market and be judicious. Should be done by telegraph.

DANIEL BUTTERFIELD.

GEORGE S. BOUTWELL.

The proposition referred to in this letter will be seen in the letter of Duncan, Sherman & Co., the writing of which was suggested by General Butterfield himself, and was that the government should loan gold to certain banking-houses, and thus relieve the market and bring down the price.

While giving this advice, and while holding, next to the Secretary of the Treasury, the most important financial trust confided to any officer of the United States, General Butterfield knew that whenever the price of gold was pushed down one cent by the action of the treasury, it would make him a profit of $7,000 on his sales through Seligman alone. In a letter to Secretary Boutwell, of October 22d, 1866, (which is made a part of the evidence,) General Butterfield writes as follows: "The charge that I have used my private means in speculating in gold, or authorized others to do so, is wholly false."

When asked by the committee whether he knew of any officer of the United States who was directly or indirectly interested in gold, he answered unqualifiedly in the negative. But when afterward confronted with the testimony of Joseph Seligman concerning his purchases of gold, he admitted that it was true.

In conclusion, the committee beg leave to call attention to the valuable facts and suggestions on the financial situation of the country in relation to gold and currency, as given incidentally in the testimony of Messrs. Low, Opdyke, Dodge, Schell, Vermilyra, Stewart, and Hodgskin, the consideration of which cannot properly form a part of this report.

CHAPTER X.

TAMMANY FRAUDS—MILLIONS STOLEN.

Party politics—Officeholders' Ring—Robbery of Tax-Payers—Political Jobs—The New Court House Job—The Armory Job—Millions of dollars stolen by the Tammany thieves—The Treasury of New York plundered—How it was done—Who got the money—The discovery—The exposure—Power of the Newspaper Press—Power of the People—Great Meeting of "Cooper Union" Hall—The Crash—The Doom of the Felon set on Millionnaires—Punishment of the Villains—Downfall of Tammany—Overthrow of the Corrupt Judiciary—Triumph of the People.

Political science is worthy of close study by every citizen. In a Republic, it is the duty of every citizen to make himself familiar with his own and his neighbor's rights, and to use such means as are provided under the Constitution and laws of the State, or nation, to assert and defend the rights and privileges guaranteed to him. If this were done, politics would not be regarded as a thing wholly unclean, and politicians would be respectable. Unfortunately for the just administration of our government, politics has become a vile art, polluting whatever it touches, and politicians, with few exceptions, are selfish, unprincipled men, if not thieves, robbers, and plunderers. Party organizations are maintained at great expense, not for the good of the people or the State, but solely for the purpose of promoting the interests of "party leaders," and their interests are "spoils."

People are sometimes tricked into the belief, that

they nominate and elect their officers. From President of the United States down to town or ward constable, neither nomination or election, with very rare exceptions, is the work of the people. There is in every State some "great man," who takes all the "bother" of choosing office holders out of the hands of the voters. He has his retainers in every county, and the county "leader" has his men in every town, township, ward, and borough. These are the men who always "fix things." The "great man," who usually resides at the State capital or in the chief city of the State, bargains with some citizen, who is ambitious to be governor of the State, mayor of the city, member of congress, senator, judge, prothonotary, treasurer, or constable. The "great man" promises to secure the nomination for his "villain," and the villain agrees to give all the "patronage" of the office to the "great man." The bargain is struck, and the "great man" then issues his instructions to his retainers in the several counties, and the county man, to his servants in the several election divisions and precincts. The instruction is always minute and positive. It sets forth who are to be nominated for State offices, county offices, township or town and ward offices. When the thing is fully "set up," the people are invited to go to the "primary elections" and ratify the work. Should the voters determine to repudiate the set up, their votes are either not counted at all, or they are counted on the side of the politicians. Thus nominations are made. The cry then is: Support the "regular nominee;" "don't go against the party;" "vote a straight-ticket."

Now it so happens that in this respect all political parties are alike, and the citizen, therefore, has no choice but to support the "regular nominee" of one of the two parties in the field. There is nothing gained by turning either to the right hand or to the left, and therefore the people must quietly submit to being crucified between "two thieves." The political maxim recognized by all parties is, "*To the victor belongs the spoils.*" By spoils is meant the money of the taxpayers. The party that wins has the privilege of stealing to the full extent of public endurance, whilst it retains power. The stealing is done by the "great man" and his retainers. The officeholders are their tools, sappers and miners, cat's paws, who gather in the spoils and pay them over to their masters, of course retaining for their own use as much as is allowed to them by the men who set them up. The lion's share always goes to the principals. This, of course, is simply organized robbery. What makes the matter worse is, the robbers are supported by the people; doubly supported; supported by the people's votes, and supported by the people's money. The taxpayers are required to pay the necessary expenses of the government, which is a small matter, and also to pay the expenses of these organizations of thieves, which is a great matter. The taxes of every State, county and city are more than double what they need be. Look at the army of idle, swaggering, drinking, swearing bar room politicians you are supporting! Look at the swarms of office seekers that run the party machinery in every county, waiting for their "turn to get into office!" These men are usually poor, shiftless, thriftless hangers on to the "great man" at the capital. Every year some of these are put into office, poor as "Job's turkey," and after a short term go out rich. Most of these, however, live in hope, deferred, and die disappointed.

Of those who succed in obtaining office some are able to conceal the mode of their rascality, and are thus held to be "respectable," because they are rich; others steal so bunglingly that they are detected, and their crime is exposed; these are held to be "defaulters."

This official and political plundering is carried on more boldly and to a much greater extent in large cities than in smaller towns and rural districts. In large cities there are larger sums of money handled by tax collectors, treasurers, department officers, contractors, and other public servants, and therefore the amount stolen is not so easily detected. There are also in cities greater facilities for covering up fraud. The machinery of government is more complex, and individual men are not so conspicuous as in the country. If a man becomes suddenly rich in a city, it is not an unusual occurrence, and therefore does not attract attention, nor excite suspicion. The multiplication of departments, as departments of water, gas, highways, education, police, public parks, &c., afford opportunities for conspiracies between officeholders, contractors, and ward politicians, to defraud the tax payers, that do not occur in the rural districts. Of course, the country people have in their midst little thieves who steal all they can from the public treasury, but they are closely watched and much more likely to be detected in their rascalities than are their greater prototypes in the cities.

The most magnificent achievements of this system of organized robbery have been accomplished in the city of New York. That being the largest field, is susceptible of the greatest results. Philadelphia, second in population, is also second in official robbery. The young and growing city of the West, Chicago, now just rising from the ashes of the great conflagration of 1871, had rapidly risen to the position of "the third city in America," had also developed not merely a third, but indeed a first-class system of organized plunder that made its public officers infamous in the eyes of all honest citizens. In the South, New Orleans, by far the greatest city in that part of the United States, is even greater in official fraud and municipal rascality than in anything else. Thus the list runs, from the greatest to the least, the growth of crime keeping pace with the increase of population and wealth.

These robberies are usually perpetrated in the name of what is rather indefinitely entitled the "Officeholders' Ring." This insures perpetual succession. The officeholders are, as has been seen, the mere tools of the organization of political manipulators, who put them in place; their successors are invariably chosen in advance, without consulting the people. The important question of candidacy is determined in the "club room," or in some private parlor, or committee room, and the electors are then commanded in the name of "the party" to ratify the choice, the chiefs of the officeholders' ring have made for them beforehand.

The officeholders' ring in the city of New York took a name, that has become infamous in politics.

Tammany Association.

The achievements of this association are in magnitude and character far beyond what had ever before been conceived possible in an enlightened community. Tammany included in its membership all of the leading politicians of the Democratic Party in the city. It ruled with imperious sway in all the departments of the city government, whose officers were chosen by the people. The people called upon the Legislature of the State for deliverance from the rule of this ring, and found relief in the passage of an act authorizing the appointment of certain "Commissioners" for the government of the city departments; in this way the rapacity of the Tammany chiefs was for a time repressed; finally, however, the Tammany influence became strong enough to elect a Governor of the State and a majority in both branches of the Legislature of their own. As soon as this had been accomplished, the charter of New York City was amended. By the provisions of the new charter and the acts of Assembly passed by the Tammany Legislature and signed by the Tammany Governor, the entire control of the government of the city and county of New York was placed in the hands of four persons. The Mayor, the "Commissioner of the Department of Public Works," the "President of the Department of Public Parks," and the "Controller of the Department of Finance." Of these four offices, only the Mayor was elected by the people, the other three were appointed by the Mayor. In effect, the new charter provided for the election of an autocrat to rule over both city and county. The Mayor appointed his aids, placing one at the head of each department. These appointees were responsible to the appointing power, but not responsible to the people.

The charter placed the Mayor and the Departments out of the control of Councils, and gave the Mayor a veto power over the acts of the Board of Supervisors. It was only necessary, therefore, under this new legistive jugglery, for the Tammany Ring to elect one of their tools to the office of Mayor, in order to capture the city. When once captured it could be plundered at will. The Mayor appointed the "Commissioner of the Department of Public Works," that Commissioner would have direct control of opening, altering, and repaving streets, of building docks, wharves, piers, bridges and all other public works, he could direct how the bills for such work should be made out, these bills, of course the Mayor would approve and the "Controller," another member of the same household, would order them paid. The same unique arrangement pervades all the business departments of the city. The "President of the Department of Public Parks," need have no anxiety about his bills, no matter how greatly disproportioned to the work done, they would be ap-

A. OAKEY HALL.

proved and paid. No report was made to the public of the transactions in the several departments. There was no statement of receipts and expenditures. All of the vast annual revenue, amounting to millions of dollars annually, was expended, millions more were borrowed and added to the corporation debt, which the tax payers are mortgaged to pay, but not a word was published in explanation of how these millions were used.

The department of Public Works was erecting a magnificent Court House, upon which millions of money were expended; but how, for what purpose, or to whom paid, were secrets locked up in the record of the Controller's office. Twelve regiments and detached companies of militia were provided with "armories," arms, drill rooms, officers' rooms, furniture &c., by the same Department, at an annual cost of millions of dollars, the distribution of which was equally a mystery. The Parks were also made the pretext for the consumption of vasts sums of money every year, spent, nobody outside of the ring, knew how. The Tammany Sachems were growing rich, powerful and bold. The poor had suddenly became millionnaires; thieves, gamblers and blackguards rolled in wealth; success in villany made the swindlers bold, reckless and careless. On the other side, taxes were increased every year, the public debt grew larger and larger, and the burdens of the tax payers became intolerable. Men cried aloud for deliverance. The fact of the wholesale plunder of the treasury was publicly known, but the method was a secret. The secret was in itself a fraud and an insult. It was a piece of just that sort of villany that eventually will break through all locks, bars and bolts, and display itself before all the world; this it did in the last half of the year 1871. At that time A. Oakey Hall was Mayor, Wm. M. Tweed was Commissioner of the Department of Public Works, Peter B. Sweeney was President of the Department of Public Parks, and Richard B. Connolly was Controller of the Department of Finance. These gentlemen constituted the Tammany Quartette. Tweed was President of the Tammany Association, and therefore the grand Sachem of the tribe. His will was supreme. Hall had been taken up and elected Mayor because he was deemed a convenient tool in the hands of Tweed. His predecessor John T. Hoffman, had proved himself to be so valuable a servant to Tammany, that he was promoted to the office of Governor. The election of Hoffman made Tweed the "great man," the power behind the throne, both in State and city, that acknowledged no superior and would tolerate no rival.

Tammany Frauds.

The public accounts of all financial transactions in the city are kept in the office of the Controller of the Department of Finance. In the summer of 1871, correct copies of these accounts were secretly taken from the books in the Controller's office. These copies were secured by the publisher of the *New York Times*, a newspaper of respectable standing, both as to circulation, wealth and power. On the 8th of July an account of the *Tammany Frauds* in the renting of armories for the militia in the city of New York, was published. This business came within the jurisdiction of the Department of Public Works, and was therefore immediately under the supervision of the "Boss," as Tweed was very appropriately named. Tweed had a partner in the chair making business, who was called into the service of his department, and appointed agent to rent lofts, stables, sheds, public and private halls, and other out of the way and generally useless rooms, at very low prices, and to sublet them to the city at very high prices. The agent discharged his duties so skilfully, that very soon the city held the leases for twenty-four armories, at an annual rental of $281,100. Now there were only twelve regiments and two companies in the city, so that ten of the armories were not occupied, that, however, was of small consequence to Tammany. The tax payers paid the rent, and the "Boss" and his agent made a large profit on each armory rented; the more armories the more profits. Tweed & Co. paid only $46,600 to the owners of the properties thus rented. The difference between $281,100 and $46,600 is what Tammany stole from the tax payers by this transaction; that is $234,500 a year.

These figures were derived from accounts copied from the Controller's books, and this fact was announced when they were published.

A few days later another instalment of accounts, showing what it cost to keep these armories in repair was made public. It appears from the discoveries made by explorers of the Tammany Camps, that the chiefs of the tribe retained in the public service a full corps of experienced mechanics and supple merchants. George S. Miller was the Tammany carpenter; Andrew J. Garvey, the Tammany plasterer; John M. Keyser, the Tammany plumber; James A. Smith, the Tammany carpet merchant; C. B. Boller, the Tammany furniture and cabinet maker; Archibald Hall, Jr., the Tammany painter; James H. Ingersoll may best be denominated the Tammany "whitewasher." There were in addition to these, here named, many others of smaller consequence, who did numerous small jobs in the way of work and supplies, for which they received very large prices. Between all these and the Tammany chief, Ingersoll acted as agent; the checks drawn on the city treasury in favor of the carpenters, plumbers, plasterers, cabinet makers, furniture dealers, carpet merchants, upholsterers, decorators and others passed through Ingersoll's hands, and many of them were endorsed in the name of "Ingersoll & Co."

The law of the State which governs the financial transactions with the city treasury provides, that whenever any claims against the city are presented for payment, each bill shall be made out in items, and accompanied by an affidavit, and that, after being passed by the Board of Supervisors, it shall be "examined and allowed by the Auditor, ahd approved by the Controller," before a warrant can be drawn for its payment. Under Controller CONNOLLY's administration of the finances, all these provisions were ignored.

To submit the Ring bills to the Board of Supervisors would have placed the latter in possession of facts, which would only have made them more restive and dissatisfied with the inglorious and unprofitable rôle to which the unscrupulous and insatiable Ring had assigned them. In addition to this, there was no occasion for submitting these bills to the Board of Supervisors. The new charter gives the Mayor absolute control of that Board—his single vote is sufficient to override the votes of all the other members. There is no law or ordinance which requires the publication of the proceedings of the Board, and hence the Mayor and the Clerk of the Board are at liberty to pass as many bills as they think proper, while the other members of the Board of Supervisors, and the public, are left in the dark as to the frauds that are being committed. The bills for repairs on armories, and for work on the new court house, are fixed up by INGERSOLL and the Clerk of the Board to Supervisors. Without any more formality they are handed to the County Auditor, who certifies that he has examined them and found them correct. The warrants are then drawn, signed by the Controller, Mayor, and Clerk of the Board of Supervisors, and then handed over to INGERSOLL, who acts as the go-between and divides the plunder among the thieves who are entitled to shares.

In many of the bills rendered, no attempt was made to show where the work was done, or of what character it was. The following is a fair sample of the bills presented, upon which millions of dollars were drawn from the treasury.

> *The County of New York,*
> *To A. J. Garvey, Dr.*
> *Repairs on the armories of the Seventh, Eighth, Twelfth, Fifty-fifth and Eighty-fourth Regiments........$39,835*

Garvey received a check for this sum on the 12th of March, 1870, and on the same day was paid on two other checks $19,343.82, and $32,250, without filing a scrape of a pen to show what these sums were intended to pay for.

On the same day, John H. Keyser, the Tammany plumber, drew from the treasury $60,702.32, on a bill rendered for "Plumbing in the several National Guard Armories."

These were the sort of statements, called by courtesy "bills," which were passed by the Auditor, approved by Mayor Hall, and paid by Controller Connolly.

The sums paid out on such flimsy and fraudulent pretexts during the years 1869, 1870, and 1871, were as follow:

To Ingersoll & Co.	$5,691,144 26
This included bills for furniture, carpenter, and cabinet work, carpets, shades and curtains, and fixtures for the new court house.	
To Andrew J. Garvey, for plastering, . . .	2,905,464 06
To Keyser & Co., for plumbing, ...	1,231,817 76
To about fifteen other persons and firms, for miscellaneous services, and goods furnished,	1,409,961 76
Making a grand total in three years, of . . .	$11,238,387 74

This sum was distributed in the Controller's accounts, as follows:

New court house,	$6,052,045 96
Repairs on new court house,	2,171,933 93
Armories and drill rooms,	2,940,473 70
Repairs on county buildings,	73,934 15
	$11,238,387 74

It is a liberal estimate to say that all the work and materials furnished for the new court house, at highest prices, would not cost over $500,000, yet the enormous sum of $6,052,045.96 was paid to the Tammany ring on this account. The building is still incomplete, and is under the hands of the workmen, yet the enormous sum of $2,940,473.70 is charged by carpenters, plasterers and plumber, for *repairs*. Andrew J. Garvey, the plumber, is able to figure his repair bill up to the princely sum of $1,294,684.73.

If there is anything in the familiar and matchless stories of the Arabian Nights equal to this in the way of conjuring, or calculation, it ought to be named as a precedent for Garvey's Exploits. As the case now stands, he has obtained the highest rank as a plastic artist; his works of imagination commanding a higher price than had ever been paid for the productions of any other—predecessor or cotemporary. The experience of the Tammany plasterer is one more illustration of the truth that "true genius is ever appreciated and liberally rewarded."

The Controller's books set forth among other things, a printing and advertising account, amounting to over a million and a quarter of dollars annually. In the years 1869 and 1870, the price paid for advertising, printing and stationery, was $2,582,129.91.

This bold robbery of the taxpayers in New York, amounting to about *fifteen millions of dollars* in three years, is only a small part of the infamous operations of the band of organized thieves that plunder the public treasury. Though the boundary of the city and county of New York are identical, the government offices and accounts are different and separate. The Tammany chiefs occupied the whole field. In order more effectually to cover up their contemplated frauds, the thieves invented a system of accounts admirably adapted to their purposes. To begin with, numerous devices were invented for raising funds beyond their regular revenues, arising from taxes, rents and other incomes. There was provision made for the issuing of "City Improvement Stocks," "Department of the Park Improvement Bonds," "New Court House Stocks," and "Repairs to County Officers' Buildings Stock." This of course gave a wide range for financial operations, but the Tammany managers were able to speedily occupy the entire field. "City Securities" soon became as abundant as Greenbacks.

Corresponding to all these sources of income to the Tammany treasury, were accounts opened in the Controller's office for the convenient covering up of the manner of distributing the spoils among the thieves. Thus the sums paid in the Armory swindle might be charged to the account of the "Armories and Drill Rooms," "County Liabilities," "Adjusted Claims," "County Contingencies," or "New York County

Repairs and Buildings Fund." Here, it will be seen, facilities were provided for every conceivable contingency. When it is considered that it was not necessary for the claimant to vouchsafe any information as to what services were rendered, or what material or goods were supplied, but merely to allege that it was "for work done," or for "materials furnished," the elasticity of the "Tammany system" is made fully apparent. Whenever Tweed or any of the Tammany Sachems required money to carry an election, to corrupt a judge, or to buy a legislative committee, or a legislative majority, it was only necessary to instruct the Tammany carpenter, plumber, or plasterer to render a bill "for work done" for the required amount, Mayor Hall would instantly "approve," and Controller Connolly would "draw a warrant" for the sum named, and Ingersoll would draw the money from the treasury, and deliver it to the "Boss." Whether the sum needed was $5,000, $50,000, or $500,000, the method of obtaining was the same. There was always money on hand for Tammany, but to other claimants the treasury was very generally empty. There was also a system for the depletion of the treasury adopted, which placed all the public money beyond the reach of honest creditors. Whenever a loan was negotiated, or an appropriation was made, warrants were immediately drawn for the whole amount, and the money was then drawn out on "special account" as needed. This effectually shut out all claimants not in the employ of the officeholders' ring.

During the first quarter of the year 1871, persons

having claims against the city found it impossible to collect a dollar; the invariable statement being that there was no money. The armorers of the several regiments who are paid $2 per day by the county—many of whose claims had been standing for eight or nine months—could not get a dollar. Claims of every description were held in abeyance until the "Tax Levy passed," and then until the "Board of Apportionment" had completed its labors. Yet, notwithstanding the scarcity of funds, the Ring managed to draw out nearly three millions on "Special account," while the amount drawn on account of appropriations, including the salaries of judges and court clerks and officers, the salaries of the commissioners, deputy commissioners and clerks of the tax office, and the salaries of the numerous employees of the Controller's office, was a little less than two millions. The following figures, copied literally from the books in the office of the Controller show the extent of these transactions: *Amount paid on special account for three months ending March 31st*, 1871, $2,804,207.05. *Total amount drawn on account of appropriations during the same period*, $1,807,846.49.

Here nearly three millions were paid out at a period when it was said that there was no money in the treasury. This amount was drawn in the same manner that the various amounts for repairs on armories and work on the new court house were drawn; was charged principally to county liabilities, and become a part of the permanent debt of the county.

By this organized system for plunder, over ninety

millions of dollars were annually handled by the Mayor and Controller, received and paid out in a manner that kept the taxpayers, the manufacturers, merchants and business men of New York in total ignorance of what was done with the money of which they are annually robbed.

The publication of the extracts from the Controller's books, wherein the enormity of the fraud long suspected to exist, was made plain to all the world, produced a profound sensation throughout the civilized world. The taxpayers of every great city felt that they were robbed by their officeholders every year out of a much larger sum of money than was required to defray the legitimate expenses of the government. The independent newspaper press in all parts of the United States discussed the subject of the New York frauds with unrestrained emphasis, and called on the people everywhere to rise and put down the infamous gangs of plundering officeholders that prey on the people's treasury.

The *Albany Evening Journal*, whose editor is a man of large and varied experience in public affairs, said:

"Utterly bad as was the reputation of the officeholders' ring of New York, its iniquities assume a still blacker character under this searching exposure. Its unscrupulous thieving has long been understood. But it is now presented in such distinct and unmistakable outlines, and expands into such stupendous proportions, that the friends of the ring are dumbfounded and its sharpest critics themselves surprised at the revelation. Such systematic, audacious, gigantic robbery transcends even the worst the imagination has heretofore conceived.

"The salient, startling fact of this disclosure is not the manner in which the appropriations are misapplied, flagrant as that is, but the cool, consummate villany with which millions are seized without a shadow of warrant. Large appropriations are necessarily made for the support of the government. Of these sums a great proportion is stolen by the ring. This has become a matter of course. The astonishing exposure is that the amounts thus realized constitute but an insignificant portion of the plunder. Considering that the regular appropriations have grown within a few years from ten or twelve to over twenty millions, that mine ought to satisfy the most grasping robbers. But it is a mere flea-bite. The rich vein is the 'special account,' which means the seizure of the public money without even the pretext of a lawful appropriation. It is precisely as if the ring pounced upon so much property and stole it by force. The method is to issue bonds for the amount, thus going entirely outside of the regular levy. If the ring-masters were the actual owners of all the property in New York, they could not handle it with more absolute and arbitrary power than they do now. What shadow of a limitation is there to their control, if, after spending the twenty or thirty millions of the regular levy, they may grasp thirty, forty or fifty millions more by the issue of bonds at pleasure?

"The figures themselves give the clearest conception of the work. Nearly $1,000,000 were paid nominally to keep ten armories in repair for a period of nine months. There is not an intelligent man in the State who does not know that most of this sum went into the pockets of the ring. To suppose that nearly $200,000 were spent for chairs, and nearly $500,000 for carpenter work to one man, would be to demonstrate the insanity of the believer. All of the money went into the hands of one go-between, who apportioned it according to the agreement. But this colossal theft was only a beginning. During the same period $4,000,000 were raised from bonds and paid to the same agent of the ring. To illustrate the beauty of the 'special account,' it need only be added that nearly $3,000,000 were drawn on that account, when less than $2,000,000 were drawn on account of appropriations for the same period.

"There is no answer to this absolute demonstration of robbery. The figures are taken from the books of Controller Connolly himself. The ring has studiously and cunningly plotted to cover its tracks. For two years the Controller refused, in defiance of law, to make any report whatever. And when finally he made a statement, it was a crafty effort to befog and conceal the true condition of the finances instead of making it plain. It could not, however, prevent the momentous fact from coming to light that the ring had *spent or plundered over one hundred millions in two years.* And it has not prevented this further exposure, which goes behind the report to the books, and shows up the ugly details. The revelation, in conjunction with previous exhibitions, cannot fail to have a profound effect."

The *Transcript*, one of the leading papers in New England, and published at Boston, thus views the situation after the exposure had been made. Tammany Hall, as a power in the country, never before received such blows as the *New York Times* is striking with each daily issue. The *Times* is not ambiguous in its statements. It singles out by name the prominent upholders of Tammany, and charges them with fraud and corruption to an extent which should make the voters of the worst portion of New York blush for their rulers. There is no mincing epithets or lack of directness in the charges. Mayor Hall, Controller Connolly, and Tweed's confidential partner are accused of crimes that should secure them speedy lodgment in the nearest penal institution; and what is more important, figures are published, which, if correct, establish the truth of the allegations. The disclosures appear to have paralyzed the accused. They never expected that the books, wherein the record of these fraudulent transactions is kept, would meet the public eye. They never dreamed of being confronted with such proofs of malversation in office; testimony sufficient to drive an honest official, who still retained some little regard for integrity of character, stark mad. They supposed the contents of the books would remain a secret with those involved in the criminality there described. But it happens that notes were taken of the various entries therein, which came into the possession of the conductors of the *Times*, who are doing a great service to the citizens of New York and the country at large in the exposure of such wholesale rascality and disgraceful breach of trust. The effect of the revelation will be to open the eyes of tax payers in New York to a wider extent than they have been opened heretofore. Throughout the Union it will render Tammany a thing abhorred, causing it to be regarded as an organization to be avoided as a pest. Democrats opposed to Tammany will use the exposure to annihilate its influence in the party upon which it is foisted, like the "Old Man of the Sea" upon Sinbad. Hartford Conventionism will be a popular motto by the side of the ism bearing the impress of the Tammany Ring. Tammany's touch hereafter will be political death. To destroy a Presidential candidate it will be only necessary to say that he is the favorite of Mayor Hall, Connolly, Tweed & Co.

The *Public Ledger*, published in Philadelphia closed an able article in this very emphatic language: "Thus much of the facts, then, must be taken as uncontroverted, if not admitted. The machinery peculiar to the government of New York City, its loose and profligate way of erecting and furnishing its 'new court houses and public offices,' and its management by irresponsible 'Commissions' and 'Rings,' have permitted the public treasury to be robbed in a few months, within two years, of more than $8,000,000. That is the appalling practical fact. That gives tremendous emphasis to all that has been said in this journal against the efforts to introduce the scandalous and ruinous system of gigantic 'Rings' and "Commissions,' with unlimited powers and no responsibility, into Philadelphia, as was attempted by the last two Legislatures, and in part effected. That should sound the full note of warning to the voters and tax-payers to beware of electing to office the men who were the instigators, the advocates, the organizers, and the willing tools of the audacious attempt to fasten that monstrous system on the city of Philadelphia."

It will be observed that only a very small portion of the public accounts were published, most of these concerned the " Department of Public Improvements" in the county work. This was Tweed's department; but even of his operations, not the half was told. Yet this partial exhibit—this mere fragment from the public accounts—proved conclusively the robbery of millions from the treasury. Intelligent tax-payers readily inferred the magnitude of the frauds that must be evolved if the whole of the public record could be given to the public. There had been enough set forth to establish the truth of the charge, that the public officers were an organized band of robbers, with the Mayor of the city as their official head, but of whom Tweed was absolute master.

These public servants had frequently been accused of extravagance in their administration and dishonesty in the use of the public money; they folded their arms in dignified composure and impudently inquired of the people " what are you going to do about it?" Now, however, they were alarmed. Mayor Hall, who is a journalist, a lawyer, and a politician, felt that it was necessary to "put in an answer" to the charges preferred against

WILLIAM M. TWEED.

him and his confederates. He published cards, wrote letters and printed editorials. Every effort at explanation only made matters worse. The charges were direct and specific. The answers were evasive and irrelevant. The "pleadings" were all by way of "confession and avoidance." The thieves confessed the robbery, but sought by subtrefuge to avoid their responsibility in the crime.

The people were not in a temper to be trifled with; they demanded instantly a full and complete exhibit of all the public accounts, receipts and expenditures in both county and city departments. This the ring dare not make. If the full measure of their villany had been exposed at one time, an indignant populace, made to suffer under high taxes to support the thieves, would havebeen excited by uncontrollable wrath to deeds of violence against their oppressors. "Down with the robbers!" "Tammany must be overthrown;" "Tweed must be crushed!" "Clean them out, were word forms employed on the streets and in public and private gatherings by the people, to express their hostility to their rulers. Soon the solid men began to move. They threw to the breeze a new banner, bearing a once popular but now long forgotten legend: "*Office holders to the rear; Tax payers to the front.*"

A call was published for a mass meeting of citizens, to be held in the Cooper Union Hall, to determine what action should be taken by the people to defend themselves against the insatiable rapacity of the office-holders. Appended to the call for that meeting were hundreds of names, and among these the most honorable, the wealthiest and most respectable merchants, manufacturers and professional men of every class. It was now evident that the giant had been aroused. The sovereign power of the municipality was about to assert itself, and to hurl from official stations the unworthy servants, who by organized fraud, violence and corruption, had fastened themselves upon the public treasury. No sooner was the voice of the people heard, than the miscreants skulked away, hiding from the indignant scorn of an outraged populace.

In secret, anxious, guilty consultation, the confederated thieves tremblingly asked, in portentious, broken whispers, "What—are *we*—going to do—about it? '

The citizens met for deliberation and conference. The great hall of the Cooper Union was crowded with an audience of intelligent, determined men. There was wisdom to determine, courage to resolve, and power to execute whatever was deemed necessary for public safety. It was a meeting of real indignation, passionately expressed. Men of all parties and all ages assembled under the call very early in the evening. Nearly an hour before the time appointed for the opening speech, no standing room remained in the hall. A score or two of women, chiefly Germans, were scattered through the vast room, but all the rest of the audience were men, and nineteen-twentieths of these were advanced in years—voters and property holders—were interested in the political redemption and prosperity of the city. The immense and enthusiastic audience was composed in every sense of substantial men, who came there with the purpose of giving free and full, emphatic, and unequivocal expression to sentiments long since formed, and to opinions now confirmed by the presentation of full proofs of the frauds of the Tammany leaders. There was no display of excitement, none either of impatience; and the vast audience awaited without demonstration the beginning of the proceedings. No one displayed any disposition to be riotous; indeed, the crowd of quiet, earnest men was not one into which the rioters in the employ of Tammany would care to venture. There was a rumor prevalent during the day that a large body of roughs had been ordered down from the Twenty-first Ward to interrupt the meeting, but it proved a false story, which intimidated no one. Tammany leaders understood too well the danger to them of interrupting a public meeting in which the whole city, the whole country was interested.

They broke up primary and ward meetings and conventions, and created considerable confusion in the outposts of the great political army of allied parties opposed to them; but they were too wise to assault the center of the phalanx itself. The efforts at disturbance were altogether insignificant, and resulted more from drunkenness than boldness. The Tammany leaders, indeed, were sagacious enough to order the police which they controlled to afford the fullest protection to the meeting. Large squads guarded the entrance, and displayed themselves in force formidable enough to intimidate within the building. Special or detective officers watched the entrances, and followed at the heels of every suspicious character who entered.

Strict orders were issued to seize the first man who made any interruption or uttered any dissent from the sentiments expressed from the stage.

Men of all parties—at least all parties opposed to Tammany—were in the audience, or rather audiences, for there were two meetings organized. One-third at least were revolting Tammany Germans, and a fair fraction was composed of the Young Democracy. The coalition between the three parties which desired the reformation of municipal rule, appeared to be perfected on this occasion.

Speech of Hon. W. F. Havemeyer.

Hon. W. F. Havemeyer, an old and universally respected citizen, was called to preside. He made an earnest and powerful address, and said:

Now, fellow citizens, you are aware that very grave charges have been made against the members of the City Government, of fraudulent and corrupt extravagance in the expenditure of the public moneys—that large sums have, in some cases, been paid to counterfeit demands; and in others, where either no equivalent, or a very disproportionate one, has been received, until the public has become alarmed, and is at last aroused to the necessity of instituting such a rigid investigation of the public accounts, as will, if the charges are false, dispel alarm for the future, or, if found to be true, will lead to such decided measures as to force the guilty parties to disgorge their ill gotten gains, and suffer the utmost penalty of the law for their larcenies.

These charges against the integrity of the members of our city government, have not yet been answered in a way to satisfy the community that they are false, or that they lack any of the elements to convict those implicated, of crime before any honest court or jury; and I must be here permitted to say, that, if what has been alleged against the officials, to whom I have referred, be true, the whole truth has not been told, and that the credit of the city is in imminent danger, by the acts of those whose duty it was to preserve and protect it. These statements cannot be weakened by flattering estimates of the value of the city property, which may be made by experts in real estate, as the mass of that property is needed for use, and is not open for sale, and any debt fraudulently incurred must fall back on the people to be paid by taxation.

The prosperity of this city is due solely to its natural advantages, its growth is in spite of the negligence, ignorance, and corruption of its government, and while commerce is shackled and burdened by unjust exactions from the moment it passes into our bay, and is seeking other marts; and capital, scared by the apparition of political receivers and referees, seeks the protection of a purer administration of justice, it still thrives. But a deadly disease is consuming its vitals. Official life, no longer honorable, has become a business. Offices are created not so much to reward political favorites as to purchase the aid of corrupt men to stamp out liberty in our midst The most exorbitant salaries are paid to the most incompetent officials. The charter of our city, as it now stands, is a mere act of perfidious legislation, conceived and framed to prolong the terms of bad men. Under it, and its attendant legislation, the government of this city has become an oligarchy. The right of suffrage is practically abolished. Elective offices are shorn of power, and scarcely the form of a democratic government remains to us in this city. Wealth, wrung in the shape of taxes from honest toil, flaunts itself in the public gaze in gorgeous array—in splendid equipages and in palatial residences—to attest, I suppose, the provident, unadulterated, incorruptible, and radical democracy of its possessors. To eradicate these evils will require the use of the cautery and the knife in the hands of bold, skilful, and faithful operators, rather than the quack nostrums or pretentious placebos of any literary mountebank.

This city, fellow citizens, so magnificent in extent, so liberal in its welcome and hospitality, and boundless in its charities, now calls her people to their duty in this time of her humiliation.

I confess, that I have been a long time surprised at the listlessness and apathy of the people of this city, and especially of the mechanical and laboring portion of our population, in not giving the subject, which now appears to excite some interest, earlier attention, when it must have been long patent to everybody who has the ability to think, or who lays claim to the least knowledge of his own interest, that every dollar improperly, not to say fraudulently, expended by the city government, must be paid by those who labor, in the increased rent of the buildings which shelter them, in the price of every garment which clothes their families, and of every mouthful of food they eat, and I here denounce, as all classes of our citizens should denounce, every act of prodigality or jobbing by the city government, as a robbery of labor, diminishing its comforts and dissipating its enjoyments, but, fellow citizens, having said these things before without exciting any attention, I will not detain you any longer than to add, that the remedy is with you; the city will be saved when the people deserve salvation; "eternal vigilance is the price of liberty" and security. To enjoy these privileges, you must pay the price in full to the uttermost farthing. The cross must precede the crown. "When men sleep, the enemy sows tares."

There are no special copartnerships in politics, any more than in religion, where one man furnishes the capital and the other does the work; to secure your reward in either, you must both work and pay, and whenever the body of our citizens each acting for himself, shall resolve that they will turn from the avocations of business, discard the interest and prejudices of party, and make an earnest and faithful effort to overthrow the wrongdoers, and establish a reform in the government of our city, the good results which you expect to flow from this meeting will be secured.

As the Mayor, in a recent communication to the Common Council, declared it to be due to their constituents, and to the public credit, to permit any unbiased, unexceptionable and unpartisan committee of tax-payers, so desiring, to participate in the labors of that body, in investigating the accounts of the city, there is reason to hope, that the duties of any such committee you may appoint for this purpose, will be rendered less difficult and protracted than might otherwise be expected, and I repeat, with sober and earnest emphasis, to the people of this great metropolis, and of this State, and especially to you here assembled, the question which has been derisively put to disappointed and dissatisfied inquirers for information concerning the state of your own affairs, when, I now ask you in conclusion—what are you going to do about it?

Speech of Judge Emott.

The question propounded by the president of this meeting is one that concerns the existence of free institutions in the world, and no man who has at heart the cause of liberty, or who has watched the progress of government, can feel unconcerned when the question is deliberately proposed to a community like this, whether a great city like this in which we live has a public conscience, and how that conscience can make itself felt.

Now we are confronted with the startling discovery that the debt of this city and county has increased until it has reached an amount at least exceeding $100,000,000; that it has increased $63,000,000 under the present government of the present Mayor, and within two and a half years past. But what is most amazing and what is most alarming is that this is a discovery; that this has been a secret and an unknown increase; that there exists a power to create debts, to issue bonds, to mortgage your property and my property to an unlimited amount, and neither you nor I can know to what extent that is being exercised. I believe, gentlemen, there is not an instance of civilized government of a State, city or county in the history of the civilized world where debt has ever been created, where bonds have ever been issued, without notice or knowledge to the people at the time when that debt was created. Why, gentlemen, you are lying in the power of men who can mortgage your property secretly and without limit, and you know not from day to day what burdens exist upon the fruits of your honest industry, nor when you may be called to bear them.

Taxes, gentlemen, are nothing. It is easy to deceive the people with the story of two per cent. a year. Even the enormous sums which seem to have been taken out of the public treasury to fatten certain favorite ones are comparatively insignificant when you consider them alongside of this great power of mortgaging the citizens' property without their knowledge and consent. Now, gentlemen, this city lies like a great whale stranded on the coast, and devoured piecemeal by sharks. The sharks are not many; they are a select few, but they are very voracious. The speaker fully reviewed the magnitude of the frauds as far as they had been discovered, and then proceeded:

Now, gentlemen, as your president has said, "What are you going to do?" I will tell you—we have come here to-night to express our ideas, and to direct public opinion. I tell you the world is waiting to see if the men of New York believe in honesty, or worship fraud. We must repeal this charter. We must compel the complete development of the acts of these men, and an entire publicity of every debt in the future which they make—we must limit their power to make these debts, to mortgage our property without our consent. We must remove the officers who have been guilty of such acts—we must punish the guilty. We must recover the money back to the city treasury.

If there be no law to do it, then persistently agitate, agitate, agitate, till at last you get a law. If the citizens of this great city are in earnest, they cannot be resisted; there is no power like the power of a people aroused—aroused and enkindled with the enthusiasm of a righteous wrath. We have seen it in this country, gentlemen; we have seen it in the war of the rebellion; let us see it again now.

Speech of Oswald Ottendorfer.

I hate, as much as any of you, the corruption and dishonesty that pervades, in varying proportions, the administration of public affairs everywhere, and corrupts to a considerable extent even the commercial intercourse between our people. I am fully convinced that it is by far the most alarming evil under which our political and social institutions suffer, and that our non-ability to arrest the further spread of this epidemic will finally result in the destruction of our rights and liberties and everything else, upon the possession of which an American citizen has heretofore prided himself. I am fully determined, therefore, to fight this gigantic evil, wherever it may appear, with all the energy I am capable of. But in order to do this, and to do it effectually, it is indispensably necessary that, in doing so, we do not deviate a hair's breadth from the path which duty and justice compel us to walk—that we act with deliberation and moderation—that we do not confound the effects of the evil with the true cause, the symptoms of the disease with the disease itself—that in dealing with persons we do not lose sight of the interest of which they are the representatives, and which, if it remains unaffected, would soon find other, and perhaps worse, exponents. Unless we do that, our struggle with the dragon of corruption may be fittingly compared with Don Quixote's fight against the windmills.

While, therefore, I fully share the conviction of the importance and necessity of a thorough examination of the finances of our city and county; while I concede, in point of public morals, that it is absolutely necessary that all who have been guilty of fraud in the administration of the affairs of the city, or in the discharge of the duties of their office, should not only be exposed to public condemnation by the publication of the proofs of their guilt, but also prosecuted to the extent of the law, I am nevertheless of the opinion that the full discharge of our duty in the premises calls for more than a mere cursory examination of the best means with which to accomplish these objects. Crying over spilt milk is never enough. The chief aim of all honest and well meaning citizens should now be to devise ways and means for preventing a recurrence of the deplorable condition which now exists here, and for establishing permanent institutions under which this great city may properly fulfil its mission as the metropolis of the Union.

I recognize the necessity of the existence of political party organizations, for the purpose of asserting and vindicating certain principles in the administration of public affairs; I know that party management often necessitates the choice of the lesser of two evils and acquiescence of measures of very doubtful expediency, in order not to jeopard the success of important questions of great bearing, for which the party is contending; I know that all relations are moulded and more or less influenced by, or made subject to, party politics, and that the reasons therefore can at all times be made to appear plausible. But, notwithstanding all that, and notwithstanding that I am ready to make all reasonable concessions to the necessities of party organizations, I cannot and will not concede the existence of any valid reason why our municipal affairs should be shaped, influenced, and even controlled by party politics. The only reason which can be assigned therefor is that the abuses exist, that they have existed for years, and that all attempts to remedy them have so far been in vain. This is undoubtedly true, but at the same time it should be considered that the evil consequences flowing therefrom have never appeared in as hideous and gigantic a form as they do since the disclosures were made which led to the call of this meeting. To consider it impossible to remedy an evil, the fatal effects of which are now clearly perceived, would involve the denial of the existence of good, sound common sense among the people, and if we are now to lack in energy and courage to effect a radical cure after the discovery of the roots of the disease which threatens to undermine the very foundations of our society, we might as well at once despair of our ability to govern ourselves.

To every attentive observer of the manner in which our municipal affairs have been conducted and regulated during a long series of years, it must have become clear that our city has been the foot-ball and target at which the intrigues of both political parties were aimed. The tax payers of New York had to furnish the corruption fund which kept the machines of both parties going. The citizens of New York are astonished at the enormous increase in the cost of the administration of the different departments and courts, over the great number of special enactments and their confused meanings, by which new loans were authorized and the adjustment of doubtful, aye, even fraudulent claims, ordered. I find nothing astonishing in all this.

As we were compelled, year after year, to submit our tax levy to the Legislature for approval, as we were placed under the necessity to procure legislative consent to every little measure affecting nobody outside of this municipality, it followed, as a matter of course, that the great wealth of New York attracted the vultures from all directions, and that this city was finally looked upon as a milch cow to support in opulence the leeches of corruption.

Even now, while this poor city, bleeding from a hundred wounds, lies prostrate under the burden of a debt amounting to over a hundred millions, the payment of which, together with interest thereon, must necessarily impose new and manifold burdens to be borne by the working classes out of their scanty earnings—now, that even the most heartless egotist should express regret at our pitiable situation, the intriguing politicians are already again at work to turn our misfortunes to the advantage of their party. This assurance is given by Horace Greeley, who interprets a manifest of the Chairman of the Republican State Central Committee in the following way:

" You speak of a formidable revolt within the Democratic party to overthrow the corrupt Tammany Ring, and that overtures were made to leading Republicans looking to reciprocal action, the revolting Democrats offering to support the Republican State ticket if the Republicans would unite in support of the anti-Tammany city ticket, and that the proposition was readily accepted."

Indeed, the spectacle offered by the Roman soldiers, in raffling at the foot of the cross for the clothes of the Saviour, can have been hardly more shoking than this new attempt to make the misfortunes of New York the basis of new political bargains. But so it has been, and so will it be, as long as we permit our municipal affairs to be influenced by party politics—as long as we do not emancipate the administration of our municipal government from the struggles of political parties. The idea is not new, but good. It is true that the feasibility of carrying it into practical effect has frequently been denied. But I do not concede the correctness of that denial; on the contrary, I maintain and insist that there never has been a more favorable opportunity for the realization of this constant desire on the part of the citizens of New York—the correctness of which in theory is universally acknowledged—than now offers itself.

The excitement caused by the discovery in regard to the corrupt management of our city affairs is as deep as it is wide-spread. Members of both political parties, inside and outside of the city, are in the greatest indignation, and are resolved to remedy the mischief, at any price, in an effective manner.

Now if the members of both parties, together with the city press, who really intend to abolish fraud and corruption in our city government, would declare plainly and unmistakably to the party State conventions ready to meet in the near future, that they will consider all high-sounding phrases against corruption, and all sorts of fine and flowing promises of honesty and frugality, mere clap-trap and vain humbug, and that they can only become convinced of the sincere intention of the parties to secure for the City of New York an honest and economical administration; if their State conventions pass resolutions in which the members of both branches of the Legislature to be elected next fall are distinctly pledged to authorize our citizens to design and adopt a charter that will contain all the safeguards against the occurrence of the abuses under which our city has suffered for many years, then I have no doubt that both parties, if not through a sense of justice, at least through self-interest, could be invited to grant this demand. A Legislature elected under this pledge could immediately after its organization pass an enabling act, by which the citizens of New York would be authorized to elect a constitutional convention to draw up a new charter, to be submitted at the general election of 1872, to the satisfaction of the people.

According to my judgment, this is the most practical and efficient way to free our city permanently from the abuses under which we now suffer. All other measures which look only to the removals of individuals, or by which one party is to be discomfited for the benefit of the other, or one faction for the benefit of another, would prove to be only temporary expedients. That much even is not quite sure, for it is idle to shut our eyes to the fact that corruption, fostered and kept alive by an irredeemable paper currency and the speculative mania resulting therefrom, has become a national evil, and as such has seized upon the political field as the one most propitious for its further extension. To endeavor, therefore, to uproot this universal evil by a series of partisan enactments would resemble the attempt made by Mrs. Partington to beat back the waves of the ocean with a broom. No doubt the citizens of New York, when they, unmolested by party considerations, assume the administration of our city, will not remain free from the pernicious influences of the general epidemic, and it will require constant vigilance to prevent its spread; but corruption will at least be prevented from using party policy as its principal ally, and misuses that may occur can, if the new charter provides for direct responsibility, be quickly detected and corrected; and I hope, nay, I trust, that our citizens possess sufficient intelligence and local patriotism to elevate our community to a position from which we can, with the same pride as the Roman pronounced his "*Civis Romanus sum*," proclaim, I am a citizen of New York.

Speech of Ex-Governor Salomon.

Has it not long since been the conviction of all thinking men in this community that the affairs of the city were in the hands of a few shrewd, unscrupulous, and bad men, banded and held together for a common purpose, that of public plunder? Has not corruption so tainted public affairs in this city that every connection with them has thrown a suspicion upon the character of a man, and that a very large proportion of the better element of its citizens have in consequence abstained from all such connection? Have we not seen the men whose names are now in the mouth of every one, grow immensely rich within a few years in the public service, and have we not been well satisfied long since that their riches were the ill-gotten gains of public plunder?

Yes, Mr. President, the people of New York City and elsewhere have known or been satisfied of all this and more long since, but there lacked the specific evidence of the specific fraud—the names and figures—to bring home to them the clear conception of the enormity of the fraud and corruption, the peril of their property, the public danger, and the necessity of some action to ascertain the whole truth, and of measures of protection. The good people of this city were all so busy with their own private affairs, and had contracted such pleasant habits of indolence, apathy, and horror of all that smacked of politics that they were like the good-natured but indolent rich young master, who knows very well that his cunning servant is constantly stealing and pilfering from him, but who settles down in the comfortable conviction that all servants will steal, and that it is a great deal better for his ease not to investigate things too closely, that he may avoid the trouble of a useless change, until one fine morning a watchful friend, who has often before remonstrated with him in vain upon this subject in a general way, startles him with the evidence, that his dear servant is in a fair way of ruining him by enriching himself and his relatives at his master's expense. So were the good people of this city recently startled out of their comfortable apathy by the revelations of the *New York Times.* There were the figures and the names procured and taken from the official accounts which had for years been carefully and illegally withheld from public inspection.

And what did these figures show? That with the

connivance, assistance, and probable participation of the men who for the past few years have been and are at the head of the city government, and who should have been its guardians, this city and county and its tax-payers had been most shamefully defrauded of many millions of dollars, and that consequently the city indebtedness had been most enormously increased! The specific evidence of these accounts thus made public relates particularly to the new court house and to the armories and drill rooms. Every item bears upon the face of it such an enormous overcharge as to be utterly incompatible with honesty.

I will only advert to one point, the attempt to explain away the responsibility of the precious triumvirate Hall, Connolly, and Tweed, in allowing and paying over $6,000,000 of bills while they were an interemistic Auditing Board. A law, procured by themselves, by the Ring, had, in very plain language which cannot be misunderstood by any honest man, given to these three men the power to audit all liabilities against the county of New York, previously incurred, and to pay the amount found to be due. In some incomprehensible and mysterious manner, the learned Mayor interprets this to mean that they have "ministerial" functions only as such auditors, and they forthwith proceed to pay some $6,000,000 of old accounts without scrutiny, upon the certificate of some other member or committee of the Ring! Oh, what a noble Roman trio is this; what immaculate and deserving public officers! Oh, ingenuity of interpretation, thy name is Oakey Hall!

There was, not long since, a proposition seriously made and entertained by the devoted friends of Wm. M. Tweed to erect a statue in some public place in this city of that noble citizen, to do justice and homage to his great deeds. Aye, Mr. President, let us have that statue now, by all means! But let it not be his statue alone; let it be a great public monument, cast in the most enduring metal that can be found, placed in front of the new County Court House, and representing, not the great Tweed alone, but also, all his great and worthy assistants and co-laborers. And let them be represented on this great monument as they now appear in public estimation, somewhat in the manner in which they were last week shown to us by Bellew in *Harper's Weekly;* chained together, two and two, and guarded by the city police! And let there be an inscription upon this monument so large that it must be seen and read by every passer-by, in these words, perhaps, "punishment for official corruption and the betrayal of public confidence!" Thus in emblematic form, at least, we might have justice done. Yes, justice! Where can we find it in this city and Commonwealth against these great wrongs and these great wrong-doers? That is the great question of the hour.

It was once the boast of the common law of England, which lies at the foundation of our jurisprudence, that where there was a wrong there was a remedy. We have improved upon this ancient system of jurisprudence in many respects, and have endeavored to make it answer the exigencies of modern times; but I trust and hope that we have not utterly lost its ancient and essential principles and remedies, by which such wrongs as we suffer from could be redressed, and such wrong-doers punished. Criminally and civilly the men that have committed these outrages against public faith, public property, and public law should be made responsible. And I, for one, have faith that with all their cunning and power, they can be so held and made to answer to the majesty of the law. In my humble opinion, there is but one thing necessary to bring these three men to justice and to rescue the city of New York from the great peril in which it now stands, and that one thing is the determination, the active, earnest, united will of the people of this city to accomplish it. Where there is a will there is a way.

No nobler, greater, or better cause ever appealed to an intelligent public than this cause to-day pleads at the bar of public opinion. It is not alone the money of which this community has been robbed, though that sum be millions and although this robbery endanger the public credit and private property; nay, it is something more that is here at stake. It is the question of self-government that is put in issue by these things. If now, at this time, under these developments and most grave circumstances, the people of New York city are found wanting, found incapable of redressing these wrongs, if they will still allow corruption, that has "boiled and bubbled until o'erran the stew," to triumph, then indeed will republican government be a failure here. You all know the old adage, that "eternal vigilance is the price of liberty." But, if it be too much to ask of a New York citizen to be ever vigilant, it certainly is not too much to ask that he should once in a great while show that vigilance, that interest in public matters which alone can save him and his property from certain ruin. And now is that time. Now or never will you throw off the yoke which has been placed upon your necks. Then, fellow citizens, let us be up and doing. The eye of the civilized world and of the Republican cause everywhere is upon us. Our own safety is at stake. We must not fail!

Speech of Robert B. Roosevelt.

To us Democrats, comes the charge of corruption against our rulers with a two-fold force, an especial horror. To hear that the chief officers of a Democratic city, who have been elected by a overwhelming majority of Democratic votes, some of whom have been chosen over and over again to various positions of trust, are venal and corrupt, is indeed almost incredible. And yet what is the evidence? The charges are direct, plain, and explicit; misappropriation of vast sums are alleged, time, place, and circumstance are all stated through the daily press with the utmost exactness. Pretended purchases, which are in their very nature impossible, are proved to have been paid for. The building and furnishing of our New Court House are made the pretext for the payment of bills which are not merely monstrous—they are manifestly fabulous. It is pretended that acres of plastering have been done and miles of carpeting furnished. The entire City Hall Park could have been plastered and carpeted at less expense, and no sane man can put faith in the pretence if it were made that the work charged for was really done. However, I must do our rulers the credit of saying that they make no such pretence. They have never denied the payments, they have not even asserted that the money was earned, while they have in every one of their lame defences impliedly admitted that the bills were extravagant, if not fraudulent. They have presumed to defy the public; they have tried to lay half the blame on the shoulders of Republicans, as if a burglar were to excuse himself by asserting that he was assisted by a fellow burglar, and they have stated that the charges were brought by political enemies and so not entitled to an answer, but nowhere has there been a straightforward, positive refutation—nowhere a denial even of any sort.

That they are guilty no man who has read the statements doubts for a moment, and no one believes that any such sums were actually expended on the Court House. Nevertheless I have been informed that this building, instead of costing $3,000,000 or $5,000,000, as is alleged, the latter being supposed to be the extreme limit, has actually cost over $12,000,000. To prove this I have been shown the figures purporting to have been taken from the Controller's books, but I hope I was deceived and that they were exaggerations. But of the facts distinctly alleged in the public press there can be no question; it is admitted by default that millions on millions of the public money have been paid to a few obscure individuals for which they neither did nor could have performed equivalent labor; while a little printing company of $25,000 capital has received $1,500,000 from the county alone in one year.

Nevertheless, shocking as are these accusations, they are but trivial in comparison with the real crimes of the accused. Money is, after all, a trivial affair; we are a wealthy nation, growing with immense rapidity, rolling up capital and adding to our resources daily; we can endure limitless peculations in our officials, and still survive; but they have stolen from us something dearer and more sacred than our wealth—they have stolen our rights, our liberties, our very national institutions. Such wrongs as I have enumerated would never have been submitted to by the the Democratic party had the individuals composing that party not been first deprived of the free expression of their will. These, our masters, have stolen our ballots, have falsified the will of the people, and have pulled away the very keystone of the arch of liberty.

What I am about to tell you I hardly expect you to believe; yet I will give you every point of time and circumstance. I will furnish you with every detail and all the minutiæ of the mode of operations, and, large as is this meeting, were I to call my witnesses together I could fill this building as full as it is now. I know whereof I speak, and in exposing these shameless iniquities rather in defence of Democracy than in arraignment of it, nothing extenuate and set down naught in malice. By a combination of certain Democratic and Republican officeholders in this city the votes of the people no longer express their will. They are falsified in three different ways, so that no matter how honest the mass of voters might be, the corrupt Ring would apparently be retained in power. To effect this three forces are brought into play. There is the use of repeaters at the polls, the manipulation of ballots as they are deposited, and the false counting of them in making up the canvass. Precisely how these schemes are managed I will explain to you.

Heretofore there has been a registry of all legal voters in this city. I can only speak of the past. I cannot tell what Tammany will do hereafter, and now that this registry law has been repealed we may be sure that matters will not be improved. There were three registers to supervise these lists, three inspectors to receive the votes, and three canvassers to count them. One of each of these boards was a Republican, and could stop all frauds if he pleased, but as the parties to be defeated were only those Democrats who were opposed to Tammany he shut his eyes with resolute determination. To begin with, gangs of repeaters were organized whose first duty was to have their names recorded in as many districts as possible, usually from a dozen to fifty; and it was curious with what childlike innocence the Republican register would receive the names of one hundred men who assumed to reside at the private dwelling of some leading Tammany Ward politician, and who pretended to camp out on some vacant lot. The repeaters are enrolled, and I have had lists of them offered to me for sale at so much a vote when Tammany did not need them.

On election day these men went to the polls in gangs, with their captains, and marched from district to district like companies of soldiers. If one of them was challenged, the result depended upon the locality; in a disreputable neighborhood, the challenger was knocked into the gutter, and probably locked up by the police for disturbing the polls. In a district where this would not answer, the accused was taken before the police magistrate, who sat all day to hear just such cases, and who let him out at once on bail, the necessary bail being also on hand for the purpose, and the repeater was usually back at the polls, and hard at work, before the challenger, and no one ever heard of such a case being brought to trial afterward.

In another way were these repeaters used. Many people, especially wealthy Republicans, do not vote. It is the duty of every man to vote; this is one of the obligations he assumes in demanding liberty, and, rather than have the duty neglected, Tammany sees that it is performed. Toward the latter part of the day it will be found that certain persons who are registered have not voted, and it then belongs to the polling officers to copy such names on slips and pass them to the proper parties outside; and it would horrify if not amuse some of our wealthy millionnaires to see what ragged-clothed, bloated-faced, and disreputable individuals represented them at the polls, and performed for them a public duty which they had neglected. This is repeating. I have given you but a hurried sketch of it; the votes polled by it count up by tens of thousands. But successful as it was, it had its defects. The repeaters began to imagine they were the masters; they thought they held the power because they were the instruments of power. To use a political slang term, they undertook to set up shop for themselves. Still repeating, when kept in its place, is not disapproved by our Ring rulers.

The manipulation of the ballots—"Ringing" the ballots, as it is appropriately called—is a very beautiful operation, and is said by those who have tried it to be perfect. It is now the favorite plan; it is simple, inexpensive and effective. When one of you good, innocent Republicans, we will suppose, is going to the polls to vote the wrong ticket or support the wrong man, as you are so fond of doing, your unwise intentions are quietly frustrated. The inspector holds in his hand the ballot you ought to deposit, and when he receives yours, quietly substitutes one for the other, and drops yours on the floor before he puts his in the box. This is a simple slight-of-hand trick, easily learned and readily applied. If, however, you are suspicious, and watch the official, if the latter is awkward and inexperienced, a man near by pushes against you or the policeman seizes you and accuses you of having voted before. Of course ample apologies are immediately tendered for the rudeness, the inspectors are indignant that so respectable a gentleman should be insulted, they abuse the rough or the policeman, you are shown out with great respect; but your ballot went down on the floor and the substitute got into the box. Repeating is expensive, false counting is troublesome, our Tammany men are not experts at arithmetic, and figures are often troublesome, as our amiable Controller will admit at this moment; but "Ringing" ballots is a complete success. It is only necessary to buy a Republican inspector, and a small place or a few hundred dollars will usually do that.

The third plan is false counting. This is done generally by transferring the figures bodily. For instance, if Jones, the Tammany candidate, gets one hundred votes, and Smith, the opposition candidate, receives two hundred, the two hundred of Smith are transferred to Jones, who gives his one hundred to Smith. This is an exquisitely simple process, but in practice it is said to work badly, and great complaint is made of it by those who have tried it. In the first place, the candidates are often too nearly equal to give Tammany its just preponderance or to overcome some persistent opposition in a district where this plan cannot be worked, for it is found utterly impracticable in some districts. Its defects can sometimes be cured by a false count. That is to say, the votes are counted by tens, one canvasser taking them up and counting ten, when he calls "tally," and slips a piece of elastic around the bundle. Of course he has only to take five votes instead of ten, and call "tally," to augment greatly the chances of his favorite. In one instance this was done so enthusiastically that the Tammany candidate had received fifty "tallies," or five hundred votes, and had a large quantity yet uncounted, when the poll-clerk felt it advisable to inform the canvassers that there were only four hundred and fifty names on the registry.

Between these three schemes the voice of the people of New York has been utterly stifled up till last Fall, when, by the "cruel and tyrannical interference of the United States Government, under the vile bayonet election law," we got a fair vote. The wrong was not so much due to Republicans, for the inspectors saw that comparative justice was secured to their party on general issues, but was allowed full scope against opposition Democrats—Democrats who believed in a pure government, and were opposed to Tammany Hall. Thus it is that Democrats have to bear the entire odium of the misrule of our city, while we Democrats still believe our party to be the honest one.

This odium we cannot endure. I speak as a Democrat to Democrats. If we would see a chance of carrying the next Presidential election, of taking the nation from the hands of those who, in our opinion, are unfit to have control of it, or restoring to general acceptation the principles we have at heart, we must vindicate our party; we must remove the load of disgrace brought on us by official corruptions in this city. Here we are in control. We have undisturbed possession of all branches of the municipal government, and an immense majority of the voters. For all frauds, peculations, venality, and iniquity in the municipal government we are responsible, and no party with such a record will ever be given the possession of the National Administration. We must crush Tammany or Tammany's dishonesty will crush us. Large portions of the money stolen from our treasury were used to bribe Republicans; notoriously the very charter under which we live was carried by the purchase of a Republican. Municipal offices and the spoil of our citizens have been divided between both parties. But none of this excuses us. We are in power; we can correct the abuses; if we do not, we ought to suffer, and we will. If Republicans are guilty, we are not blameless. Already we are threatened with the loss of the German. That economical people will not submit to have their houses mortgaged by the issue of municipal bonds in order to give to corrupt men wealth and luxury. From all sections of the country come complaints from the Democrats that they have to defend the iniquities of Tammany Hall, and that they are beaten by the bad record of our city rulers. If Democracy would survive, it must put down with a strong hand these abuses. We can still do so. The people are not so entirely helpless as our masters would have us believe. They cannot defy an outraged and indignant community with the impunity they hope. The power is still with us if we are willing and determined to exert it. In times of great excitement the usual barriers are swept away, and the people rush along in a mighty current which carries all before it. Those who would resist it are overwhelmed and perish, but the corrupt always cower before it and are most earnest to conciliate it. So will it be here. Canvassers, inspectors, and registers, be they Democrats or Republicans, are as fond of their lives as though they were honest men; and no one appreciates the danger of irritating the people more than they. An aroused and outraged public is not patient, and Judge Ledwith laid down good law when he told his friends that if they saw an inspector tamper with their ballots they could shoot him on the spot. The man who cheats a nation out of its birthright has committed the highest of crimes, and deserves no mercy. We are living under a wrong system. To allow a Mayor, elected for two years, to appoint all other municipal officials for five years may be Tammany Democracy, but it is not ours. That system must be changed; a proper mode of selecting polling officers must be established; every protection must be given to the ballot, and, incidentally, to these reforms; the Ring which has secured control of Tammany Hall must be put down, and then not only will our city's fame be redeemed, our taxes lightened, our business affairs improved, our commerce increased, and our metropolis made what it should be, the grandest city in the world; but Democracy and Republican institutions will be relieved from the discredit which has been brought upon them.

Speech of Judge Pierpont.

In this vast concourse of my fellow citizens, is there any one here who does not wish an honest Government? Is any one here who believes that the Government of the City is honest? The public journals upon which we are accustomed to rely tell us that the City is in the hands of knaves; and they charge specific facts as proof of the assertion. They tell us that a few men, whom you have intrusted with the sacred functions of official power, are robbing you; that these men, from recent penury, have become enormously rich, living in princely splendor and wanton luxury. Are these things false? Then why do the fearful statements go unchallenged and unpunished? Show us the accounts which are unlawfully concealed—they will refute these charges if false. Produce the accounts, you who are charged with the grossest frauds. The law requires them to be published. Why have you concealed them so long? Why do you conceal them now? Why do you not deny the specific charges of the specific bills, and produce the accounts to prove the charges false? Are these things true? Then who so very a coward that he dare not speak his honest mind on the side of right? How happens it that these official men have grown so vastly rich? By what magic power were their sudden millions made? Not out of their salaries sure! It is given out, through simple dupes, that these vast fortunes came of "investments in real estate!" This is all a cheat; the records have been searched, and they prove that your rulers have not realized any considerable sums by the sale of real estate. That pretext is as false as the fraudulent bills they paid. On the 1st day of January, 1869, the debt of the City and County of New York was $34,407,-047.91. Between that date and July 31st, 1871, the treasury received from taxes and other sources $72,-457,112.11. Enough, you will say, to have carried on the Government honestly, and to have paid off the debt. But the Controller reports the astounding fact that on the 31st of July last the debt was $100,955,-383.33. Thus by an increase of $66,548,335.42 in the debt, and from $72,457,112.11 of the revenue, your rulers have paid out $139,005,447.53 in two years and seven months! So much is known; when the unknown is explored, we shall see what it will reveal. What has been done with this money? Why have the city officers concealed the accounts of these years, in direct violation of law and of former usage? We begin to see why. Certain fraudulent bills getting before the public, have made us cease to wonder why the accounts have been unlawfully suppressed.

The charges are public, specific, long-made, reiterated, and not denied, and all can see that the city is plundered, and that the toil, and labor, and self-denial, and industry of the people avail them not, because they are deprived of their honest gains, which go to enrich a few. Men laughed a hollow laugh, and smiled a false smile, and shrugged their coward shoulders for a time as these things were told. They have ceased to smile, and begin to look sober. They ask, "Where is this to end? Will it not bring riot, anarchy, bloodshed, and loss of property?" Yes, all this; and the day is not very distant. The American people are patient, law-abiding; they love peace, and industry, and thrift. But they have a deep sense of justice, with a strong love of property, and they will fight for their rights; and when they once begin they do that kind of work so thoroughly that war for the same object never comes but once. People have to meet occasionally to learn the "time of day;" and often surprised, they find that the dial hands on the great horologue of time have moved onward. They found in England once that the clock struck the hour when old Cromwell was to cut off the head of a tyrant King, and put an end to the impious mockery about "Divine right." They did not expect all this! A little further on, and Kings and Queen, and nobles, and the divinities which hedged them about, passed under the guillotine and perished forever. Not long ago we "took the time o'day," and found that the hour had come when the horrid hydra, slavery, was to die. He died hard, and crushed in his expiring folds three hundred thousand of our youth; but he died. He will never live again. The frauds and corruptions in our city government seem to be conceded, and we are insolently asked, "What are you going to do about it?" Great wrongs are always insolent, just before they die. In the Senate of the United States a Massachusetts Senator said that slavery was a great wrong. "Well," replied a slave Senator, with great arrogance, "What are you going to do about it? I will call the roll of my slaves on Bunker Hill." Not long after, that Senator heard the roll-call of Massachusetts soldiery in the citadel of Charleston, and his slaves were free? What are we going to do about it? That is the question upon which I propose to speak to-night. I have very definite views upon that subject, and I shall leave it to my fellow citizens to judge whether the views are sound or not.

Out of this million of people there are but few who participate in, or who profit by, these frauds. All who do not share in the plunder are injured by the robbery. There is but just so much of property in the city, and just every dollar which your rulers have wrongfully taken you have unjustly lost. Every laborer must have some roof for his family. If the house is taxed $200 when it ought to pay but $100, this extra $100 is first paid as rent to the landlord, who is obliged to pay it over to the fraudulent tax fund, and thus the poor man is robbed to enrich those who are his rulers. Or the laborer owns a little farm charged with a tax of $200, which ought to be but $100. He is defrauded of his $100 all the same. It makes not the least difference whether it is paid in rent or in tax, it comes from the laborer's toil and goes to the same foul pool. You cannot escape by hiring, for the rent must, in great measure, be governed by the tax.

Invest $10,000 in a house, the annual interest is $700, the insurance and repairs $150, requiring a rent of $850 to save the owner whole. Now, whatever tax is added must come from the tenant, or no man will build a house to let. It is the occupier of the house who suffers from the fraudulent tax, whether he occupy as tenant or as owner. Tenants of this great city—numbered by hundreds of thousands—the landlords will gladly abate from your rent every dollar which the tax-gatherer will deduct from the tax. The owner derives no benefit from the tax which he collects from you in the shape of rent. He is but the unwilling agent, compelled by law to pay it over into the tax office, where the larger part is distributed among a very few of the public defrauders; and thus the substance of your business and your labor is taken from you.

A few years ago our complaint was that no one was responsible in the city government. We now know who is responsible—no mistake about that. The power and the responsibility are in the same hands, and we know the heads which move the hands.

Not ten in two hundred thousand of our citizens profit by these frauds—the vast multitude are fast impoverished by them. Have we no remedy? Are five hundred thousand citizens to be plundered by a handful of dishonest men, who have no army at their back, not even the Governor of the State, nor the sentiment of their own political party, to sustain them? But the question recurs—"What can you do about it?" If your neighbor takes from you fifty thousand dollars by fraud, have you any doubt that you can recover it back? If your city officers appropriate to their own use, or to any fraudulent use, the funds of the city, have you any doubt that the money can be recovered back? Yes, every dollar of it. But I hear loud whispers that the judges cannot be trusted. I deny the charge. I have as good an opportunity to know as most men; and I here pledge, that if the Governor will order suits to be brought to recover back the public money which has been fraudulently appropriated, the judges of this district will be swift to aid in any such recovery; and that, in any legal proceeding instituted to protect the city, the judges will do their duty to the uttermost. I speak advisedly, knowing whereof I speak. Let a committee of citizens whom you can trust be appointed; let them be taken from each political party; let them take up these charges and if found true, let them wait upon the Governor and Attorney General; and if the Governor acts, all well; if he refuses to act, report back his refusal to the assembled people, and then take such measures as the emergency may require. Perhaps we shall then be ready for an argument a little rude; if so, we shall make the argument. Do you suppose, if the officers of this city are stealing its funds, that the Governor cannot find means to arrest the theft and suspend the fraudulent officers from power? The way is plain if the will goes with it, and only difficult when the will is wanting. The Governor knew how to revoke the orders of the city officers on the 12th of July, and he will be made to see what he can do now in a time of great peril to the city. But that is a small part of what we need to do.

We must look to the Legislature for Relief.

We must look to the Legislature. There lies the radical and permanent relief, and to that I direct your chiefest attention. Their power is ample. Be not diverted by doctrinaires and metaphysicians who demonstrated that a State could not be coerced, that the rebellion could not be put down, and that slavery was eternal; we have done with that kind of nonsense. In the Legislature there is every necessary power to correct the evil. Let each party vie with the other in selecting honest men for the Legislature, who will go against corruption. The next Legislature will be against corruption. The time has come, dishonest rulers, betrayers of the trust reposed in you by a trusting people, plunderers of a treasury which you should have defended with your lives; will you show those accounts? We shall get at them. "The wicked shall not always rule." The time has come, you may be sure of that. A new Senate is also to be chosen. It lasts for two years. It will vote upon the next United States Senator. It will not be a Senate of corruption. But few voters have profited by corruption, and the voters are tired of being the slaves of corrupt masters. Remember that we elect by districts, and not by general ticket, and if they count up a hundred thousand of fraudulent votes it will do them no good. Corruption is doomed. By the next Legislature it will be destroyed.

The idea has been thrown out and circulated in other States that these great frauds have been perpetuated for the purpose of raising a Presidential fund for Democratic use. No truth in this whatever. The Democratic party will never see a dollar of this money—it has already been divided, and those who have it care no more for the future of the Democratic party than they do for the laboring voters whom they plunder and deceive.

Let all or every party in favor of good government

join to secure an honest Legislature, and then we begin the reform in earnest. But some very far-seeing, doubting citizen says, "But suppose the Governor won't act; suppose you don't secure the Legislature; suppose the corruptionists buy up enough of the members to destroy the anticipated good; then what are you going to do?" Well, that is a fair enough question, only it is a little permature. I would rather wait until the Governor acts or refuses to act; until the Legislature is lost or corrupted. But you will agree with me that these frauds upon the people are a fearful evil, and that they ought to be redressed. I have pointed out to you the peaceful ways to right these wrongs. But if these ways will not do, and if, emboldened by success, yet new men come into the field of fraud to plunder you still more, as they surely will, then I need not tell the other way. You will hear it in the yells of an infuriated mob, in the fire and rapine and slaughter, in the noise of musketry and of cannon. Order will be restored, but some despot will put his iron heel upon a people too sordid, too corrupt, too craven for liberty!

These extracts from the speeches delivered by some of the ablest and wisest citizens of New York, clearly set forth both the situation of the public affairs and the means proposed by the citizens to overthrow the corrupt power of the city rulers. General John A. Dix who was unable to attend the meeting wrote as follows:

"It is not in my power to attend the meeting this

evening, in reference to the financial condition of the city, but the movement has my cordial concurrence. The disclosures which have been made show that the municipal treasury has been plundered to an extent and in a manner unparalleled in the history of popular government. Such a perversion and currupt use of powers would, under a despotic system, lead to revolution, and would justify revolution under any system which should be found not to contain within itself the means of redress. It is a duty above all party considerations to probe the iniquity to the core. No intelligent man can doubt, and no fair man will deny, that millions have been fraudulently paid out of the treasury, and if individuals belonging to both the great political parties shall be found to have participated in the frauds, each should be more anxious than the other to expose and renounce the unworthy followers who have dishonored it. The wrong to be redressed is not to the tax payers alone, whose contributions, wrung years ago from the earnings and hard industry, are thus squandered; there is a wrong to the city as a corporation, by impairing and threatening to destroy its credit. It is vain to point to the value of our parks and public buildings as ample security for the payment of our debts, unless capitalists have further assurance that the city government is honest and prudent. No man will lend money unless he has confidence in the integrity of the borrower. There is a further and a deeper wrong to popular government which cannot be upheld for any length of time, if such frauds can be perpetrated with impunity. Free institutions do not always secure perfect purity of administration, but if they shall be found not to have the sufficient force of protecting those who live under them from plunder, one of the chief motives for maintaining them will be lost. If, in this contest against venality and public abuse, any co-operation which it is in my power to lend will be of any value, it shall be freely given, as a duty which every good citizen owes to his country and to himself."

Among the resolutions adopted, there was one which put into form the sense of the meeting, and provided for systematic work on the part of the citizens against the officeholders. It provided that "an Executive Committee of seventy members be appointed by the President of this meeting, whose duty will be to take such measures as shall be necessary or expedient to carry out the objects for which we are assembled; to demand a full exhibition of all the accounts of the city and county, and an explicit statement of all the persons to whom and the pretences upon which the large payments of the past two years and a half have been made; to enforce any remedies which now exist to obtain this information if it is refused, and to recover whatever sums of money have been fraudulently or feloniously abstracted; and also to press upon the Legislature and the Governor of the State such measures of legislation and action as may be necessary or proper to enforce the existing laws, and to supply their defects, and to remove the causes of the present abuses, and finally, to assist, sustain and direct a united effort by the citizens of New York, without reference to party, to obtain a good government and honest officers to administer it. And the said committee are hereby authorized to call upon all citizens interested in good government to contribute such funds as may be needed to execute the powers intrusted to them, and also to fill vacancies and add to their number."

This committee, which was known as the "Committee of Seventy," met, organized and determined on a plan of action. Meanwhile a citizen petitioned the court, and obtained an injunction against Tweed, Hall, Connolly and Sweeney, restraining them from using the public money and from the payment of all bills except wages to the laboring men employed on the public works.

As soon as the Committee of Seventy had fully matured a line of policy, suits were instituted against all the "Tammany chiefs in office." Warrants were issued for the arrest of the four members of the "great quartette." Hall and Sweeney gave bonds promptly and were released on bail. Tweed skulked about the city, from one hiding place to another to avoid arrest; after weeks of misery, fear and exile he finally surrendered himself to the sheriff, and finally succeeded in giving the required bonds for his appearance. Poor Connolly, "Slippery Dick," was lodged in jail and held there several weeks, when his friends also succeeded in procuring his release.

The "grand inquest for the county of New York found true bills" against all of the accused office-holders and returned them to be tried before juries of

THE CORRUPT JUDICIARY.

the citizens they have so greatly outraged and voraciously robbed. They were forced to resign their offices, and successors were appointed by the Committee of Seventy. Thus Tammany was completely and utterly overthrown. The question only a few months previously so insultingly propounded by "Boss" Tweed, "What are you going to do about it?" was triumphantly answered by the people.

As soon as this work had been accomplished, the committee next gave its attention to the corrupt judiciary; the basest, vilest, most abominable of all Tammany tools. The "New York Bench," from the Supreme Court down to the office of Police Magistrate, had fallen so completely under the control of Tammany and Erie, that all applications for relief or protection from the wrong inflicted or sought to be inflicted by the members, associates or servants of these rings were invariably refused. It was the sheerest folly in any one to appeal to the courts for protection or relief when the wrong was perpetrated by the minions of Tweed or Fisk. They owned the courts, and the judges dare not do aught against their masters. When an appeal was taken to the court of last resort—the high court of the people—all the cases were reviewed. The thieves, robbers, plunderers and murderers were brought to punishment, and the corrupt "bench" was overthrown.

The citizens of New York have fully demonstrated the practicability of a republican government for great cities. Crime may more readily find shelter in densely populated communities and corruption spread more rapidly in great cities. The plunder of tax payers is more easily accomplished in large commercial and manufacturing centres; official intrigue and robbery finds greater facilities in the midst of a city comprising a great floating population, made up of accessions from all parts of the world. But in these large cities there are also a preponderance of stirring, active, honest, successful men, intensely absorbed in business affairs. They meet each other "on change," in the street, in the great mercantile, manufacturing and financial operations; they know and trust each other in matters that involve vast sums of money daily. Now, let these men be aroused to a sense of common danger; show them a public enemy, domestic or foreign, and instantly they stand together, give battle, wage war, exterminate the foe. The work is short, sharp and decisive. Business men of great cities do not trifle; they meet, deliberate and act. Their power is irresistible wherever it asserts itself. It was this class in New York that has settled the question for all time, that a Republican form of government is applicable to the population of one of the largest cities.

The danger is that men become so deeply absorbed in their private affairs, that they wholly neglect their public duties. Politics is turned over to those who make it a profession, and who live and grow rich by office holding. It is only when the robbery of their rulers becomes so glaring, and the sums of money stolen so enormous, as to excite very general alarm. that the real dignity and power of citizenship asserts itself, and demands from the public servants an account of their stewardship. "Short settlements make long friends," is a maxim as true in politics as in trade. A more general adherence to it will save millions of revenues annually to Nation, State and municipality; for it is not the money required to defray the legitimate expenses of any government, that imposes high taxes, but the systematic, organized robbery of the public treasury by officeholders, that consumes the earnings of the poor and lays burdens upon the rich. The lesson of the Tammany frauds is one that may be studied with profit by the people in every community in the United States. Tax payers take courage! Officeholders take warning!

CHAPTER XI.

FISK'S ASSOCIATES.

Daniel Drew, the Leader of the Bear Clique—The magnate of Erie—Cornelius Vanderbilt, the leader of the Bull Clique—The king of railroad managers and manipulator general—Jay Gould, "Fisk's bosom friend" and business partner—President of Erie—William M. Tweed—"Boss" of the Tammany Ring—The most powerful leader among the robbers who plundered the tax paxers—Peter B. Sweeney, the Brain of Tammany—Mayor Hall—Richard B. Connolly, Comptroller of Finance.

If an attempt were made to judge Fisk by the company he kept, he would appear even a greater enigma than when judged by his public acts. It has already been recorded, that in Vermont he bore a good name as a boy, a man and a merchant. In Boston he was a conspicuous man in that "middle class," which in-includes by far the largest proportion of what is called good in society. He was an active, thriving, rising young merchant—was so recognized and classified. The single circumstance of his admission to a partnership, after due trial, into one of the most respectable business houses in New England, is in itself evidence of good standing.

His first venture in New York was a failure. It is not worth while, therefore, to notice it. Upon his return to that city, the reader will recollect, he carried with him a letter of introduction to one of the leading men in the metropolis—leading as a banker—as a steamboat proprietor—as a railroad manager—as a stock broker—as a Methodist. Daniel Drew was pleased with Fisk, and gave him opportunities which were employed to the best possible advantage. He set Fisk up in the brokering business, and took him into his confidence, and finally put him into the "Erie Board." Of course no one will accuse Mr. Drew of having led Mr. Fisk into temptation, nor attempt to hold him responsible for Fisk's acts. It is true, however, that the heavy operations in Erie stock, the flight to New Jersey, and a considerable part of the increase to the Erie stock and debt, and also the "Currency Corner," were perpetrated by the joint efforts of Drew and Fisk.

The association between Fisk and Vanderbilt was not so long continued, nor so intimate; it was rather a dealing with each other, standing face to face; in Drew's case it was side by side.

Fisk and Gould met in the Erie Board, of which both were chosen members at the same time. They were peers—warmly attached to each other—partners in business, standing firmly together to the end.

When Drew retired from the Erie management, Fisk, with his partner, Gould, fell into the jaws of Tammany. He became an associate plunderer with Tweed, Sweeney, Hall and Connolly, names that have become notorious throughout the civilized world, and in the city of New York. Biographies of these men are given, in order to more fully illustrate the business associations of Fisk. The social relations, recreations and episodes in his life are treated of in other chapters.

Daniel Drew.

Daniel Drew was born in Carmel, Putnam county New York, in July, 1797. His father, who was a small farmer, died when his son was fifteen years old. Daniel had received such education as a country school in those days could afford to a lad of his age. After the death of his father, he worked the farm for his mother three years, and then, in 1815, went to New York City in search of more lucrative employment. As is the case with thousands of young men going from country to city, seeking an easy livelihood, this young man met with disappointment. He finally returned to the country and engaged in the business of buying cattle and driving them to the city. He gave five years to this work, without realizing satisfactory profits. In 1820, he settled permanently in New York, and became the proprietor and keeper of the Bull's Head tavern in the Bowery. This house was at that time the chief resort of drovers and butchers, and proved to be a source of considerable profit to its proprietor. Drew formed a copartnership in the "droving" business for the purpose of buying cattle in the southeastern counties of New York, and driving them to market in the city. The business being profitable, extended rapidly and soon spread into adjoining States, and finally reached the far West. Drew and his associates were the first to drive cattle from the country west of the Allegheny mountains to New York. The first attempt was made with a lot of two thousand head, divided into small droves of about

DANIEL DREW.

one hundred each. The trip from Ohio to New York occupied nearly sixty days, and proved to be a very profitable venture. During the fourteen years that Drew gave to this business, he accumulated a considerable sum of money, which was the foundation of the immense fortune he has since amassed.

In 1834, about the time Drew was preparing to retire from the cattle-driving firm, a circumstance occurred that wholly changed the course of his life. He was by public accident placed in a position to be assailed by a young, vigorous, rising man. Opposition called into requisition the powers of the man, and he proved himself a worthy foe. The steamer "General Jackson," owned by Jacob Vanderbilt, a brother of Cornelius Vanderbilt, and running on the Hudson river, was blown up. Drew was induced by one of his friends to invest a thousand dollars in the "Water Witch," a boat put in the trade to take the place of the "General Jackson." Cornelius Vanderbilt controlled the river business, and he was unwilling that an opposition line should be encouraged, he, therefore, resolved to drive the "Water Witch" out of the trade. He put on a new steamer, the "Cinderella," and reduced the freight and passage between New York and Albany to a price below what was necessary to defray expenses. The "Water Witch" sank about ten thousand dollars in the first season, and was then sold to Drew, Kelley & Richards. Vanderbilt warned Drew not to invest in Hudson river boats. The warning was unheeded. Drew naturally concluded that, if the river trade was so profitable as to induce Vanderbilt to fight so vigorously for a monopoly, it would pay to look after. He, therefore, determined to make an effort to divide it with his rival.

This was the beginning of an opposition that will be terminated only by the death of one of these remarkable men, both of whom have lived eventful lives, and have now arrived at ripe old ages. Drew and Vanderbilt were brought face to face, and have stood so, with numerous shifting of scenes, during more than a third of a century. They stood opposed to each other in the steamboat trade, they have been rivals in railroad management, and in the fiercest battles of Wall street, where the opposing cliques fought valiantly and desperately over stocks, gold and currency. The army of "bears" was led by Drew, and the army of "bulls" was commanded by Vanderbilt. In these encounters, millions of dollars frequently changed owners in an hour. Other men were made bankrupt and disappeared, some lost heavily and dragged out a precarious living through an unceasing struggle against poverty and want, but the heroes of all these battles, Drew and Vanderbilt, have ever met with unyielding power the most withering blasts of every storm.

Drew and his associates placed a new steamer on the Hudson in 1836. Other boats were added to the new line, some making day trips and some night trips, so as to accommodate the public to the fullest extent. In 1840, Drew formed a partnership with Isaac Newton, then a successful boatman on the Hudson; the new firm placed on the river the celebrated "People's Line." A new era was inaugurated in steamboating; new vessels were constructed, larger and more elegantly finished and more comfortably furnished than those in use prior to that time. Among the boats placed on the river by this company, the "Isaac Newton," the "New World," the "St. John," the "Dean Richmond," and the "Drew," are cited as examples of the most magnificent achievements in steamboat architecture. The affairs of this company have been conducted with such skill that the profits have annually increased, and during a period of over thirty years, it has held an unimpaired control of the trade. Numerous powerful and persistent efforts have been made to break the power of this "line," but all have been unsuccessful.

In 1847 Drew and George Law established a line of steamers on Long Island Sound, running between New York and Stonington. This was to form part of a "through line" to Boston, in connection with the Stonington and Boston Railroad, which was controlled by Drew and Vanderbilt, for though these great rivals generally were face to face, they frequently in "outside operations" were associated.

But now a new event approached—the Harlem Railroad was drawing to completion; it was to be opened for travel and freight in 1852. After that, of course, "Drew's steamboats would be laid up." "The railroad would do all the business between Albany and New York, and steamboats would no longer be patronized by through passengers and freight." Thus said the enemies of Drew; his friends even were not without fears for the future success of his business. Drew saw farther and knew more. Transportation by water must ever be cheaper than transportation by rail. Everybody and everybody's things are not in so much haste as to be willing to pay twice as much to get into New York at midnight, as they would to be delivered there at daylight next morning. Moreover, Drew foresaw that the development of the great West and the North would increase the business to such an extent that there would be enough to give active and profitable employment to both railroad and boats. Advancing years have justified this opinion. Two railroads and many more steamboats are now pressed with business that is annually increasing. Drew continued his interests in steamboats, and has been eminently successful in all ventures in that direction.

At about the same time that he entered into the steamboat business, he contributed to establish the banking house of Drew, Robinson & Co. in Wall street. This has been one of the strongest and most reputable houses in the city. Through his banking operations, Drew was drawn into dealing in railroad stock and from that easily glided into railroad business in all its departments. From 1855 to 1857 he endorsed bonds of the Erie Railroad Company to the value of a million and a half of dollars; a performance that took New York financial circles utterly by surprise. This was a demonstration of financial power that at once placed Drew in the very front ranks of the wealthy men of New York. The boldness of the risk was unprecedented. The year 1857 was a very depressing one, and carried disaster into many corporations. The venture, however, proved to be a profitable one. In that year Drew was elected a director of the Erie Railway Company, and soon thereafter was chosen treasurer of that company. He was one of the principal managers and stockholders. His position gave him facilities for dealing in Erie stocks that he was not slow to improve. In Wall street he was the leader of the "bear clique," and having the power to issue Erie certificates almost without limit, he was always able to "carry his point" against all combinations that could be organized against him.

He has of late years withdrawn from active participation in railroad management, and now gives his attention to the business of his banking house.

He owns a magnificent estate in Putman county of over a thousand acres, including the old family homestead. His farm is one of the best managed and most profitable in the State.

Mr. Drew is an active and honored member of the Methodist Episcopal Church. He has given large sums of money towards the erection of church buildings; has made liberal endowments to schools, and finally established the "Drew Theological Seminary" at Madison, New Jersey, at a cost of nearly a million dollars. He also contributes largely to missionary and other charitable objects. He is estimated to be worth over twenty millions of dollars, and is regarded as one of the most liberal in his donations and private charities of all the New York millionnaires. Though quite advanced in years, he is a hale, hearty old man, active in business, of a lively and cheerful disposition. He is the father of two children, a son and a daughter, the latter the wife of a Baptist clergyman. Daniel Drew is perhaps the most conspicuous example of a "self-made man" in the country. He started life without education, lost his father at an early age and was forced to make his own way unassisted; he went to New York a green country lad, and by virtue of innate personal force, rose from poverty and obscurity to wealth and position. To do this he never found it necessary to use profane language, or to drink intoxicating liquors.

Cornelius Vanderbilt.

Cornelius Vanderbilt was born at the old family homestead on Staten Island, May, 1794. Like the great majority of country boys, then and now, he was not inclined to appreciate the utility of schoolroom education. Going to school was wasting time. He was an active, energetic lad, fond of boats and horses. His father, whose name was Cornelius Vanderbilt, owned a sail boat which made daily trips to New York. There was then no steam communication as now. The son spent his time on this ferry boat and on his father's farm. From early youth he evinced the characteristic traits of his life. Whatever he undertook he accomplished, or proved that it was beyond his power to compass it. He never shrunk from difficulties, but by skill and labor overcome them.

At the age of seventeen he earned the use of one hundred dollars, which his mother promised to lend him if he would plant in corn one of the roughest ten

CORNELIUS VANDERBILT.

acres in his father's farm. He set to work earnestly to plow, harrow and prepare the field to receive the seed, and at the proper season planted it. His mother thereupon gave him the money which had been promised. With this borrowed capital, Cornelius purchased a small boat, with which he intended to embark in the carrying trade in New York harbor.

It was the good old custom in the days when Vanderbilt was young, for boys to aid their parents until they were arrived at the age of twenty-one years. In accordance with this law which was soundly observed in all proper families, though Cornelius had set up business for himself, what he earned belonged to and was fairly claimed by his parents. He was still a member of the family, and whilst he held that relation the idea of withholding his profits for his own use never entered his mind. Until he was twenty-one years old he was a "boy," and of course his time, skill and energy belonged to his parents, and to them he honestly and cheerfully carried every dime of his income. The parents, however, finding that the son was working day and night, and with remarkable success, generally permitted him to retain for his own use a portion of what he earned. There were at the time when young Vanderbilt entered the business, nearly fifty boats in the trade in New York harbor, and many of his friends endeavored to discourage the young man, by the declaration that "the field was already occupied;" "many of those now running scarcely earn a living;" "half of them are in debt for more than their boats are worth;" "you would do much better to stick to your father's farm." All this shortsighted counsel was unheeded. Cornelius saw that the majority of the men in the trade were dull, lazy, shiftless spendthrifts. They worked without spirit during the day, and spent the evenings in drinking saloons, where they spent their earnings for rum and lost it in gambling. The ambitious and well trained youth saw that by energy and skill he could do more work during the working hours than his drinking and gambling competitors, and that he could save what they spent in the saloons. When this theory was reduced to practice its results far exceeded the highest expectations. In the face of great competition, as far as numbers in the trade were concerned, he entered the carrying trade, and during the first three years saved annually one thousand dollars. When, therefore, he attained the age of majority, he was able to leave the service of his parents, after having added something to their stock, in possession of a very prosperous and profitable business, with a good boat with which to carry it on, a reputation for skill, industry and integrity that rapidly carried him forward to wealth and position.

The war of 1812 was in progress when Cornelius entered business. This circumstance offered a favorable opportunity for a young man of character, intelligence and indomitable energy such as he possessed. In the winter of 1813, he married Sophia Johnson, the daughter of one of the neighbor's to his father's farm. She was one of the most beautiful young ladies on the island, and proved herself a noble and worthy companion for the man destined to attain a notable position in the commercial society of the country.

During the second year of the war, New York City was threatened with invasion by a British fleet. The whole military power of the State was put in readiness for immediate service. The militia of New York City and vicinity was mustered and ordered into camp. About the time of the enrolment Vanderbilt was awarded a contract for carrying military stores from the city to the several ports in the harbor. This exempted him from other military duty, at the same time that it drew from the trade the other boatmen, who were drafted into the army. This gave to the ambitious young man an extraordinary field for enterprise, which he proved himself able to cultivate. There were in the harbor six military stations, to each of which he was required to deliver one load of supplies weekly. He arranged his business so as to receive a load at the foot of Whitehall street every evening at six o'clock, and delivered the stores during the night. Thus he labored night and day. Serving the Government according to his contract while others slept, and during the day run his boat in the regular carrying trade, which was then very active and profitable. All competition had been removed, leaving the entire business to Vanderbilt. This rich harvest of good fortune continued during three months, and enabled the reaper to gather enough to pay for the building of a splendid schooner, which he named "Dread." He built the schooner Charlotte in 1815. This vessel sailed in the harbor trade, during the summer, and in the winter made trips southward to the Carolinas and Georgia. This trade was very profitable in the way of gaining money, nearly ten thousand dollars having been realized in three years; but it also made the name of the young trader favorably known in all the principal ports on the south Atlantic coast of North America.

Steam navigation was introduced soon after the close of the war, and among the first to embark in it was Cornelius Vanderbilt. He foresaw the complete revolution of river, harbor and coastwise trade. He sold out his interest in the sailing vessels, and accepted the position of captain of one of the first steamboats that was built for the New York waters. He entered the employ of Thomas Gibbons in 1818, at a salary of one thousand dollars. The boat he commanded ran between New York and New Brunswick, on the route between New York and Philadelphia. In those days there were no great railroad lines, with main trunks extending from the Atlantic to the Pacific, and with arms stretching out to every seaport. "Camden and Amboy" was then not dreamed of; the locomotive engine had not been heard of in America, and not a foot of iron rail had then been laid. Marvellous progress! wonderful achievements! Here in the centre of business, strong, vigorous, hale—active in corporation management, powerful in finance—owning thousands of miles of track, with roads fully equipped, with engines, cars and machinery to make them, is one who was a full grown man, and who had been long enough in business to earn a fortune and a name before railroads had an existence, before locomotives were invented, and before steamboats were constructed. Within two-thirds of this man's lifetime how the traffic of the world has changed! Ye dwellers on Manhattan and adjacent shores, think of it. Cornelius Vanderbilt, now the most considerable man in your midst, when a young man, ferried passengers and merchandise from shore to shore in a sail-boat, because steamboats were not then in existence. The whole of steam navigation, the vast system of steam transportation, on land and on water, has been developed from nothing to measureless extent within the lifetime of many now living.

At the time when Cornelius Vanderbilt was captain of a steamboat, passengers from New York to Philadelphia went by steamer from New York to New Brunswick; from New Brunswick by stage coach to Trenton, and from Trenton to Philadelphia by steamboat on the Delaware. Passengers going either way, between these cities, spent the night at New Brunswick. There was but one hotel at this place, it had never been the source of profit to its owners; but Vanderbilt had the foresight to see that it would pay, when the steamboat began to carry passengers by that route. He therefore leased it, and whilst he ran the boat, Mrs. Vanderbilt ran the hotel. This lady proved herself to be a very popular hostess, and made her house a place of note on the principal line of travel in America.

Vanderbilt continued in the employ of Gibbons eleven years, and in that time, by the aid of his wife, had accumulated a fortune of thirty thousand dollars. He then, in 1829, determined to set up in the steamboat business for himself. He built a small boat, called the "Caroline," and run it between New York and the towns on the bay and the river. The competition had become active, and a powerful effort was made to drive the young adventurer out of the trade. This cost Vanderbilt nearly all of his previous savings, but he maintained himself against all opposition, and gradually rose to wealth and power as a "steamboat man."

The building of the noted ocean steamer "North Star" was an important event in his life. He made a voyage to Europe in that vessel, and attracted much attention in the old world. At that time the "Collins Line" of steamers controlled the carrying trade between New York and foreign ports. Collins evinced so much jealousy towards Vanderbilt that, by his own acts, he forced his young rival into a sharp competition. When the "Arctic," one of the Collins line, was lost, Vanderbilt immediately proposed to run the "North Star" in the place of the lost vessel, but this Collins flatly refused to permit him to do. Captain Vanderbilt then resolved to compete with Collins for the ocean commerce. He built a line of steamers, and proposed to carry the United States mails without demanding a subsidy. He urged his proposition with so much energy, that the National Government was compelled to withdraw its large subsidy from the Collins line, and to award a carrying of the mails to Vanderbilt. This effectually bankrupted Collins, who drew his vessels from the trade. His success as a manager of a large fleet of river and ocean steamers, won for him a high name and title, and he is now known as the "Old Commodore."

When the war of the rebellion had increased to such vast proportions as to tax the full powers of the National Government, Commodore Vanderbilt selected his best ship, the "Vanderbilt," and fitted it up as a war vessel, and offered it to the navy department at a fair price. He soon discovered, pecuniarily, what each man discovers, both in times of war and in times of peace, who has anything to sell to the Government; that is, between the seller and the buyer, there are troops of "sappers and miners," thieves, robbers, plunderers, men who demand a "commission" for "negotiating" the sale. If the "Vanderbilt" was worth, for example, half a million dollars, the Government must pay three-quarters of a million, so that the difference between the value and the price, two hundred and fifty thousand dollars, may be divided among the thieves both in and out of public offices. That is the way "things are managed." Tax payers are robbed, and officeholders are enriched. If it were not so—if officeholders received no more than the legitimate salaries designated by law—there would not be such a desperate struggle for place and power. It is the stealings men are after, and it is the stealings that make officeholders rich. No man ever becomes rich honestly by holding office. The salaries are too small, and the expenses too great, to admit of the accumulation of wealth in office. The old Commodore was a patriot; he would not take advantage of the nation's necessities to rob its treasury. He spurned the advances of these middlemen, withdrew the offer to sell, and *presented his noble ship a free gift to the nation.*

After having achieved great success as owner and conductor of steamship lines both to foreign and domestic ports, Vanderbilt gradually withdrew his capital and attention from ships, and applied money and time to railroads. He soon gained control of the New York Central, connecting the Hudson river at Albany with the lakes at Niagara Falls and at Buffalo. He was not long in adding to his possessions the Hudson River Railroad and also the Harlem. With these three lines firmly in his grasp, his only rival was the Erie, then controlled by Daniel Drew. Vanderbilt was ambitious to own all the railroad connections between New York City and the West. He made several very desperate efforts to capture the Erie Road. He employed strategy first; that failing, he went into the stock market, using his millions of capital to buy up Erie stock, in order to control the election of directors. This also failed. His wily oponent was quite too fertile in resources to be cornered even by Vanderbilt. The Commodore resorted to injunctions to restrain Drew from issuing new stock, and to prohibit him from using the stock held by the Erie company, as collateral, but all to no purpose. Drew was more than a match for Vanderbilt, and fairly outwitted him in every move against the Erie directors.

When Drew retired from the Erie board and the management passed into the control of Fisk and

Gould, Vanderbilt organized a second series of efforts to gain the much coveted prize. Fisk, the old Commodore supposed, was young and inexperienced in the arts, and unlearned in the profound sciences whereby great capitalists in New York make themselves richer and everybody else poorer. He hoped, therefore, to "negotiate" the Erie Railway out of Fisk's possession and into his own. In this he was greatly mistaken. Fisk had far too much natural shrewdness to be taken in and done for by even the most successful of metropolitan operators. Vanderbilt then resolved to crush out all opposition. He put down the price of freight and passage between New York and Lake Erie over his road so low, that the receipts could not under any circumstances pay expenses. He lost hundreds of dollars by every train that passed over his road. In this way he expected to bankrupt the Erie treasury. The "Central" could afford to sink millions in the fight, "Erie" could not afford thousands; this Vanderbilt well knew, and therefore, relying on his financial advantage, determined to push his rival to the wall. Though the plucky little Vermonter had less money, he possessed a genious for invention and a fertility of resources that gave him personal power whereby the sharpest and most potent of New York money kings were utterly baffled in every assault. Fisk instantly comprehended the whole of Vanderbilt's new scheme; he compassed the full extent of the dangerand prepared to meet it. Who but James Fisk, Jr, would have turned impending disaster into a fortunate opportunity; who but this inimitable manipulator would have ventured to become the chief patron of his enemy, in order to reap a golden harvest from his own parched and withered fields?

Fisk maintained regular rates on Erie and ran trains to meet all demands of travel and transportation. He secretly despatched agents to the West with orders to purchase thousands and tens of thousands of cattle, sheep and hogs, and to ship them over Vanderbilt's roads at the reduced rate of charges. On every head carried eastward Vanderbilt lost money, for it cost more to carry than the railroad charged for the carriage. What Vanderbilt lost Fisk gained. The sum which thus changed hands was about $150,000. But this was not all. Fisk's live stock came upon Vanderbilt's rolling stock, like the lean kine upon the fat; they overran and swallowed up all his trains; every car and engine on the road was pressed into service to move this live freight; to such an extent was this so, that regular merchandise could not be transported. This more profitable and agreeable traffic was therefore sent to the Erie road, and was carried at regular paying rates. When the old Commodore discovered how he and his road were paying into the treasury of his rivals, he was filled with unbounded wrath. The evil machinated for others had descended upon himself. The sum total of his last move was loss to himself—loss counted by hundreds of thousands. Even that reflection was bad enough, but when all that loss was gain to his enemy—when dollar for dollar, lost by him was added to the treasury of Erie, the great financier was unconsolable. All the swearing he had learned as a harbor boatman, a steamboat captain, a Wall street broker was called into requisition on that occasion. The performance demonstrated that of "the army in Flanders" he would have been a worthy commander. Fisk chuckled, rubbed his thighs, rammed his hands deep into his pantaloon pockets and danced gleefully around the treasury box of "Erie."

From this disastrous experience Vanderbilt turned his attention to the affairs of his own roads, leaving his rivals to manage theirs undisturbed. He applied to the Legislature of New York for the passage of an act of consolidation, providing for the union of his three roads, the Central, Hudson and the Harlem into one grand corporation. The process of special legislation is the same in all the States. Large corporations asking special favors from the people's representatives are everywhere expected to pay liberally for it. Vanderbilt made a careful "inventory" of the Legislature with the "selling price" set opposite to each name. He purchased what he thought sufficient for his purpose and "ticked off" his property so as to distinguish it from the rest. This done, his bill was reported and put on its passage in the regular way. The prospect of consolidation had the effect to enhance the value of Harlem stock; the price advanced rapidly and soon reached a very high figure. Here there was an opportunity for a "corner" on Vanderbilt. The Wall street gamblers and the legislative "Roosters"* combined in

* "Rooster" is a term applied to a legislator who refuses to vote until he is paid; that is, a member who sits on his perch and refuses to come down, until he sees the *corn in the trough.*

order to swindle the railroad companies asking for the passage of the bill. It was well understood that if the consolidation should be defeated, the price of Harlem stock would instantly fall to a low figure. The members of the Legislature who had promised Vanderbilt to vote for his bill, secretly agreed with New York brokers to vote against the bill. The brokers, therefore, sold Harlem stock "short;" that is, they sold large quantities at the price as it was on the day of sale, with the understanding that the stock was to be delivered at some future day named in the bill of sale. The brokers, of course, knowing that the consolidation bill would be defeated, knew also, that stock would be low at the time of delivery agreed upon; they could then buy what they needed to fill their contracts at a very low price and demand of the purchasers the high price as stipulated for before the final vote on the bill. Large quantities of Harlem stock was thus sold by the brokers and friends of the dishonest legislators. Of this infamous piece of treachery the old Commodore received early knowledge, and he instantly resolved on swift punishment for the official thieves and their rascally confederates. He instructed his broker to buy and lock up every share of Harlem stock that could be found in the market. This order was promptly executed and the crafty financier complaisantly awaited results.

The bill came up on its final passage, and was rejected by a very decided vote. The public was taken by surprise; the dishonest legislators and their brokers were in high glee over their success, and already began

THE GRAND CENTRAL DEPOT

to estimate the extent of their gains. The joy of the plunderers was short-lived. Harlem, to the astonishment of everybody not in the secret, did not fall. During one day it remained firm. The old giant had put his broad shoulder under the load; in order to steady himself, he had braced his arms on his knees. Thus he stood the first day. On the second day, finding the load after all not very heavy, he began to straighten himself. "Harlem is rising!" was the cry of dismay that flew through the ranks of the robbers. It rose steadily day after day. Those who had purchased now demanded delivery. There was no stock in the market. Delivery was impossible. The speculators were, therefore, compelled to settle with their customers by paying the current value of the stock in money, and this carried well-merited ruin to every member of the infamous combination. Subsequently a more honest legislature gave the required legislation, and the three roads controlled by Vanderbilt were consolidated. In 1871 the "Grand Central Depot" was completed in New York, for the accommodation of the united roads, including also the New York and New Haven railroad now under the same management. A new road was constructed to connect the Harlem and Central roads, called the Spuyten Duyvil and Port Morris railroad. It connects with the Hudson River road at Spuyten Duyvil, and follows the northern side of Harlem river, in Westchester county, until it joins the Harlem road, about a mile and a half north of Mott Haven.

The ground selected for the depot building at Forty-second street and Fourth avenue, is suffiently removed from the fine mansions of the avenues to prevent any annoyance from smoke and noise. The depot proper is in the shape of a half cylinder—the immense ribs of the roof, which reach the ground on both sides, taking that form. The ornamental buildings on the south and west sides are quite extraneous to the main depot, and follow, for the most part, the architectural style of the Renaissance. The pressed brick of all this outside work is finely set off. by the white iron facings, which, when kept well painted, are a good imitation of marble. An entire square, extending from Forty-fourth to Forty-fifth street (five acres), is covered by the building, which is 692 feet long and 240 feet wide. Although the front is not more imposing than that of some Western depots, the appearance of the whole, as seen from the southwest, is more striking than that of any similar building on this continent, and probably in the world. As to size, it is unsurpassed. The depot of the great Midland road in London is of exactly the same width, but is five feet shorter. The towers of the front (the central tower is 130 feet high and the others 110 feet—the three towers of the west side 110 feet), together with a few patches of nearly perpendicular roof, are covered with slate. All the main roof is covered with glass and iron. Even the sheds over the sidewalks, where passengers most frequently enter the building, are half covered with glass.

The west side presents a curious succession of towers, interspersed with sections of frontage, resembling isolated mansions. There are many doorways on this side, giving access to the saloons on the first floor, the great rooms in the basement—which are to be rented to various tenants, who will be of use to passengers—and the long suites of business offices in the upper stories. The north end is entirely devoted to giving ingress and exit to the railroad trains—the whole space being taken up by iron doors and doorways. The view from any point inside the great dome-like roof is very grand. The intricate network of iron arches and rods, half covered with thick glass, seems, when the sun shines upon it, like a gigantic cobweb in the sunshine after a rain. The twelve tracks are divided into groups of two by elevated walks.

Commodore Vanderbilt is the father of thirteen children, four sons and nine daughters. His wife died at an advanced age in 1868. He is distinguished for his liberality to worthy charity and for well known generosity. He is in every sense a conspicuous example of the American gentleman of the "real old sort," enjoys excellent health, has recently married a young wife, and now, at the age of seventy-eight, is as active, correct and prompt in the despatch of business, as a man in the prime of life.

Jay Gould.

Jay Gould was a banker and broker of considerable standing on Wall street, at the time Fisk made his first appearance in New York. He was in the confidence of Commodore Vanderbilt, and frequently participated in the profits of the great financial operations that were organized and put through by that gentleman. Gould was a careful, safe operator, a man of sound judgment and deliberate action, rarely embarking in any enterprise without having first calmly surveyed the whole scheme and arrived at a conclusion that it would pay.

When Fisk returned to Wall street and resolved upon "making it pay," he, as has already been explained, settled down under the protecting shadow of Daniel Drew. In the struggle of Vanderbilt and Drew, wherein each labored to capture the Erie railway directorship, in 1867, Gould was a candidate on Vanderbilt's ticket and Fisk was a candidate on Drew's ticket. They were, therefore, brought out in opposition to each other. It will be recollected, that a compromise was effected between the two great leaders in such manner as to give each a fair representation in the new board. On the combination ticket appeared the names of both Gould and Fisk. That ticket was elected, and these gentlemen came together as directors of the Erie Railway company. Fisk liked Gould and Gould liked Fisk. The two men were opposites in every thing. Gould is tall, slender and dark; Fisk was short, stout and of light complexion. Gould was cautious, cool, calculating, slow —Fisk was reckless, impetuous, impulsive, instantaneous. These men at once united their fortunes and their forces. Gould planned and Fisk executed. Gould gave to the firm respectability, Fisk gave courage. The operations of the house and of the men who were in it are elsewhere told in detail. Gould rose to the

JAY GOULD

position of President of Erie, and held it three years. He was made Fisk's representative by the will of the latter, and therefore became the great power in the Erie Board. The same policy that had made that company notorious and its management the object of much contention, was continued by Gould and his associates. The opposition to the Gould management, under the leadership of Gen. Daniel E. Sickles, finally succeeded in forming a combination of sufficient strength to displace Gould from the office of President, and to even force him out of the Board, from which he resigned on the 14th of March, 1872. That was the end of the "Erie Ring."

William M. Tweed.

The most extraordinary character in his way, the most unscrupulous political juggler, the most reckless plunderer among American officeholders is "Boss Tweed." He was born in New York of Irish parents, and was reared among the vilest associations of the lower stratum of life in that city. In his youth he was apprenticed to the chairmaking trade, and worked for a short time at that business; but, finding the excitement and vulgarity of the fire engine houses more congenial to his nature than the atmosphere of a mechanic's shop, his work was neglected, his bills were not paid and presently he failed. He was then free to "run with the machine" and loaf with the corner loungers, to spend the day in the street and the night in low dens talking politics to such as were in need of such instructions as he could give. He soon worked into ward politics, attended the precinct primary meetings and ward conventions; became a leader of a gang of "shoulder hitters," then foreman of a fire company. Having earned recognition he was appointed to a small office, and from that beginning worked up by diligence and tact step by step. He was at one time a member of the Board of Supervisors, after that he was elected a member of the State Senate, and finally gained the important and responsible position of "Commissioner of Public Works." The precise value of this office to a man like Tweed is not known. One of the leading newspapers,* published in March, 1870, thus suggests of what advantage it had been to the "Tammany Boss."

"Mr. Tweed was worth less than nothing when he took to the trade of politics. Now he has great possessions, estimated all the way from $5,000,000 to twice as much. We are sorry not to be able to give his own estimate, but, unluckily, he returns no income. But at least he is rich enough to own a gorgeous house in town and a sumptuous seat in the country, a stud of horses, and a set of palatial stables. His native modesty shrinks from blazoning abroad the exact extent of his present wealth, or the exact means by which it was acquired. His sensitive soul revolts even at the partial publicity of the income list. We are tossed upon the boundless ocean of conjecture. But we do know from his own reluctant lips that this public servant, who entered the public service a bankrupt, has become, by an entire abandonment of himself

* The "*World.*"

to the public good, 'one of the largest tax payers in New York.' His influence is co-extensive with his cash. The docile Legislature sits at his feet, as Saul at the feet of Gamaliel, and waits, in reverent inactivity, for his signal before proceeding to action. He thrives on percentages of pilfering, grows rich on the distributed dividends of rascality. His extortions are as boundless in their sum as in their ingenuity. Streets unopened profit him—streets opened put money in his purse. Paving an avenue with poultice enriches him—taking off the poultice increases his wealth. His rapacity, like the trunk of an elephant, with equal skill twists a fortune out of the Broadway widening, and picks up dishonest pennies in the Bowery."

Peter B. Sweeney.

Peter B. Sweeney, President of the "Department of Public Parks," is recognized as the brain of the Tammany Ring. He was born in New York; the son of an Irishman, who kept a drinking saloon in Park Row. His father's saloon was the rendezvous of low political tricksters, and it was in such company that the lad received his first ideas of the sublimity of republican liberty and the science of American politics. From this rare school he was promoted to the position of errand boy in a law office; he afterwards became a student and was in due time admitted to the New York bar. Law as put on as a cloak, Sweeney's profession was from the beginning, politics. He was first chosen "Counsel to the Corporation;" while in this office he demonstrated such consummate skill as a manipulator that he was at once admitted to full membership in the ring that ruled and robbed the city. He next became District Attorney, enjoyed the emoluments, and left others to do the work of the office while he travelled in Europe. Upon his return to New York he resigned the District Attorneyship to accept the office of City Chamberlain, to which place he was appointed by the Mayor.

In the city of New York the Chamberlain was formerly the custodian of all the public moneys, in fact, the treasurer. It is the almost universal practice, for such officers as State Treasurer and City Treasurer, to use the people's money in private speculations. In some cases the money is simply deposited on interest and the interest money is stolen by the treasurer. To this general practice New York had not been an exception. But, strange as it may seem, Mr. Sweeney astounded the tax payers of New York by accounting fully to the public for all the interest money during his term of office, and paid the whole amount into the treasury. He, however, fully rewarded himself for this parade of honesty. If the whole truth were known, it would doubtless appear that in many of the heaviest stock operations in Wall street the people's money was used at high rates and in sure investments, solely for the benefit of the clique that controlled the treasury. The testimony before the Committee of Congress in the investigations of the operations of the Gold Ring divulged the fact that Sweeney was very deeply concerned in that notorious conspiracy. As

PETER B. SWEENY.

President of the Park Commission he controlled the disbursing of vast sums of money and thus became one of the most active members of the Tammany Association.

A. Oakey Hall.

The climax of its infamy, and the downfall of the Tammany power in New York, was attained while A. Oakey Hall was Mayor. Hall was born in New York in 1825. He was educated for the profession of law; after having gained admission to the bar, he went to New Orleans and, for awhile, was in the office of John Slidell, in that city. He returned from New Orleans, where he had not met with much success, to accept the post of Assistant District Attorney for New York, under the late Nathaniel Blunt. Upon the death of District Attorney Blunt, Hall was made the candidate of the Whig party for that office and was duly elected. By a succession of re-elections, he held that office for about twelve years, and at the end of that time was elected Mayor.

To be able to hold office during so many years in such a political atmosphere as that which pervades New York, is by no means an ordinary feat. Hall is a lawyer of considerable ability, and of great cunning. As a member of the firm of Brown, Hall and Vanderpool, he has enjoyed a large and very lucrative practice. In politics he has ever exhibited a versatility of character that has made it an easy matter for him to accommodate his professions, not being hampered with such a thing as principles, to the public demands, whatever they chanced to be. He began public life as a Whig, was a dark-lantern Know-nothing in 1856, and when Know-nothingism waned, he cast his boat on the rising tide of Republicanism, and then, turning Democrat, became a member of the "Tammany Hall Ring."

It has been the fortune of Hall to change front at the most favorable time, so as to keep him on the winning side. Men who make politics a trade, and office-holding a business, are usually so utterly devoid of convictions that it is an easy matter for them to turn for their allegiance from a losing to a winning party. As a Whig and a young man, he attained quite a reputation for ability and honesty in public affairs. As a Know-nothing, he was one of the most violent of the leaders in hostility to foreigners. As that new party rose into power he saw instantly in it an opportunity to gain power. When the bubble burst and the froth vanished, Hall was not found in the ruins. He had snuffed afar the coming disaster, and permitted no delay in the transfer of his allegiance to the ranks of the young giant, Republicanism. The city of New York, with the base and corrupting influences, the facilities for sheltering, the opportunities for plundering, the chances largely in favor of concealment, and the avenues of escape, ever wide open, was not the sort of ground on which Republicanism would be likely to thrive for any considerable time. The party was new then, and, like all new parties, was sound in its doctrines and honest in its administrations. Virtue and honesty are deemed vulgar in the political circles of great cities. Parties organizing in the interest of the people for the protection of tax payers, are usually strangled in infancy or captured in early youth. Every great city has its great political "Rings," whose members farm out the offices among themselves. The tax payers are robbed, and the thieves defend each other.

In New York, the old ring was too powerful for the young party. Hall had the shrewdness to discover this, and instantly resolved to join the plunderers; he became one of them, and has fared most sumptuously ever since. He entered the Tammany camp soon after the beginning of the war in 1861, and in 1868 was elected Mayor of the City. He has been a most pliant instrument in the hands of the men who have, during many years, manipulated the ballots, and plundered the finances of New York; and has lent his aid and countenance to the most monstrous frauds, systemically organized, that have ever disgraced the administration of public affairs.

Richard B. Connolly.

Connolly was perhaps the least active of the Tammany quartette. In 1870, he was appointed Comptroller of the City Finances; an office at that time of small consequence, but which, under the new city charter, concocted and passed by the Tammany Ring, became of the first importance to the plunderers. It also proved to be the magazine of information, which ultimately exploded and spread all the rascality of the city officers in official figures before the people.

Connolly was born in Cork, Ireland; his father, a village schoolmaster in the "ould counthrie," gave his son a "good education," which unfortunately was applied to bad purposes. Richard came to America with an elder brother, and very soon became a popular leader among his countrymen in ward politics. He was at one time elected to the office of county clerk in New York. Next he was sent to the State Senate. Though the salary of a State Senator is little in excess of the board bills at a first-class hotel, yet it not unfrequently happens that Senators go to the State Capitol poor, and after remaining there one or two sessions, they come away men of great wealth. There is some secret about this that is not generally understood by the public. A man is elected a member of the Legislature of some State, and draws a salary of about one thousand dollars for each session, and pays about six hundred dollars for board and incidental expenses. At the close of the session it becomes known to the friends and associates of the member or Senator, that his wealth has increased during his term of services, sometimes to the extent of five, ten, twenty, or even fifty thousand dollars. This is a great mystery, and it is because of this mysterious increase of wealth that so many men of doubtful reputation and incapacity for business pursuits are so exceedingly anxious to "permit their names to be used" as candidates for the office of legislator.

This was the case with Mr. Connolly at Albany. By some accident, not accounted for, he was in possession of a considerable sum of money at the close of

RICHARD B. CONNOLLY.

his term, that did not belong to him at the beginning of it. Thereafter he was called " slippery Dick," and was entitled to membership in the Tammany Association; he was accordingly admitted and was appointed by the Tammany Chiefs, Comptroller. How he administered the affairs of this office so as to aid the thieves and plunder the tax payers is fully set forth in another chapter.

The proof of the frauds was derived from Connolly's records; and of the infamous qnartette, he was the first to break and surrender to the people. He was arrested, and in default of sufficient bail, was committed to prison, and held there during several weeks. The amount of bail required was afterwards reduced, and he was permitted to go forth to a very unenviable freedom, to await trial and the decree of the court in his case.

CHAPTER XII.

NEW YORK LIFE, PEN SKETCHES.

Fisk as a Showman—How he amused New York—Managing Theatres Four Establishments at once—Social Life in New York—Free Love —Free Lust—Woman's Rights—Social Crimes—The fruits of False Teachings—The Wages of Sin—Death.

FISK was a natural showman. When a boy at Brattleboro, he was ever ready to entertain a crowd of spectators by his "performances." He was a perfect mimic and a good clown. While serving the hotel as a waiter-boy, an opportunity to travel as a showman with a menagerie and circus presented itself, and James eagerly embraced it, and made a trip through the Eastern and Middle States as a "showman." The passion for getting up amusement for others remained and grew with him. As soon, therefore, as he had gained a firm footing in New York, he turned aside from his regular business to try an experiment at theatre management. His first venture in this line was a bold one. He purchased in 1868, Pike's Opera House, on Twenty-third street, and named it the "Grand Opera House." Soon after this he took possession of the Fifth avenue Theatre, on Twenty-second street, and so thoroughly reconstructed it as to give it the appearance of a new and very elegant establishment. He made it one of the most attractive places of amusement in the city. In May, 1869, he leased the new Acadcmy of Music, the largest establishment of the kind in New York.

This was one of his most erratic and inexplicable manias. He expended money by thousands and tens of thousands of dollars to refit, and refurnish buildings, and to import star performers. Neither effort nor expense were spared to give to the theatre goers of New York first-class entertainments. English, German French and Italian companies were organized and put in training under the best possible management, and the New York public were invited to the best entertainment that money, energy and experience could produce.

Strange as it may seem, the efforts of Fisk were not appreciated. The public did not give a liberal support to his lavish preparations. He lost heavily at every performance, and was compelled very soon to divide his companies and send some of the star actors travelling through the country to play in the leading cities. At the end of the first year he gave up all the theatres with the exception of the "Grand Opera House." He so reconstructed that building as to make it available for the offices of the Erie Railway Company. The price paid for the house is reported to have been eight hundred and twenty thousand dollars. The Erie officers occupy the second floor; they are fitted up and furnished in massive black walnut, trimmed and mounted in silver. They are among the most elegantly furnished business rooms in the United States. Here, in the midst of his Erie associates, surrounded with many attendants and superfluous luxuries, "Prince Erie" reigned in imperious sway. The audience room of the theatre was kept intact and was used as a place of amusement during the lifetime of its owner. Fisk's greatest success as an *impressario*, was achieved in the French Opera Bouffe. He sent Max Maretzek, one of the most able managers in this country to Europe with full powers to organize a company for the Grand Opera House; the commission was promptly and successfully discharged, and the new sensation was brought out under the most favorable circumstances. The venture proved to be a success, and the Opera Bouffe found a permanent home in New York. Fisk, however, had a most unfortunate faculty for quarrelling with his managers. He always selected the best, but very soon lost their services. He tried Brougham, Bergfeld, Tayleure and Maretzek, all men of acknowledged ability in their profession, but neither of whom could agree with the erratic proprietor; with Maretzek he actually came to blows; a disgraceful knockdown scene was enacted in the presence of the entire troupe at rehearsal in the Grand Opera House, much to the alarm and terror of the ladies, who were unaccustomed to that kind of "acting." Nevertheless, in the face of all difficulties, he sustained the performances at the Opera House to the last. The fact that he received from the Erie company an annual rent of seventy-five thousand dollars, made it comparatively easy to carry on his place of amusement without pecuniary loss.

To this Opera House Fisk was in the habit of inviting his friends to spend the evening. On several oc-

EIGHTH AVENUE CO

casions he took the "Ninth Regiment" there to witness the performances. He never lost an opportunity to get great men, distinguished visitors and notorious characters to accompany him to the plays, and ever took delight in claiming the establishment as his own.

His private rooms, his domicile in New York, were in an adjoining building, and not far off was the residence of the notorious woman he had raised up, established and supported in defiance of decency, law and morality, in violation of his vow at the altar and against the repeated advice of his best friends. Here, in this small circle of New York territory, he lived, transacted his business and satiated his wicked lusts. To this place was carried from the Grand Central Hotel his lifeless body, to receive the last tribute of his friends and associates, to await obsequies. Hence he was carried out from the city, so multifarious in its social influences, so prolific in crime, back to the quiet village, in the purer atmosphere of the Green Mountain State; back to the scenes and innocent surroundings of his youth; back to the place of his birth, there to be burried.

What a life is this! From the cradle to the grave, less than forty years.

> "Placed on this isthmus of a middle State,
> A being darkly wise and rudely great;
> With too much knowledge for the sceptic side,
> With too much weakness for the stoic's pride,
> He hangs between; in doubt to act, or rest,
> In doubt to deem himself a god, or beast;

In doubt his mind or body to prefer;
Born but to die, and reasoning but to err;
Alike in ignorance, his reason such,
Whether he thinks too little, or too much;
Chaos of thought and passion all confused;
Still by himself abused, or disabused;
Created half to rise and half to fall;
Great lord of all things, yet a prey to all;
Sole judge of truth, in endless error hurl'd;
The glory, jest, and riddle of the world!"

Social Relations.

Much of the crime in New York high life is directly traceable to the false teachings of the disciples and advocates of the doctrine of what is called FREE LOVE. It might with much greater propriety be called *free lust.* There is neither love, virtue nor decency in the doctrine or practice There is a numerous class of restless, rattlebrained, indigent persons in every great city, that ever seeks to escape the restraints of the recognized laws of social relations. They imagine themselves "enslaved by custom," deprived of their "natural rights by a false idea of propriety." "Every woman has a perfect right to choose for herself who shall be the father of her children," say these co-called reformers. "This is a fundamental necessity." Be it so. But having once made her choice, the stability of society and the good of the State require that she shall abide by her own decision. With this, however, the restless spirits are not satisfied. They insist that, as all men are fallible, full of error and liable to make mistakes, it is monstrous to compel two persons, uncongenial to each other, to live together a lifetime. After two have been wedded for a time, one or both of them may discover that the other is not congenial; he or she ought, therefore, to be permitted to forthwith leave the presence of the other and go out to seek another companion on whom to experiment. This going together and separating at will should be allowed to proceed until every man and woman has found his or her "affinity."

This doctrine effectively breaks up the family, the most sacred institution on earth. It disintegrates society, lowers the standard of public morality, breaks down the barriers of virtue, destroys domestic felicity, makes the marriage tie a bond of sand, abolishes the obligations of paternity, and extinguishes love.

In return for all this, these false teachers would give us liberty in crime, unrestrained lewdness and licentiousness in its lowest form.

New York City is peculiarly the centre of this school of "reformers." The baneful effects of its teachings are not confined to its own members. It is felt in all circles of society. Familiarity with these false theories beget a general looseness of thought, that speedily leads to laxity of conduct and to crime.

Scarcely a week passes that New York papers do not give accounts of the workings of these doctrines in the overthrow of some domestic shrine. Sometimes it is only "scandal," sometimes "abandonment," sometimes "infidelity," sometimes "elopement," sometimes it is "suicide," sometimes it is "murder," sometimes it is "assassination." The cause is always the same.

The effect is changed only by reason of some local or individual circumstance. The doctrine of "Free Love" leads to a total disregard of the obligations of marriage. In this school the women are far worse than the men. They go out in quest of "affinities" and are not long in finding them. They ply their art insidiously, by dexterously exposing their charms so as to entrap men. Few men can escape the arts of a designing woman. Men who are generous, frank, liberal and benevolent are easiest subjected to the power of an intriguing clique of women, skilled in the arts of fascination.

The murder of a noted author and journalist in New York in 1870, is a conspicuous illustration of this truth. He was a large hearted, liberal minded, generous, kind man, brimful of good impulses. He sought only to help the weak, to assist one struggling to rise to a higher and more independent condition. He was surrounded by those who had designs conceived in error and brought forth in sin. He was led dumb as a sheep to the shearing, and as an ox to the slaughter. He died a victim of the doctrines of "Free Love." A true appreciation and a lawful respect for the marriage tie, in the company he kept in the metropolis, would have led him from and not intocrime and death.

The assassination of James Fisk, Jr., is another sacrifice made to the same demon. One divorced woman, ambitious, recklessly abandoned—two married men, faithless to their vows most solemnly given at the altar—sinful affections, base loves, sensuality, jealousy, assassination. That's all.

Then there is the scandal about Victoria C. Woodhull and her sister, Miss Tennie Claflin, with two men, Flood and Andrews, fastened upon them and Theodore Tilton, a gentleman for many years associated with good men in New York, disgracefully mixed up with their shame. All of these parties hold marriage to be a thing of convenience, to be taken on and laid off at pleasure, without incurring obligations or invoking censure. Some day will bring an explosion in this "happy circle;" some respectable family will be ruined, some unwary suitor will be shot, and New York will have a sensation of three days' duration.

Travelling on the same road, some slower, some faster, some near to, some remote from the disgraceful end, is the whole company of those who call themselves "Woman's Rights Advocates." Unhappy in domestic relations, and eager to get away from obligations rather than anxious to discharge them, is the secret cause of all the chafing, ranting, fuming and swaggering, that characterizes the discontents who hold conventions to assail the established usages of good society. One after another these men and women, who rant and whine about woman's wrongs, sink and fall away into the belief and practice of "free lovers," and are lost. Some see the error of their way and retrace their steps; others grieve, fret and die young, and escape the humiliation, disgrace and crime to which their vile theories tend.

It is the story of moderation and excess over again.

"Moderate drinking" coupled with respectability, leads to excessive drinking and drunkenness. Just as every moderate drinker protests that *he* will never become a drunkard, so every "Woman's Righter" insists that he will never become a "free lover." In the first case one begins in moderation and ends in excess—in the second case one begins in moderation and ends in excess. "Things that are equal to the same thing, are equal to each other." The remedy in each case is the same—*total abstinence.*

In every movement, whether good or evil, there are some, both leaders and followers, who are honest and sincere; nevertheless they err and are responsible to society for the consequences of their acts. So in the "Woman Question," there are many honest and virtuous men and women who imagine that woman is grossly wronged, and that the panacea for all the ills she is heir to, lies in the ballot; as is their right and privilege in this country—they, therefore, advocate the extention of the right of suffrage to women. But a very large class of the "Woman's Rights" advocates, war against "usage," and clamor for a liberty in social affairs that amounts to licentiousness. This branch of the champions in this movement is kept so prominently before the public, and their peculiar views are so persistently thrust upon society, that the taint of vulgarity pervades the whole, and the influence of the movement is, therefore, totally bad.

It is a notable and instructive fact, that not one of the respectable and pure women engaged in this loose and rambling discussion of the marriage relation, has ever yet given to the world a single, clear and comprehensible statement of what they understand or mean by Free Love, or precisely what they want in exchange for the existing order of domestic unity. There is no lack of excited and intemperate denunciation of what is, but nowhere is there suggested a practical theory of life to take the place of that founded on the marriage which they seek to abolish. The few pure and ethereal creatures, who have been "carried to the skies" on the gauzy wings of incomprehensible logic, never come down from their nebulous heights to face the brutal facts of existence, and to declare in all seriousness what they propose to do with men and women, when, by destroying marriage, they have destroyed the family.

When they are told that the theories in which they clothe their lives of innocence, are by others made the soiled cloaks wherewith to cover their unclean lives, they fly into a passion and deny the statement with an earnestness which conclusively shows that they are too pure and too ignorant to suspect their allies or to comprehend the force of their own teachings. They consider themselves personally accused and cry out bitterly against the injustice and brutality of men.

Now if Free Love means anything, and is not a mere form of words with which these idle women amuse themselves, with no object but pastime, it means that the obligations of marriage are not binding as against the momentary inclinations of the parties married. In place of those ideas of conjugal duty, with which society has succeeded for some centuries, we are to accept a "higher truth" and the "inner consciousness" of each individual as his only rule of action in social matters. People are to pair like birds or beasts at the bidding of irresistible impulse, and the obligations of fidelity are to last no longer than the impulse. This, stripped of its vail of mysticism, is the doctrine preached by these new teachers of social ethics; and there is but one word to describe this doctrine; it is beastly. The good ladies who profess it may sit in their balloons, far above the things of earth, tossing up their half-dozen meaningless phrases like the gilt balls of a juggler, and laying down an unsubstantial law for men and women, which might suit very well if the race were like cherubs, with nothing but heads and wings. But see what work the real men and women make of it when they take hold of it! Two married men, whose souls reject the tyranny of marriage, find their affinity in the same soiled dove, and eliminate each other with revolvers from the embarrassing problem. Another pretty free lover, who uses in her letters the very slang of the platonic sisterhood on this coast, is so devoted to the purity and sacredness of her emotions that she murders her ex-lovers to save them from falling back into the slough of matrimony, and gets visited by leading apostles of the sisterhood from New York in consequence, and deluged with their sympathy.* When these events are cited as the natural result of indulging in those restless impulses of revolt against the social

* Mrs. Fair, the California murderess, was visited by Susan B. Anthony and Mrs. Stanton.

and moral laws, which many find theoretically so irksome, these good women "recoil with affright," and protest that this is not what they mean by Free Love. Of course, it is not. But this only proves that they do not know what they are doing nor whither they are drifting. Because they are virtuous, they know nothing of the quality of the cakes and ale they are serving out to greedy and vulgar buyers.

One of the most brilliant and accomplished of the advocates of this new doctrine, and a lady whose personal qualities entitle her to perfect respect, thus sets forth what in her judgment is required to set in order the domestic machinery of human society:

"Where marriage is sanctified by love, there Free Love obtains and rules. So far for the morale of this question. The next point is, who shall determine where marriage shall exist, the man or the woman? I hold that woman shall make the laws (if we must have them) to govern the affections, not man. On woman falls all the burdens of marriage. She bears and nurses the children. If there is to be legislation here, it is hers by right, by a great law of nature. Is it a logical conclusion to say that marriage is only a civil contract, and at the same time hold it a sacrament, as does the Catholic church—indissoluble? I am not afraid to trust human nature in freedom. Love will find its own way to take care of children. These contingencies which trouble you so much will take care of themselves when marriage is sanctified by 'Free Love,' not compelled by 'Circumstance,' that unspiritual god."

"I propose, first, that woman shall be made politically man's equal; that she shall have a voice in making the laws by which she is governed—second, that as you did by the negro slaves, you shall do by her; aid her to gain education and pecuniary independence, removing from her the necessity of marrying for a home, and thus at the very altar perjuring her own soul. I propose that man at the altar shall not perjure himself in the vow he makes as he places the ring upon the bride's finger, endowing her with all his worldly goods, and then keeping her forever a pauper. I propose that children shall not be born in homes of discord, hatred and strife, to die in infancy, or grow up in crime to fill our prisons and our penitentiaries, and to make our cities unsafe to live in. I propose that the instinct of parentage shall rise above the mere animal instinct, which is sufficient for propagation, but not for improvement of even the lower orders of animals. I propose that it shall be dignified by sentiment and by scientific knowledge. I propose that when two persons find that they have made a sad, bitter mistake, the fatal one of their lives, that the woman shall not be placed under a ban, if she seeks relief from this bondage, any more than a man is who easily slips the knot, and is ready for a new life."

Precisely what all this means to the lady who brought it forth, it is impossible to imagine, but what it means to the hundreds of families, wherein black discontent and base longings have superseded peace of mind and active love, is painfully evident.

To the world of restless and reckless spirits, married

and unmarried, these propositions mean that a marraiage which can be violated by either party, is not a marriage. That if love is "free love" it is not love. That if in marriage differences arise, it is evident that it is an unnatural mating and must be instantly renounced. A pulpit philosopher instructing his flock concerning vital piety, said: "If you have it you cannot lose it; if you lose it you never had it." So reason these senseless theorists: "If you are married and desire separation, you are not married." There are no bonds stronger than caprice. There are no moral obligations, no social restraints. When a man and woman are together, and either one of them takes a fancy for another, it is a sign that they are improperly joined. If two men have an "affinity" for the same woman, one must shoot the other.

There is deadly virus lurking in these disjointed and illogical "catch words," that sinks with baleful effect in innumerable hearts and manifests itself all over the land in thousands of discontented women, whose listless minds have been poisoned by these confused rhapsodies put forth in violent and inharmonious strains.

This is the bare and revolting bestiality stripped of its swaddling metaphors, which these good and pure women—misled and deceived by years of silly playing with phrases and by able and insidious leaders of their own sex, whose purposes are vile, are now daily preaching to the world. It is not a matter to dismiss with a word, to trifle with or to wonder at.

It is sowing in hundreds of families the seeds of

discord and ruin. The ignorant and impressible women whose principles have been shaken by this insidious propaganda, become the easy prey of the first plausible scoundrel who can persuade them of his sympathy. A school which is capable of preparing so baleful a harvest of foulness and misery, cannot claim the immunity of being considered respectable.

HELEN JOSEPHINE MANSFIELD.

CHAPTER XIII.

HELEN JOSEPHINE MANSFIELD.

Biographical sketch of "Fisk's Woman"—Who she is—Where she came from—Her early life—Education—Training—Associates—From Boston to San Francisco—Marriage in California—Divorce in New York—Introduction to Fisk—Fares sumptuously every day—Her home in Twenty-third street—Who went there—How she entertained Fisk's company—The presentation of Edward S. Stokes—That correspondence—The result—The fruits of sin—Quarrel among the debauchees—Jealousy—Rejection—Revenge—Death.

MISS MANSFIELD was born in Boston, in the year 1840. The early part of her life was spent in that city; there she received her education, in the public schools, and is still held in the memory of her young associates.

She is described as having been an exceedingly attractive girl, remarkably stylish in figure, and giving promise of developing into a slight, graceful and elegant woman. The surroundings of her youth were such as to admirably fit her for her subsequent career. She lived in publicity, and was entirely without the guardianship of prudent counsellors.

Her family moved to California in 1852, and settled in Stockton, San Joaquin county. Joseph Mansfield, her father, was a practical printer. He served his apprenticeship in the office of the Boston *Journal.* Shortly after his arrival in California he went to work as a compositor on the Stockton *Journal*, at that time edited and published by William Bliven, a brother of Rasey Bliven, who was with General Crabb at the Cavorca massacre. In the early part of 1854 the *Journal* passed into the hands of John Tabor, who edited it as an organ of the Whig party. Mansfield at this time started the San Joaquin *Republican* as a Democratic journal. It was in this year that the celebrated contest between John Bigler and George S. Waldo, for the governorship of this State, drew out the full strength of both parties. The most rancorous partisan feeling was exhibited on both sides. Tabor espoused the cause of Waldo, and Mansfield was an equally strong advocate of the claims of Bigler. The columns of these papers daily teemed with abuse of the two candidates, and finally the editors began to abuse one another.

A challenge to mortal combat followed. On the morning of August 6th, 1854, Tabor and Mansfield, with their seconds, went across the Mormon slough. They selected a plot of ground about three hundred yards back of the State Lunatic Asylum. Colt's revolvers were the weapons. They were to stand ten paces apart, and after the first shots had been exchanged at that distance, they were to advance and fire at will and without the word of command. The first shots proved harmless. The two then advanced on each other. Mansfield was excited, and hence his aim was uncertain. On the other hand, his antagonist was cool and collected. At the third round Mansfield suddenly threw up both arms, his pistol dropped, and he fell backward on the sod. The surgeon, Dr. Norcoin, was quickly at his side, but too late. He was dead! The ball had pierced his heart.

As Mansfield was very much esteemed and respected by men of both parties, his death created excitement, and for a long time the friends of Tabor, fearing that he might be killed, would not allow him to appear in public. When the estate of Mansfield was settled there was but a pittance for his widow and child.

In 1855 Mrs. Mansfield removed to San Francisco, and rented a house on Bryant street. Josie was at that time fifteen years old. She was just budding into womanhood, and was possessed of rare personal attractions. James D. Carter was the owner of the property adjoining the residence of Mrs. Mansfield. Carter did an extensive trucking business, and, although a young man, had accumulated a fortune. He had become acquainted with Mrs. Mansfield and her daughter. The personal charms of Helen Josephine had made a deep impression on him, and he proposed marriage. Mrs. Mansfield objected on account of her daughter's youth. Carter then proposed that Helen Josephine should go to the convent of Notre Dame at San Jose, about fifty miles from San Francisco, and finish her education. He offered to pay her expenses until she was of age, and then marry her. Helen Josephine was sent to the convent. After she had been an inmate of that institution about two years her mother married a Mr. Warren. About one year after the marriage of her mother the theatrical company which had been playing in Maguire's Opera House went to

San Jose to fill an engagement. Attached to this company was Frank Lawler, a young and promising actor. Lawler was a tall and handsome young man—just the person to attract a young and thoughtless school girl. During the company's stay in San Jose, Lawler and Helen Josephine became acquainted. This acquaintance ripened into love, and in less than ten days they eloped and were married. When the news of the marriage was communicated to Carter he was for a time inconsolable, and his friends were compelled to keep a close watch on him to prevent his committing suicide. Time assuaged his grief, however, and six months afterward he married another. Lawler and his wife, on their return to the city, went to board with the mother, who was then living in Sutton street, and Lawler resumed his connection with the opera house company. His wife was a regular attendant at the Saturd y afternoon matinees. She was an incorrigible flirt, and when at the theatre was always surrounded by a circle of admirers.

Among these admirers was D. W. Perley, an Englishman, a law partner of Judge David S. Terry, who killed Senator David C. Broderick in a duel. Perley was wealthy, and for him Helen Josephine showed a marked preference over all other admirers. The intimacy with Perley gave rise to scandal and family trouble that involved Mr. Lawler and his wife in public disgrace, so that they were compelled to leave the State. They therefore sailed for New York, where they arrived in 1864.

The domestic affairs of the Lawlers were not conducted in a satisfactory manner. There was little love and much hate. It was a run-away-match, which at best is a very poor match. People who marry in haste usually repent at leisure. With repentance comes the birth of discontent and the death of love. Then follows a dissatisfaction with what is, and a longing for what is not. To this general course of events the life of the Lawlers was not an exception. After their arrival in New York each seemed to take a separate course. Mrs. Lawler travelled about from New York to Albany, to Boston, to Philadelphia, Baltimore and Washington, finding associates and making acquaintances not calculated to lift her into greater respectability. This sort of roaming brought its proper fruits.

In 1866, Mrs. Lawler obtained a divorce from her husband, and thereafter assumed the name of Mansfield, by which she is best and most widely known. After the divorce, she made an effort to support herself by appearing as an actress, but met with poor success. At this time she became acquainted with Miss Annie Wood, an actress living in New York, according to whose statement Miss Mansfield requested an introduction to James Fisk, Jr., saying she had not "a single change of clothes, and had nothing to live upon but her handsome face, and she must make the most of it." Miss Wood gave her the introduction, though, as she says, with some reluctance; and, meeting her shortly afterwards, Miss Mansfield, according to Miss Wood, stated that her circumstances had very much improved, and she "had now plenty of good things; that she meant to get all the money she could out of Fisk, and then let him go, as he was not really the kind of man she fancied." But, before this introduction, Miss Mansfield's friends had appealed to Mr. Fisk's sympathies on her behalf, claiming that she was a worthy actress, laboring under difficulties, and he sent her several sums of money before he had ever seen her, and when he had no expectation or desire of becoming acquainted with her.

She, very soon obtained a strong hold upon Mr. Fisk, and early in 1868, he provided a house for her on Twenty-fourth street, and for more than two years defrayed all her expenses. One night, in the fall of 1868, a few gentlemen, meeting at her house, played cards with one another, and agreed to make her a present of all their winnings, which amounted to some twenty-five hundred dollars. This money Mr. Fisk advised her to let one of the party take and invest in Erie, which he knew was bound to rise the next day. She did so, and the money being invested as a margin, the entire amount realized, which, including the original investment, was about fifteen thousand dollars, was paid over to Miss Mansfield two or three days afterwards by the gentleman who managed the speculation. This money she invested in government bonds until Mr. Fisk purchased a house for her in Twenty-third street, when she sold out the bonds and deposited the proceeds in the hands of Mr. Fisk. When the deed was ready for execution he paid out this money, and a little over four thousand dollars more to the seller of the house, the price of the house being

THE INTRODUCTION.

forty thousand dollars, subject to a mortgage of twenty thousand dollars. He then spent ten thousand dollars more in improvements upon the house. From this time forward she was entirely dependent upon Mr. Fisk, who paid all her bills and kept her constantly supplied with money, although he refused to make any permanent settlement upon her, which was a point upon which she greatly insisted, and on account of his refusal to grant which, she, on one or two occasions, pretended to leave him, although she very speedily returned.

Miss Mansfield is a woman of prepossessing appearance, and is skilled in the art of making herself attractive. She is much above the medium height, having a pearly white skin, dark and very large and lustrous eyes, which, when directed at a judge, jury, or witness, have a terrible effect. This, it is said, was the case in the celebrated court trial in which she was engaged before the assassination of Mr. Fisk.

She is thus described when appearing in court in Yorkville:

"Her delicate white hands were encased in faultless lavender kid gloves, and over her magnificent tournure of dark hair was perched a jaunty little Alpine hat, with a dainty green feather placed thereon. Her robe was of the heaviest black silk, cut *à la imperatrice*, and having deep flounces of the heaviest black lace over Milanaise bands of white satin. At her snowy throat, the only article of jewelry on her person, a small gold pin glistened and heightened the effect. Her hair was worn *à la Cleo-*

patra, and a superb black velvet mantle covered her shoulders. Sitting there, this superb women was the impersonification of coolness and proud disdain."

Fisk became so deeply involved with this woman, that he not only supported her in grand style, but made a confidant of her; made her the custodian of business secrets, wrote frank, foolish letters to her, took his friends and associates to her house to dine and to spend the evening in playing at cards, and thus placed himself almost wholly in her power. The truth was he loved Helen Josephine Mansfield. He told her so—and, alas! he *wrote* her so. She retained his letters, and, afterwards when they quarrelled, she threatened to publish them.

Fisk foolishly endeavored to prevent her from so doing—tried to "buy her off,"—then invoked the power of the court to get an injunction against their publication.

But his death has dissolved the injunction, and certain of the letters have been published.

Whether these letters are all of the Fisk-Mansfield correspondence, remains to be seen. His friends say they are the whole. His enemies say they are *not* the whole. Time will show. Meanwhile, the letters have attracted a great deal of attention. They are less learned than elegant, less sentimental than some of their historic precedents; but they are "funnier" than any other correspondence of which the world has any knowledge.

In her wanderings previous to the time when she met Fisk, Miss Mansfield met in Philadelphia a young man of prepossessing appearance, gay, affable, bold, reckless and liberal in spending money. After she was settled in New York, this young man, then also residing in that city, became a frequent visitor to the house—was in fact a formidable and successful rival to "Prince Erie" in the affections of this woman.

Edward S. Stokes, the young man here referred to, had an interest in a large oil refinery in Brooklyn, in which Fisk became part owner. Fisk and Stokes were active, earnest friends. Jealousy made them bitter unrelenting enemies. Fisk advised Stokes not to go to Miss Mansfield's house, and plead with the woman to have nothing to do with the man. He was laughed at—he remonstrated; his affections were trifled with, and he, therefore, commanded that his wishes must be respected. He was defied by both; and was finally altogether rejected by the ungrateful woman he had lifted from poverty to affluence, and, he, therefore, resolved to be avenged.

A disgraceful quarrel arose, which has been dragged through the courts of New York to the disgust of all good people. Stokes was arrested and imprisoned on a charge of having embezzled certain stocks, preferred by Fisk. Fisk was threatened with the publication of his correspondence with Miss Mansfield. Several suits were brought on various charges against all parties; these required the expenditures of large sums of money, greatly to the inconvenience of Stokes and Mansfield. They, therefore, attempted to force hush money out of Fisk; and thus new complications and more law suits arose.

In order to prevent the publication of the silly and disgraceful letters held by Fisk's enemies, he had resource to that infallible remedy for every ill in New York—an injunction. A legal notice was served on Stokes and Miss Mansfield, forbidding them to publish the letters they threatened to use to damage Fisk. As specimens of this incomparable epistolary literature, a few of the letters are here inserted, It will be seen that the favorite pet names were "Josie" and "Dolly."

For the surrender of these letters it is said Stokes and Miss Mansfield demanded of Fisk, the comfortable sum of $200,000. The letters are as follows, beginning with a note written on his visiting card to "Josie" when she lived in Lexington avenue.

MRS. JOSIE LAWLER, 42 Lexington avenue:

Come. Will you come over with Fred and dine with me? If your friends are there bring them along.

Yours, truly,

J. F., JR.

Have not heard from you as you promised.

On the back of the card was the following:

Come. Fred is at the door. My room, eight o'clock. After many good looks I found Mr. Chamberlain. The understanding is now that yourself and Miss Land are to go with me, say at half-past nine o'clock, and the above gentleman is to come at eleven o'clock, as he has some matters to attend to which

HER FIRST VISIT TO THE OFFICE OF THE PRINCE OF ERIE.

will take him until that time. Answer this if you will be ready by half-past nine o'clock.

Yours, truly,

JAMES FISK, JR.

As soon as Miss Mansfield became established in the keeping of Fisk, she availed herself of every possible opportunity to display her good fortune. She drove out in fine style, and appeared on the street and in the park dressed and attended as a lady of great consequence.

One day she went to the office of the Erie Railway Company in the Grand Opera House, and called on "Prince Erie," to the surprise and astonishment of himself and his employees. This visit called out the following note:

Strange you should make my office or the vicinity the scene for a "personal." You must be aware that harm came to me in such foolish vanity, and those that could do it care but little for the interest of the writer of this.

Yours, truly,

JAMES FISK, JR.

He soon attoned for this scold. In January, 1868, he wrote:

FIFTH AVE. H.

DOLLY:—Enclosed find money. Bully morning for a funeral!

J. F., JR.

Next came this:

DEAR JOSIE:—Get ready and come to the Twenty-third street entrance of the hotel and take me down town, and then you can come back and get the girls for the Fulton dinner to-day.

Yours, truly,
SARDINES.

Josie was going off on a journey, and Fisk provides for her like a devoted lover:

DOLLY:—The baggage sleigh will call at one o'clock, and you can leave in my charge what you see fit. You have no time to lose.

J. F., J

By proxy due notice was sent:

MISS MANSFIELD:—The sleigh will call for you at two P. M.

Yours,
J. FISK, per J. C.

He explains short comings in a formal and business-like note.

My people are partaking of New York, in the shape of "White Fawn," and two or three other different matters. I may not be able to see you again to-night. If not, will take breakfast with you—the best I could do.

Yours, truly,
February 5th, 1868. JAMES.

The head of the family gives minute instructions:

DEAR DOLLY:—Get right up now and I will be down to take breakfast with you in about thirty minutes. We will take breakfast in the main dining room down stairs.

Yours, truly,
JAMES FISK, JR.

Wednesday Morning, February 6.

To-day Fisk sent "Dolly" some money, saying:

Have the kindness to acknowledge.

Yours, truly,
February 22, 1868. J. F., JR.

DEAR JOSIE:—I have got some matters to arrange and cannot call for you until it is about time to go. I will be there twenty minutes before eight. Be ready.

Yours, truly,
February 26, 1868. JAMES.

Here is a very excellent opiate and one that patients would no doubt be willing to take quite often:

DOLLY;—Enclosed find $50. Sleep, Dolly, all the sleep you can to-day—every little bit? Sleep, Dolly! I feel as if three cents' worth of clams would help me some.

Yours, truly,
J. F., JR.

"Josie" is reminded that there are other ties, and that "my family" does not include her:

Monday Morning.

I am going to the San Francisco Minstrels with my family. If Mr. L. was here I should ask him to take you. Shall see you to-morrow evening.

Yours, truly,

J. F., Jr.

How he made amends for preferring his family for one night only, appears from the following sent to "Josie" next day:

Dolly:—Enclosed find——. I am wrong, but am bothered. I will come right. When I don't come don't wait. You shall not be placed as you were to-night.

Yours, truly,

JAMES FISK, Jr.

Wednesday Evening.

Have the kindness to acknowledge.

Yours, truly,

J. F., Jr.

Feb., 22, 1868.

Hon. William M. Tweed, "Boss" of Tammany, and the partner of Sir Morton Peto, the great English financier, are to dine at "Josie's" with Fisk. No doubt the gentlemen felt highly honored by the privilege of such extraordinary company.

187 West Street, *Tuesday Oct.* 13, 1868.

My Dear Josie:—James McHenry, the partner of Sir Morton Peto, the largest railway builder in the world, Mr. Tweed and Mr. Lane, will dine with us at half-past six o'clock. I want you to provide as nice a dinner as possible. Everything went off elegantly. We are *all* safe. Will see you at six o'clock.

JAMES FISK, Jr.

Pater familias orders his valise packed:

Monday Aug. 2, 1869.

Dear Josie:—Send my valise, with two shirts, good collars, vest, handkerchiefs, black velvet coat, nice vest, patent leather shoes, light pants. I am going to Long Branch to see about the calerye. Inclosed find twenty-five dollars. Be back in the morning.

J. F., Jr.

More money sent:

St. James Hotel, *Sunday Oct.* 18, 1869.

Dear Josie:—Inclosed you will find one hundred and forty-three dollars.

Yours, truly,

JAMES.

The following is rather an humble inquiry. There must have been some little jarring. Fisk evidently was penitent, wanted to make up and be on good terms with his "Dolly." He wrote like one who had been locked out in the cold over night and did not enjoy the exposure and exile from home:

February 10, 1869.

My Dear Dolly:—Will you see me this morning? If so, what hour?

Yours, truly, ever,

JAMES.

Whether "Dolly" saw him, or not is a matter unrecorded, but judging from the following dispatch four days later and the enclosure made in March, the presumption is that the difference was duly healed.

WORCHESTER, MASS.

[Received at Thirtieth street, *February* 14, 1870.]

To H. J. MANSFIELD, 350 West Twenty-third street.

On the three o'clock train from Boston. Shall be in New York at twelve.

J. F., JR.

(13 D. H.)

March 10.

DEAR DOLLY:—Inclosed find seventy-five dollars, which you need; do not wait dinner for me to-night; I cannot come.

Yours, truly, ever,

JAMES.

Miss Mansfield was a shrewd, far-sighted, sharp, calculating woman of the world. She knew that any moment some new attraction might arise that would transfer Fisk's affections to another. She, therefore, determined to "make hay whilst the sun shone." She demanded of her suitor a "settlement." The little sums of money received from time to time were well enough in their way; they provided for present needs, but made no provision for the future. On the 28th of January 1870, "Josie" renewed her demand for a settlement on her of the sum of $25,000, and threatened to leave "Prince Erie" if he refused compliance.

On the following day "Josie" wrote him a letter suspending their relations until Fisk granted her request. To this letter Fisk made a studied, formal, weak, foolish, reply as follows:

Sunday Evening, Feb. 1, 1870.

MY DEAR JOSIE:—I received your letter. The tenor does not surprise me much. You alone sought the issue and the reward will belong to you. I cannot allow you to depart believing yourself what you write, and must say to you, which you know full well, that all the differences could have been settled by a kiss in the right spirit, and in after days I should feel very kindly toward you out of memory of the great love I have borne for you. I never was aware that you admitted a fault. I have many—God knows, too many—and that has brought me the trouble of the day. I will not speak of the future, for full well I know the spirit you take it in. "You know me," and the instincts of your heart will weigh me out in the right scale. I will give you no parting advice. You have been well schooled in that, and can tell chaff from wheat, and probably are as strong to-night as the humble writer of this letter. The *actions* of the past *must* be the right way to think of me; and from them, day by day, I hope any comparison which you may make from writing in the future will be favorable for me. A longer letter from me might be much of an advertisement of my weakness, and the only great idea I would impress on your mind is how wrong you are when you say that I have "grown tired of you."

Wrong, wrong! Never excuse yourself on that in after years. Don't try to teach your heart that, for it is a lie, and you are falsifying yourself to your own soul.

No more. Like the Arabs, we will fold our tents and quietly steal away, and when we spread them next we hope it will be where the "woodbine twineth," over the river Jordan, on the bright and beautiful banks of heaven.

From yours, ever,

JAMES.

Josie repented, receded and sent for Fisk to come and see her; the quarrel was made up and pleasant relations resumed. Four months later the correspondence began afresh.

MY DEAR JOSIE:—Enclosed find your request. I will send to the Fifth avenue for the things. I cannot go to the house as much as I would like to.

Yours,

JAMES.

May 6, 1870.

COMPTROLLER'S OFFICE, ERIE RAILWAY COMPANY,

NEW YORK, *May*, 1870.

DOLLY:—What do you think of this man? I told him you would talk to him, and then tell him to come back to me next Monday, and I will talk to you about it.

Yours ever.

JAMES.

A new trouble arose, however, when Montaland arrived from Paris, "Prince Erie" paid court to her, to the neglect of Miss Mansfield, but then "Josie" had a new suitor in Edward S. Stokes, and should have been satisfied. She, however, was not, and revolted, scolded and threatened Fisk with separation, Fisk apologized:

August 1, 1870.

MY DEAR JOSIE:—I send you a letter I found to my care on my desk. I cannot come to you to-night. I shall stay in town to-night, and probably to-morrow night, and after that I must go East. On my return I shall come to see you. I am sure you will say, "What a fool!" But you must rest and so must I. The thread is so slender I dare not strain it more. I am sore, but God made me so, and I have not the power to change it.

Loving you, *as none but you.*

I am yours ever,

JAMES.

Fisk discovered a plotting against his "peace of mind" and reports his discovery to "Josie."

August 4, 1870.

DEAR JOSIE:—I found on my arrival at my office that the following dispatch had passed West last night:

E. S. Stokes, Buffalo and Saratoga Springs.

Pay no attention to former dispatch. Come on first train. RANE.

Of course *it means* nothing that *you are aware of.* But let me give you the author of it and my authority, and you will see how faithfully they have worked the case out after my departure last evening. Miss Pieris drove directly to Rane's office; from there to the corner of Twenty-second street and Broadway, where the above dispatch was sent, and from there to Rulley's. A third party was with them, but who left them there? Rane and Pieris, why should they heed Stokes? "Comment is unnecessary"—a plotting house and against me. What have "I done" that Nully Pieris should work against my peace of mind.

Yours truly, ever,

JAMES.

P. S.—Since writing the within I understand a dispatch has reached New York that he is on his way.

JAMES.

Fisk, though offended, is still willing to help "Josie" pay bills:

August 14, 1870.

Enclosed you will find $400 for your little matters. You told me when I saw you last you would send me your bills, which I would be pleased to receive and they shall have my attention at once. Your letter would require a little time to prepare a right answer to, so I will answer it more fully by to-morrow, when I can look it more carefully over. I am very happy to know that you have acted from no impulse in leaving me, but that it was a long matured plan. I hope you have made no mistake.

Yours truly, ever,
JAMES FISK, JR.

Miss Mansfield finally failed to obtain from Fisk a large sum of money as a maintenance, and therefore gave him notice that she would discontinne his acquaintance. There were undoubtedly some sharp letters passed which have not been preserved. Here however is one from "Josie" that tells the whole story:

JAMES FISK, JR.—

That your letter had the desired effect you can well imagine. I am honest enough to admit it cut me to the quick. In all the annals of letter writing I may say it eclipsed them all. Your secretary made a slight error, however, in supposing that Mlle. Montaland was mentioned. The only prima donna I referred to was "Miss Pieris." As you say, Mlle. has nothing whatever to do with my affairs. I have always respected her, and only thought of her as one of the noblest works of God—beautiful and talented and *your choice* —never referring to her in my letter in thought or word. I freely admit that I never expected so severe a letter from you. I, of course, feel that it was unmerited, but, as it is your opinion of me, I accept it with all the stings. You have *struck home*, and, I may say, turned the knife around. I will send you the picture you speak of at once. The one in the parlor I will also dispose of. I know of nothing else here that you would wish. I am anxious to adjust our affairs. I certainly do not wish to annoy you, and that I may be able to do so, I write you this last letter. You have told me very often that you held some twenty or twenty-five thousand dollars of mine in your keeping. I do not know if it is so, but that I may be able to shape my affairs permanently for the future that a part of the amount would place me in a position where I never would have to appeal to you for aught. I have never *had one dollar from any one else*, and arriving here from the Branch, expecting my affairs with you to continue, I contracted bills that I would not otherwise have done. I do not ask for anything I have not been led to suppose was mine, and do not ask you to settle what is not entirely convenient for you. After a time I shall sell my house, but for the present think it best to remain in it. The money I speak of would place me where I should not need the assistance of any one.

The ring I take back as fairly as I gave it you; the mate to it I shall keep for company. Why you should say I obtained this house by robbery I cannot imagine; however, you know best. I am sorry that your associations with me were detrimental to you, and I would gladly, with you (were it possible), obliterate the last three years of my life's history; but it is not possible, and we must struggle to outlive our past. I trust you will take the sense of this letter as it is meant, and that there can be be no mistake I send this by Etta, and what you do not understand she will explain.

To this and other letters, Fisk made the following reply:

NEW YORK, *Oct.* 1, 1870.

MRS. MANSFIELD:—There can be no question as to the authority of the letter which was handed to me yesterday by your servant, in this respect differing from the epistle which you say you received from Miss Pieris, and which, in your opinion, required the united efforts of herself, Mlle. Montaland and myself. Certainly the composition should be good if these two parties had combined to produce it. But the slight mistake you make is evident from the fact that the letter referred to was never seen by me, and I presume Mlle. Montaland is equally ignorant of its existence, as it is not likely she troubled herself about your affairs. I can scarcely believe that she assisted Miss Pieris in composing the letter, and the credit is therefore due to Miss Pieris for superior talent in correspondence. As far as the great exposure you speak of is concerned, that is a dark story upon which I have no light, and as I fail to see it I cannot of course understand it. I have endeavored to put your jumbled letter together in order to arrive at your meaning, and I presume I have some idea of what you wish to convey; but as your statements lack the important element of truth they cannot, of course, have any weight with me. You may not be to blame for entertaining the idea that you have shown great kindness to Miss Pieris and others, and that they are under great obligations to you for favors conferred. The habit of constantly imagining that you were the real author of all the benefits bestowed upon others would naturally affect a much better balanced brain than yours, and in time you would come to believe that you alone had the power to distribute the good things to those around you, utterly forgetful of him who was behind the scenes utterly unnoticed. Can you blame, then, those from whose eyes the veil has fallen, and who see you in your true light as the giver of others' charities? I would not trouble myself to answer your letters, and I do not consider it a duty I owe you to give you a final expression of my opinion. In venting your spite on Miss Pieris (with whose affairs, by the way, I have nothing whatever to do) you have written a letter, in answering which you afforded me an opportunity of conveying to you my ideas respecting the theories which you have taken every opportunity to express to those around you, and which many people have considered merely the emanations of a crazy brain. I could not coincide with this view, for crazy people are not inclined to do precisely as they please, either right or wrong, and so long as they are *loose* I consider them sane, and therefore I could not put that construction on your conversation. As for Miss Pieris being "a snake in the grass," I care but little about that. She can do me neither harm nor good. I have done all that has been done for her during the past year. She comes to me and says: "Sir, you have been my friend; you have assisted me in my troubles, and I thank you from the bottom of my heart." That is a full and sufficient recompense for me for any good I may have done her, and she can return. If she be a snake in the grass I know full well her sting is gone and she is harmless. But what think you of a woman who would veil my eyes, first by a gentle kiss, and afterward, night and day, for weeks, months and years, by deceit and fraud, to lead me through the dark valley of trouble, when she could have made my path one of roses, committing crimes which a devil incarnate would shrink from, while all this time I showed to her, as to you, nothing but kindness, both in words and actions, laying at your feet a soul, a heart, a fortune and a reputation which had cost by night and day twenty-five years of perpetual struggle, and which, but for the black blot of having in an evil hour linked itself with you, would stand out to-day brighter than any ever seen upon earth. But the mist has fallen, and you appear in your true light. I borrow your own words to describe you, "a snake in the grass," and verily, I have found thee out; and you have the audacity to call your sainted mother to witness your advice to me. "A dog that bites," &c., &c.

You accuse her of leading you on and of ever standing ready to make appointments for you. The tone of your letter is such that you seem willing to shoulder the load of guilt under which an ordinary criminal would stagger. I believe you have arrived at that state when no amount of guilt will disturb your serenity or prevent your having sweet dreams, and we still shall see you crawl "a snake in the grass."

How I worship the night. I said, "Get thee behind me, Satan!" The few weeks that have elapsed since that blessed hour, how I bless them for the peace of mind they have brought me! Again the world looks bright and I have a being. You imagined I would pursue you again, and you thought I would endeavor to tear down the castle you had obtained by robbery. God knows that if I am an element so lost to every feeling of decency as to be willing to link itself with you, I will assist and foster it, so that it will keep you from crawling towards me and prevent me from looking on you as a snake, as you are, and from raising a hand in pity to assist you, should trouble again cross your path. So I have no fears that I will again come near you. I send you back a ring; and, were I to write anything about it, the words would be only too decent for the same, were they couched in the worst of language. So I say, take it back. Its memory is indecent, and it is the last souvenir I have that reminds me of you. I had a few pictures of you, but they have found a place among the nothings which fill the waste basket under my table. I am aware that in your back parlor hangs the picture of the man who gave you the wall to hang it on; and rumor says you have another in your chamber. The picture upstairs send back to me. Take the other down, for he whom it represents has no respect for you. After you read this letter, you should be ashamed to look at the picture, for you would say, "With all thy faults I love thee still," and what would be merely the same oft-repeated *lie*. So take it down. Do not keep anything in that house that looks like me,

If there are any unsettled business matters that it is proper for me to arrange, send them to me, and make the explanation as brief as possible.

I fain would reach the point where not even the slightest necessity will exist for any intercourse between us. I am in hopes this will end it.

JAMES FISK, JR.

Four days later, Fisk sent the following:

NEW YORK, *Oct.* 4, 1870.

After the departure of Etta to-day I wasted time enough to read over once more the letter of which she was the bearer from you to me, and I determined to reply to it, for the reason that if it remained unanswered you might possibly think I did not really mean what I said when I wrote; and, besides, I was apprehensive that the friendly talk carried on through Etta, at second hand, between you and me, might lead you to suppose I had somewhat repented of the course I had taken, or of the words I had penned. It is to remove any such impression that I again write to you, as I would have the language of my former letter and the sentiments therein expressed stamped upon your heart as my deep-seated opinion of your character. No other construction must be put upon my words. I turn over the first page of your letter; I pass over the kind words you have written; have I not furnished a satisfactory mansion for others' use? Have I not fulfilled every promise I have made? is there not a stability about your finances to-day (if not disturbed by vultures) sufficient to afford you a comfortable income for the remainder of your natural life? You say you have never received a dollar from any one but me, and you *will never* have another from me, until want and misery bring you to my door, except, of course, in fulfilment of my sacred promise, and the settlement of your bills up to three weeks ago, at five minutes to eleven o'clock.

You need not have any fear as to my sensitiveness regarding your calling on any one else for assistance, as I find the word "*assistance*" underlined in your letter to make it the more impressive on my mind. That of all others is the point I would have you reach; for in that you would say, "Why, man, how beautiful you are to look at, but nothing to lean on!" And you may well imagine my surprise at the selection of the element you have chosen to fill my place (Stokes). I was shown to-day his diamonds, which had been sacrificed to our people at one-half their value, and undoubtedly if this were not so, the money would have been turned over to you, that you might feel contented as to the permanency of your affairs. You will therefore excuse me if I decline your modest request for a still further disbursement of $25,000. I very naturally feel that some part of this amount might be used to release from the pound the property of others in whose welfare the writer of this does *not* feel unbounded interest.

You say that you hope I will make sense of your letter. There is but one sense to be taken out of it, and that is an " epitaph," to be cut on the stone at the head of the grave in which Miss Helen Josephine Mansfield has buried her pride. Had she been the same proud-spirited girl that she was when she stood side by side with me—the power behind the throne—she would not have humbled herself to ask a permanency of one whom she had so deeply wronged, nor would she stoop to be indebted to him for a home which would have furnished a haven of rest, pleasure and debauchery without cost to those who had crossed his path and robbed him of the friendship he once felt. The length of time since I had her and the kind words she spoke left my mind ill prepared for the perusal of your letter at that time, and it was not until after her departure, when I was seated quietly alone, that I took in the full intent and meaning of your letter, and felt that it was " robbery" and nothing else. Now, pin this letter with the other. The front of this is the back of that, and you will have a telescopic view of yourself and your character as you appear to me to-day; and then I ask you to turn back some pages of your life's history, counting each page one week of your life, and see how I looked to thee then, and ask your own guilty heart if you had not better let me alone; and instead of trying to answer this letter from your disorganized brain, or writing from the dictation of those around you to-day, simply take a piece of paper and write on it the same as I do now, so far as we are now, or ever may be, "Dust to dust, ashes to ashes. Amen."

J. F., Jr.

Fisk maintained that after Josie left him and went with Stokes, that Stokes ought to pay the bills, and Fisk thus writes to Josie:

(J. F., Jr.) [monogram.]

Oct. 19, 1870.

MADAME:—Enclosed I send you bill of Harris receipted, and I also beg to hand you $126.29, being the honest proportion of the Bassford bill which belongs to me to pay. I should have made the word "honest" more definite, for had not Mr. Bassford to put the dates to the bill, as he had received instructions from Miss Mansfield to have the bill all under the date of June 8th, 1870, although ($146. 26) the amount of the goods, as bought by you or your agent, was sent at a much later date? I should not suppose you would care to place yourself in the light that this bill puts you, knowing as as I do the instructions that you gave Mr. Bassford. I had supposed you "honest," but I find that a trace of that virtue does not even cling to you.

I am, yours,

J. F., JR.

DEPARTMENT OF FINANCE,

NEW YORK, *Oct.* 20, 1870.

MADAM:—You know I would not wrong you and I would take back all my acts when there could be a shadow of doubt that you were right and I was wrong; and let me speak of the other harsh letters I have written. I wrote them because you had wronged me positively, because you had placed between me and my life, my hope and my happiness, an eternal gulf, and I felt sore and revengeful, and on those letters I am now the same. It would be idle for me to write aught about them or abont *us*, when I could talk to you there. You did not listen. I presume it to be the same now. The entire connection is like a dream to me, a fearful dream, from which I have awoke, and, while dreaming, supposed my soul had gone out; and the awakening tells me I am saved, and, from the embers of the late fire, there smoulders no spirit of revenge towards you, for you acted right, and the *wrong* only came to me from you because you did not act sooner, and I would not believe that any power on earth would make any question of money, influence us or come between me and the holy feeling I once had for you. I sent John to Bassford's, and they told him what I said, or he told me so, that you left word that the dates of the bill should not be changed. But what does it matter whether it is so or not? I cannot *feel* that you would do it, and something says to me this was one of the things she was not like. So I pass it by, and if the letters of last night or to-day are not like me you can wash the bad act out from your memory, and leave but the one idea that I want to do my duty and fulfil every unsettled relic. At least in my heart rests no remorse, for the memory is too deeply seated, and I would cherish all that is good about you, and forget forever the bad. Of late you have thought different from me (this may be imaginary on my part), for which I think you give me all the credit you can. We have *parted forever*. Now, let us make the memory of the past as bright and beautiful as we can; for on my side there is so little to cherish that I cling to it with great tenacity, and hope from time to time to wear it off. You *know* full well how I have suffered. *Once* you knew me better than any one on earth. To-day you know *me less.* It is the proper light for you to stand in. It is *all* you desire on your side. It is all you deserve *on mine.*

This letter should remain and be read only by you. Should you see fit to answer it, the answer will be the same way kept by me. There has been a storm. The ship, a noble steamer, has gone down. The storm is over and the sea is smooth again.

Little ships should keep near shore;
Greater ships can venture more.

"My ship is small and poorly officered."

I am yours, ever, etc., etc.,

J. F., Jr.

P. S.—I would have liked to have answered your letter in full, but, as you say, I have not a well-balanced brain, and I know I could not do justice to a letter of that kind, so refrain, and content to let the sentiments of it "know and fret me."

There was then an unsuccessful attempt at reconciliation, after which Fisk writes another letter.

October 25, 1870.

Why should I write you again. Shall I ever reach the end. There comes another and another chapter, until I get weary with the entire affair. I would forget it, and no doubt you would the same. The mistake yesterday was almost the mistake of a lifetime for me. Who supposed for an instant that you would cross my path again in a spirit of submission, and with a contrite spirit? You have done that you should be sorry for, and I the same in permitting it. This cannot be, and I shall write you the final letter, and I shall see you no more. I told you that much yesterday evening, and still I write it to you again. Yes, for the reason I treated you falsely last night, and I left you with a different impression, and I would put that right. You acted so differently from your nature that I forgive you, and even went so far as to bring my mind to bear how I could take you back again. First, the devil stood behind, and my better reason gave way for the moment, and I came away, telling you I would see you no more. When your better character comes in contact with mine we are so much alike that much of what is said, like that last night, had better been unsaid. All now looks bright and beautiful, and my better nature trembles at ideas that were expressed last night. But that I should have left on your mind an idea that you could control me is erroneous. There are truths in this affair, and they must be spoken. You have gone out from one element and have taken another (Stokes), and for you to turn back, either when you are situated that way, or when even you could say that element had gone, should make no difference to me. It was you that took the step and you should and shall suffer the consequences. Supposing the part you took last night and yesterday afternoon was one of truth, if not, and I——.

Again, if you were not dealing from your heart in what took place, and I hope it was not true, then there are no consequences and no suffering for you to endure. Why, it has been many a long year since I could say to myself that I had committed such a folly. To find another like yesterday would bring me back almost to childhood. To imagine that I should have again crossed your threshold, and crossed it, too, deliberately knowing that the same facts existed that had given me all my trouble and made me this sorrow —why, it is devilish. I told you that I had passed the realm where I had forgiven you all the sorrow you had made me, and that I would not murmur; I would not find fault with all that I saw. I would fain tear your image from my mind, and I will. Why, I thought all night last night, and all day to-day of your saying, "I would rather be a toad," etc., etc. Was that written to apply to me? I should say so. Yes. Who knows what you would not conceive? No one but yourself. And I must weigh you carefully, for I have nothing but a great character to deal with, and I must meet things carefully. You might suppose you could love two and, perhaps, more elements, and make them hover near you. Certainly you did last night, and, for shame, I was one of them. But it will *never* occur again. For once let us be honest. You went that road because it looks smooth and pleasant, and mine looked rugged and worn. Now, a mistake can-

MISS MANSFIELD'S RESIDENCE.

24

not be found out too soon. Travel further along, and don't try to turn so soon. I can see you now, as you were last night, when you talked of this man (Stokes); and do not deceive yourself—*you loved him.* Yesterday there was nothing but the breaking up of strong pride and the giving way of wilfulness. Cling to that one. Leave me alone; for in me you have *nothing left.* Why ask me to weaken yourself with him? All this you must study; but I pledge you to-night that *I will not* countenance even your impression on my mind until the door is closed behind forever. For what you can gain from me you probably cannot afford to do that: so let me advise you—nourish him and be careful. Nothing is so bad for you as changes. He loves you; you love him. You have caused me all the misery you could. Cling to him. Be careful what you do, for he will be watchful. How well he knows *you cheated me.* He will look for the same. And now, as I know precisely how you stand from your own lips, I will treat him differently. Although you would not protect him I will. While he is there and until his memory is buried forever, never approach me, for I shall send you away unseen. Ever be careful that you do not have the feeling that you can come back to me, for there is a wide gulf between you and me. I would not hold a false hope out to you. I shall not trouble you more in this letter. You have the only idea I can express to you. You know when you can see me again, if ever. The risk for you is too great. Loving, and suited as you are, cling to him for the present, and when your nature grows tired of that throw him off. And so long until it is time for you to be weary and for you to be "put in your little bed" forever, you must rest contented. Don't begin plotting to-morrow. Take to-morrow for thought, and be governed by this letter, for the writer has much of your destiny in his hands.

Notwithstanding their last farewell letter, Josie still clung to Fisk. She asked him for favors, asked him for money, which Fisk, in his good nature, almost always gave, as we see by the letter following:

November 1, 1870.

MISS MANSFIELD:—I have taken the steps for the corn doctress' removal to a southern clime, where her business should be better, as vegetables of that class thrive more rapidly there than on our bleak shores. I presume it will take from two, or say four days, before I get the passes, when they will be sent to you. Should she call on you say to her to come back in four days and you will have them for her. I sent you a package by Maggie for what you desired on Saturday evening, with a little surplus over for trimmings, which I hope you received. I am of your opinion regarding not only Dr. Pape, but all of the doctors. You are well; let nature take its course. You are in too good health to tamper with a constitution as good as yours. This is important for your consideration.

Yours, truly,

JAMES.

November 10, 1870.

Enclosed find $300. Please use. I am very sorry we could not have arrived at a more satisfactory conclusion last night. I did all I could, and the same feeling prevails o'er me now. With a careful and watchful manner you should look at all our affairs. You should make no mistake. You told me I should hear from you when you came to a conclusion. Therefore I wait upon your early reply, and until then I must of course pursue the same course I have for the last six weeks. I hope we shall mutually understand each other, for the thing could be made, as it should be made, satisfactory to you.

I am, yours,

JAMES.

More Money to Josie.

Fisk sent $1,000 to Josie in November, with this memorandum:

Erie Railway Company, Treasurer's Office, November 7th, 1870, receiving desk—$500.

WM. H. B.

Erie Railway Company, Treasurer's Office, November 10th, 1870, receiving desk—$500.

WM. H. B.

Please acknowledge receipt.

JAMES.

November 11, 1870.

Enclosed you will find the order on Miss Guthrie, which have Etta or you present and it will be all right.

Mr. Comer gave them an order not to deliver anything only on my written order, to stop the "opera bouffers;" but present this enclosed order and it will be all right. Mrs. Reher was here this morning and I gave her transportation for self and Michael to Charlestown by steamer. Enclosed you will find box at theatre in order to get the same, as it was sold. I have convinced myself that I desire you and yours to come.

Please answer the note, that I may know you are to come.

Yours, truly,
JAMES.

November 12, 1870.

Enclosed find the letters. I was not aware Miss Jordan was to come until I saw her pass the gate-keeper, but that is nothing astonishing, as she is one of our regular customers. Of course I did not send her the box, for she is not in a mood that I presume such civilities would be received from Fisk, Jr. I am glad you were pleased. I would have been glad to have you seen "Le Petit Faust." At the "Duchesse" we used old clothes and scenery, while in "Faust" all was new. We play "Faust" this afternoon. Shall I send you a box? And on Monday night we give the world "our diamond," "Les Brigands," all new. Surely the world is machinery. Am I keeping up with it? is the question.

Yours, truly,
JAMES

Fisk was completely melted again and still in love with the woman to whom he had written very severe letters. Josie never gave him up. She kept in his way. By and by Fisk's love came back. The love notes were again written friendly as ever :

November 4, 1870.

DEAR DOLLY:—Do you really wish to see a "brigand" at your house to night; if so what hour, or from what hour and how late should I call? for I might be able to come at eight or perhaps not till ten. Say what hour and how late is your limit after the time you first say?

JAMES.

November 15, 1870.

Enclosed find box for to-night. Should you find you cannot use it, send it back to me in the letter. Do you feel as I said you would this morning? The box, of course, is for whoever you may invite,

Yours ever,

JAMES.

November 16, 18—.

DEAR DOLLY:—Don't feel that way. Go riding, and to-night, darling, I will take you to rest. I shall go out at half-past three, and you can safely look ahead, darling, for rest. It will come, and we shall be happy again.

Yours, truly,

JAMES.

November 18, 1870.

Shall go to the race to-day, and this evening I am engaged until late, and I am afraid you would get tired waiting for the ring of the bell or the ring of the door. So I will not ask you to wait my coming unless it be your wish, in which case I will come as early as I can. Yours, &c.

Enclosed find the Leidunnor Ball.

Yours, truly,

JAMES.

Monday Morning.

Not time to come up.

J. F., JR.

The Stokes Suit.

After Fisk and Josie had "made up," Stokes entered the field again. He persuaded Josie that the letters which Fisk had written were of immense value to him, and that he would pay any price rather than have them exposed to the gaze of the public. So in a fatal hour Josie consented to "go back" on Fisk.

Fisk remembered his private correspondence with the woman whom he had once loved, whom he had taken from poverty and made rich, with a feeling of remorse. He fully comprehended the object of his enemies, and met their attack at once.

Stokes failing to get a settlement from Fisk for his $200,000 claim, offered to enter upon an arbitration, and selected Clarence Seward to arbitrate the matter. Fisk agreed to this. Clarence Seward decided that Stokes' claim was null and void, but that Fisk ought to pay Stokes $10,000 damage for the night which he spent in the Tombs. This Fisk agreed to do, provided Stokes would give up the letters which he had written to Josephine Mansfield. Stokes agreed to do this and received the $10,000 from Wm. H. Morgan, Fisk's attorney, on the 30th of June, 1871. Stokes also wanted Fisk to pay his attorney, Ira Shafer, $5,000. This Fisk agreed to do. So he paid in all, to get these letters out of Stokes' hands, $15,000, and Stokes sent the letters to Peter B. Sweeney, with this letter:

HON. PETER B. SWEENEY:

DEAR SIR:—Mr. Buckley informed me of your desire to have possession of Mr. Fisk's letters, approved, &c. I herewith send them all to you.

Yours, respectfully,

E. S. STOKES.

A release and award, which was to forever close the dispute, was given by Stokes to Fisk.

In his efforts to defeat the schemes of Stokes and Miss Mansfield, and to counteract any publication that might be made derogatory to his reputation, Fisk induced one of the servants from the Mansfield mansion to make a statement under oath of what he overheard in that house. This extraordinary affidavit was published in the newspapers and created a lively sensation.

It was as follows:

Supreme Court.—James Fisk, Jr., against Edward S. Stokes, Helen Josephine Mansfield, and others—City and County of New York, ss.—Richard E. King being duly sworn, says: I am 22 years of age, and am by occupation a waiter; from about the 18th of October, 1870, to the 20th of March, 1871, I was engaged in my said capacity as waiter in the house of Helen Josephine Mansfield and Edwin S. Stokes, at 359 West Twenty-third street, in the city of New York. I took the place of John Marshall, who left the employ of the said persons about the time I commenced my engagement there, and got the position in answer to an advertisement upon my own application; when I went to live at the house of Mrs. Mansfield and Mr. Stokes, I was told to keep away from John Marshall and all Mr. Fisk's party, and Mr. Fisk, and have nothing whatever to do with them, and that that was a condition of my keeping my place; when I went there to live, I found that Mr. Stokes and Mrs. Mansfield were living there together as man and wife; they both made that house their home; Mr. Stokes had his meals there almost invariably with Mrs. Mansfield; they occupied the same room when they retired at night, and in all respects conducted themselves toward one another as is customary for married people to do; and the said Stokes never failed to my recollection to come there and stay all night with said Mansfield at least twice a week, to-wit, Saturday or Sunday nights, and Wednesday or Thursday nights.

The principal subject of conversation between Mrs.

Mansfield, Mr. Stokes, and Mrs. Williams, who, I believe, is a cousin of Mrs. Mansfield, and resided with her from the time I went there to the time I left, was the manner in which they proposed to make money out of Mr. Fisk by means of letters from him to said Mansfield, which she said she had, and statements by said Mansfield by conversations between Mr. Fisk and herself, by selling the same to newspapers, or compelling him to pay the money to prevent the same being made public, and they said that they could get a large amount of money out of Mr. Fisk in that way. I waited upon them at table at dinner, and after dinner in their rooms, and heard much of their conversation upon the subjects stated in this affidavit; and among other matters said Mansfield said to said Stokes in my hearing, 'I have the letters, and I will give them to you and let you use them to your best advantage, and make all you can out of Mr. Fisk. So you take care of me and stick to me through life, I will do all I can to assist you in this matter; all I wish is just to get satisfaction out of that fellow, now the dog won't look at me. I have to depend on all that you can make, and it worries me to death." Another time she said, "Now, Ed., I have given you these letters; you have got them and they are yours, and now I want you to put them to the best advantage, make all you can and take care of me." He said he would; that he had talked the matter over and knew there was money in it, and he was going right into it heavy. She laughed and said, "'Bully for you." He said, "When he finds out this, it will make him open his eyes." Then she said, "Then we will lay back and draw the greenbacks. Now, Ed., if we become victorious I will then buy a new carriage and dispose of my horses and get a new pair and have a jolly time with my balmoral and you. But, Ed., what will some person else, your wife, say?" Stokes said, "I was talking with her yesterday, and she put on so many airs; she showed me her father's picture; I looked at it slightly, and pushed one of his eyes clean out; she raged; she got all to pieces; I told her lightly, I did not care." One night, about 11.30 o'clock, I was called up from my sleep in the kitchen by Mrs. Williams, who said she wanted me to sign some papers; I said I did not want to sign any papers unless I knew what it was; she said it would not do me any harm, "and Mrs. Mansfield requests you to sign it;" I said, "I don't know what it is; I don't like to sign it." I commenced to read it to see what was in it, but she took it from me and would not allow me to read it, and said again: "Mrs. Mansfield requests you to sign it, and it won't do you any harm;" I signed it, but I don't know what it is, except that I saw it had some reference to Mr. Fisk coming there; I would have never signed it in the world without reading it except from the way Mrs. Williams talked. I was sure I would be discharged if I did not. One night Mr. Stokes said to me at the table, in the presence of Mrs. Mansfield and Mrs. Williams, "Richard, have you ever been in court on any occasion?" I said, "No, sir." He said, "You have not?" I replied, "No, sir." He then said,

How much money would you take to swear to a lie; would you take $30?" I said, "No, sir." Then he said, "Would you take $3,000; would you?" I said, "No, sir; I would not take anything; I would not swear to a lie for anything." He left after he could not get me to the point, and found he could not get me to swear to a lie, and said, "Well, I believe you."

RICHARD E. KING.

Sworn before me, October 30, 1871.

FRED. E. BARNARD, Notary Public,
New York County.

The publication of this statement induced Miss Mansfield to institute against Fisk a suit for libel. The suit was brought before Justice Bixby in Yorkville, a district in New York City. The case came up for trial on Saturday, November 25th, 1871. The occasion was one of unusual excitement and attracted a large crowd to the court room long before the hour fixed for calling the case.

At length a buzz of admiration was heard in the lower part of the court-room, and Miss Mansfield, her cousin, Mrs. Williams, and Mr. E. S. Stokes, preceded by the sergeant of the court squad, made their way through the crowded audience and assumed seats in front of the bar. There was not the slightest doubt but that Miss Mansfield looked extraordinarily handsome. Imagine a woman, young and vivid, with full, dashing figure, yet not gross, with deep, large, almond-shaped black eyes, luxuriant purple-black hair, worn in massive coils—tempting mouth, lips not too prominent, and yet not not insipid, magnificent teeth, clear pearl and pink complexion, oval face, and nose not retroussee and yet not straight—with a quiet, lady-like walk and action—soft voice and winning smile. Dress such a woman in dark silk, flounced with deep Valenciennes, a flowing silk jacket, beautifully embroidered with white braid, with a plain gold cross to set off the exquisite contour of her neck, and a dark green Tyrolese hat falling partially over her forehead, surmounted by a waving ostrich feather, and you have Miss Helen Josephine Mansfield as she appeared in court.

Mrs. M. A. Williams, the cousin of Miss Mansfield, though *distingue* in appearance, possesses but a tithe of the beauty of her fair relative. She is a pleasant-faced girl, with dark brown hair arranged in braids, blue eyes, and a short piquante nose. She was dressed in a dark purple silk, elaborately flounced, a sealskin jacket cut almost to the figure with Brussels lace collar, and jockey hat. Her demeanor through the whole proceeding was perfectly unconcerned, and no one laughed more heartily at the quips and snarls of the opening counsel than she. In this respect her cousin, Miss Mansfield, though more severely tested, was not far behindhand.

Mr. E. S. Stokes, the alleged cause of the present bitter Trojan war between James Fisk and the fair Helen, was attired sumptuously in the height of the prevailing fashion. He wore a light cream-colored overcoat over a blue diagonal suit, ruffled shirt, large diamond pin, crimped hair, artistically curled moustache, and straw-colored kids. Such was Mr. Stokes' admirable costume. He appeared very unconcerned, and laughed very heartily at Col. James Fisk when he entered the court.

Col. Fisk was attired in the simplest and most tasteful fashion. A short navy jacket of that peculiar hue which Mr. Samuel Weller, Sr., regarding Mr. Job Trotter, denominated as "mulberry," enveloped his not adipose form. This jacket was ornamented by a multitude of gold buttons of various sizes and shapes, but all impressed with the magic monogram, "Narragansett Steamship Co." Underneath this garment was a suit of sober black cloth, and in the centre of his black Bond street neck-tie sparkled Col. Fisk's immense diamond. The Col. wore dark olive kid gloves and carried a gold-headed cane. Add to this picture a batch of keen, sharp New York lawyers, and you have the scene as it was enacted.

The first, and indeed, the only witness called on that day, was Helen Josephine Mansfield. She answered to a most formidable array of questions. She proceeded to relate the leading events of her life, from her school days in Boston, through her travels, her marriage, her divorce, her efforts as an actress, to her relations with Fisk and Stokes, These facts were substantially as before stated.

The passages between the lawyers were often brilliant and keen. At one point, in arguing for the admissibility of a question, Charles S. Spencer, Fisk's enior counsel, said:

"I expect to show that Mr. Fisk found this lady without a dollar; that after lavishing upon her means enough to have satisfied Cleopatra herself, when the supply ceased, means were resorted to for the purpose of renewing them, among others this very proceeding. In other words, our defence is that this prosecution has no basis in good faith, no basis in the interest of public justice, no basis in anything good, nothing but an attempt to extort money. And have I not a right to show, if such be the fact, that finding this lady without a dollar, and having enriched her—although like most riches obtained in that way, it is rapidly disappearing—that she has had resort to this means to replenish her treasury? Cleopatra—aye, like unto her; for as the Egyptian syren queen is spoken of by the grandest of poets, 'age cannot wither her, nor custom state her infinite variety.'"

Before the examination of the witness was concluded the court adjourned to the 9th of December, and was subsequently continued to Saturday, the 6th of January, 1872. On this day, the court-room was again filled with a crowd of spectators with all the accompanying surroundings that were present at the opening of the case.

The examination of Miss Mansfield was resumed and concluded, after which Mr. Edward S. Stokes was put on the stand and subjected to a very severe and humiliating cross-examination. The witness was required to describe very minutely the relations between himself and Miss Mansfield. The truth was very damaging. Mr. Stokes was of good family and was married into a very respectable and wealthy family in New York, and his confessions that he lived a life of guilt, of low disgusting crime, was humiliating in the highest degree. He was stung with a deep sense of shame and left the court-room after the case was adjourned over for a week, in a very excited state of mind. He was too weak to be a man of honor, and yet too strong to be an unblushing debauche. At the conclusion of his testimony, the trial was continued until the next Saturday, and the crowd dispersed.

The principal actors in the shameful drama of life separated—parted not again to confront each other until summoned before that Tribunal whose judgments consign the arraigned, by decrees unalterable and irrevocable, to an everlasting fate. One goes, how unprepared! to his long home—one goes to the solitary gloom of a murderer's cell—one to a life of deep, dark, ungovernable remorse.

THE ASSASSINATION

OF

JAMES FISK, Jr.

THE OBSEQUIES.

THE ASSASSIN.

WHAT FOLLOWED.

CHAPTER XIV.

ASSASSINATION.

Fisk, Mansfield and Stokes—Wilful Assassination—Jealousy—Feud Revenge—Death—Fisk shot on the Stairway of the Grand Central Hotel—Full Description of the Affair—The Wounded Man Taken to a Room—The Assassin Arrested—The Scenes at the Hotel—The Scene in the Death Chamber—The Will—A Night of Agony—The Dying Man's Statement—Public Feeling—Mrs. Fisk Arrives from Boston—The Last Moments—The Death—Viewing the Body—Removal of the Body.

Crime and its Fruits.

In the midst of this life of rapidly shifting scenes, this whirl of business and operations unnumbered, Fisk was overtaken by this most disgraceful and disastrous *amour*.

The woman and the preferred suitor failing to overcome their victim by blackmail or by prosecution for libel, were driven to utter desperation. Fisk, more fortunate in his petitions to the "Courts of Justice," had procured the indictment of Stokes by the Grand Jury on a charge of perjury and conspiracy. An order had been issued on Saturday for the arrest of Stokes, or at least such was the report which came to his ears. He felt himself defeated at every point and driven at bay by his powerful enemy. The moment of desperation was at hand. The measure of endurance was full to the brim. The chief actor in this shameful drama had completed his engagement; the work was ended, and the workman stretched forth his hand to receive his wages—the wages of sin.

On the afternoon of this day, January 6th, at about half-past four o'clock, Mr. James Fisk, Jr., was shot in the Grand Central Hotel, Broadway, by Mr. Edward S. Stokes.

At the hour above indicated Colonel James Fisk's private coach drew up in front of the Grand Central Hotel, on Broadway. It was about the time that New York's great thoroughfare presents the pleasantest sight. Men of business were walking leisurely homeward, troops of ladies were lingering among the glories of the shops, stately carriages lined the curbstones awaiting the pleasure of their mistresses, and the color and sound of life were more subdued and harmonized than at busier hours of the day. The rumble of the vehicles was not so noisy, for the heavy drays and trucks had done with their incessant dragging hither and thither, and had left Broadway, going home through the by-streets.

As Mr. Fisk's carriage dashed over the pavement before reaching the hotel, guided dexterously through the tide of other conveyances, a coupé, at some distance in the rear, was observed following in a mysterious manner. On the box of this coupé sat an upright and sturdy-looking man. He held the reins with a firm hand, and seemed to be looking continually at the back of the head of the coachman who was perched upon the stylish equipage of the Prince of Erie. All the way down Broadway this curious proceeding was continued. A few blocks from Bleecker street the door of the coupé was

GRAND CENTRAL HOTEL.

flung open and a man sprang quickly out, reached the sidewalk and ran swiftly through the moving crowd of pedestrians in the same direction in which the carriages had hitherto been going. This man was Edward S. Stokes, known to the world by this time as the bitterest enemy of the man who had been riding in advance of him in his glittering carriage and challenging public observation of himself. Darting the crowd he ran for some distance until he reached the entrance of the Grand Central Hotel. He passed into the main corridor just as the carriage of Fisk stopped in front; then went up the stairs, and it was observed by those who saw him that he was pale and much agitated. No one fancied, however, that there was much significance in this fact, and so the momentary surprise at his hurried egress passed only like a ripple over the minds of those lounging near the door.

Stokes ascended the stairs to the first floor and then went down the ladies' private stairway. He reached the first landing.

Fisk had entered the vestibule and was going up seven steps which led into the hall. When he reached the last step, Stokes, above him, standing near the balustrade, rested a revolver on the rail and fired at Fisk. The shot struck him in the left arm; another immediately followed it striking in the abdomen, and Fisk cried out,

"For God's sake, will anybody save me?"

The impassioned Stokes glared at him fiercely,

fired two more shots and turned and ran up the stairs.

At the top of the stairs he was met by a gentleman, who had heard the reports and was hurrying to find what was the matter. He passed Stokes and saw nothing singular in his appearance. Fisk was still crying,

"For God's sake, will anybody save me?"

This gentleman, who is a resident of Boston and a surgeon, lost no time in putting his arm under the head of the prostrate man, who was gasping. The people in the hotel and those in the street at the time crowded around in intense excitement, and gazed and listened breathlessly and with some horror at the sight of blood that was running out of Mr. Fisk's sleeve on the floor. The question was asked him,

"What is the matter?"

He said, with an effort,

"I'm shot."

He was then lifted and carried up the stairs into the ladies' parlor. There he was put upon a sofa, but it was thought better to take him into another room across the corridor. Here he was laid upon a bed. A messenger was hurriedly dispatched for a surgeon. Some one asked him,

"Where are you hurt? How many wounds are there?"

"Two or three of them."

His coat was quickly removed, but it was found

STOKES WAITING FOR HIS VICTIM.

more difficult to get his shirt off; so it was cut into pieces, and in this way the wound in the arm was disclosed, the blood from which was running in a great stream.

The Colonel looked at it bravely and without any apparent shrinking. The shot had passed completely through the flesh, leaving a large, ugly-looking hole like one made by a bullet used in a navy revolver.

Fisk was asked if that was the only wound, and said, "No." He said he had another one, and pointed to his stomach. The physician who had arrived uncovered the wound and found it a large one, like the other, with very little blood visible. After the doctor had finished his examination for the time Mr. Fisk asked for some "brandy and water." After he had drank it the doctor probed the wound, but found that he had no instruments long enough to reach the ball, if it could be reached at all. While the operation was proceeding and a large number of persons were around him Fisk maintained his composure, the muscles of his face never quivering, and watching the movements of the surgeon with the greatest coolness.

After it was through he said to Dr. Triplet, who was the first to attend him: —

"Doctor, if I am going to die I want to know it. I'm not afraid to die; but then if I am going to die I would like to know beforehand."

The Doctor replied :—

"Colonel, you are not going to die to-night, and not to-morrow either, I hope."

The gentleman who had first found Mr. Fisk after he was shot asked him who it was who attacked him.

He answered, "Stokes."

Captain Burns in a few minutes entered the room, and after saying a few words to the Doctor went out again. Then he returned with Edward S. Stokes, well guarded between two policemen. He was made to approach the bed. He wore a rigidly dignified air, with a face perfectly immovable, expressive only of intense passion strongly suppressed. There was a singular light in his eyes, which he fixed upon the man whom he had assassinated.

He was asked by the Captain,

"Is that the man who shot you?"

Fisk looked at Stokes and said—

"Yes, that's the man who shot me. That's Stokes."

Some one asked him if Stokes wanted to kill him.

"Yes, he wanted my life."

Fisk was soon surrounded by a number of doctors; and the corridor which opens into the ante-room to the chamber in which he was lying was quickly filled by his friends and associates. The news of the assassination had circulated very rapidly, and nearly all of the directors and officers of the Erie Railway Company were there. A policeman closely guarded the door, and at the foot of the main stairway a waiter permitted none but privileged persons to pass.

Stokes, the assassin, after discharging the pistol, ran down the stairs that he ascended a few moments before, and went up to Mr. Powers at the desk, saying,

"There's a man shot at the ladies' entrance!"

When he had said this he seemed to have lost all control over himself, and to have been overcome by a panic. He looked about wildly and confusedly, as if to escape, and then suddenly ran towards the barber's room, from which he knew there were doors opening into Mercer street. Mr. Powers had watched him suspiciously after hearing his startling announcement, and gave the alarm. He shouted, "Stop that man!" Stokes was seized with the assistance of several persons, the guests who were receiving the soothing ministrations of the *coiffeurs* starting from the chairs with the towels around their necks and their faces covered with white lather; Stokes was taken back to the foot of the stairs; and made to sit down in one of the waiters' chairs; while sitting here a man observed that he very nearly fainted away.

Mr. Powers sent immediately to the Fifteenth Precinct Station House, and Captain Burns and officer McCadden soon arrived and took the prisoner into their custody. Vigilant search was then made through the halls and parlors for the revolver or pistol which Stokes had used, as it was not found in his possession. Mr. Crockett and all the servants looked anxiously in every imaginable place, until, just after the identification of Stokes by Fisk, a young lady discovered it in the parlor near the head of the stairs, lying under a chair, where Stokes had flung it in his haste and excitement. The prisoner was then taken by Captain Burns and the officer to the station house.

Here he walked calmly up to the desk and gave his name, residence and occupation. He was then taken to a cell below, in which he was placed. But it did not suit him, and as he spoke of such treatment in a deprecating way, he was ordered to be brought up to the Captain's room.

The prisoner was again removed to a cell, this time to pass the night there. The cell is like all others in police stations—small, low and narrow, with a wicket door of latticed iron work, to which is fixed a strong lock. The walls are whitewashed to a ghostly whiteness; the interior is dark and gloomy, and at the further end is a narrow slab against the wall, the nightly couch of the unfortunate who is immured as a consequence of misdemeanor.

Stokes appeared very sullen when going to the cell, and, when the door shut behind him with a clang, turned around abruptly and looked at the officer. Then he commenced walking restlessly up and down the small space and called roughly for cigars. They were brought him, and he commenced

THE ASSASSINATION.

smoking fiercely as if for life. Cigar after cigar was lighted and flung away. In the course of this restless reverie he suddenly asked of the policeman who stood outside the door, with a betrayal of nervousness in his tone:—

"What do you think, is the man seriously injured?"

The officer said that he did not know.

Stokes resumed his nervous movement and kept it up until the reporters left at a late hour, smoking and muttering to himself.

In another part of the station house was locked the boy who tends the door of the ladies' entrance to the Grand Central Hotel. He was closely guarded from the reporters until taken away to be examined by the Coroner. His name is Redman, and he witnessed the shooting of Fisk by Stokes. He, knew both of the principals in this fearful tragedy, he had frequently admitted them into the hotel through the "ladies entrance." He had, a few moments previous to the assassination, opened the door for Fisk and saw him shot down, almost at his side. Now, under the system of "justice" in practice in New York City, he was as much a prisoner as the man who had fired the shot. Stokes was in prison as a murderer, Redman as a witness. Redman, however, soon gave in his testimony and was released. The story of this servant is the only account of an eye witness, as he alone saw the whole scene enacted.

Diagram of Scene of Shooting.

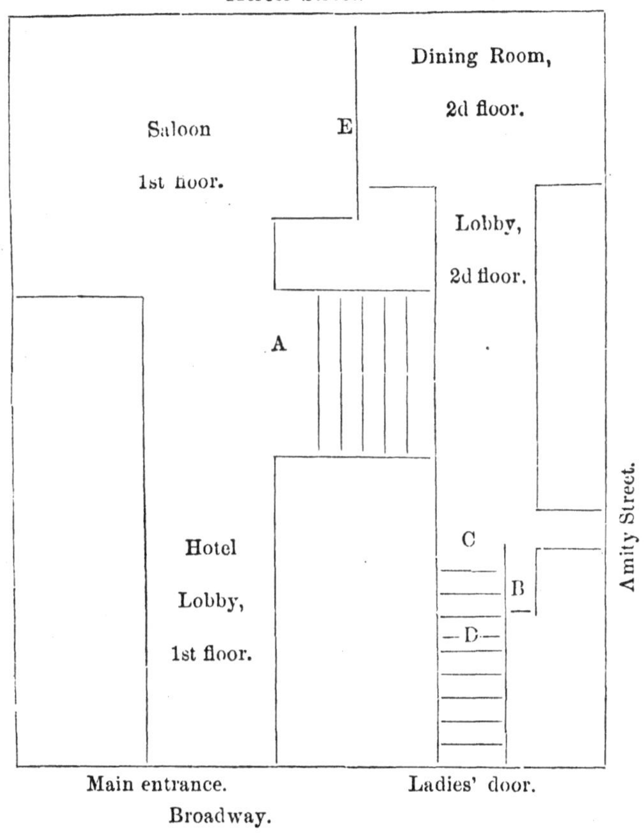

A. Stair-case by which Stokes ascended.
B. Position of Stokes while waiting for Fisk, Jr.
C. Position of Stokes when he fired.
D. Position of Fisk, Jr., ascending the stairs when first shot.
E. Position of Stokes when captured.

Clinging to a Thread of Hope.

It was hoped that, as the Colonel was very fat, the intestines might have escaped fatal injury. As the Colonel had recently suffered from a bilious attack, and used cathartics to good effect, it was thought that he might stand a better chance for life than would another man in his position.

About half past five the Colonel's colored servant entered the room.

"What is the matter, Colonel?" he asked.

Col. Fisk—I have been shot, but I think there is a good chance of my life, and I hope it won't amount to much.

The Arrival of Friends.

Mrs. Morse and her two daughters, on whom Col. Fisk was about to call when Stokes shot him, entered the room. They did everything in their power to soothe his sufferings.

As the moments flew hope for his recovery vanished, and the fearful truth, that the wounded man must die, sank deep into the hearts of his friends, who had gathered in large numbers at his bedside and in the halls of the hotel. A telegraphic dispatch had already carried the sad intelligence to Mrs. Fisk, in Boston, and she immediately hastened to the scene of her heart-rending sorrow.

His Will.

For some hours after the shooting he maintained complete composure and full possession of his mental faculties, and with the assistance of his principal lawyer, Mr. D. D. Field, made his will.

After Fisk had given his attornies general instructions, they retired and drew up a will, which, when it had been read to the dying man, he approved and signed. It is as follows:

I, JAMES FISK, Jun., of the city of New York, being of sound mind and memory, do make, publish, and declare this my last will and testament, hereby revoking all former wills by me made.

1. I give, devise, and bequeath all my estate and property, real and personal, except the special legacy hereinafter mentioned, to my beloved wife, Lucy D. Fisk, subject, however, to a trust to pay to my dear father and mother jointly, or to the survivor of them, $3,000 a year for their support during the life of them or either of them; and further, to pay to Minnie F. Morse and Rosie C. Morse each $2,000 a year during their lives, respectively, until marriage, when the annuity of the one marrying shall cease; the property and estate aforesaid to rest absolutely in the said Lucy and her heirs forever, subject only as aforesaid; and the said trust shall not affect her right freely to dispose of and transfer any such property.

2. I give and bequeath to my sister, Mrs. Mary

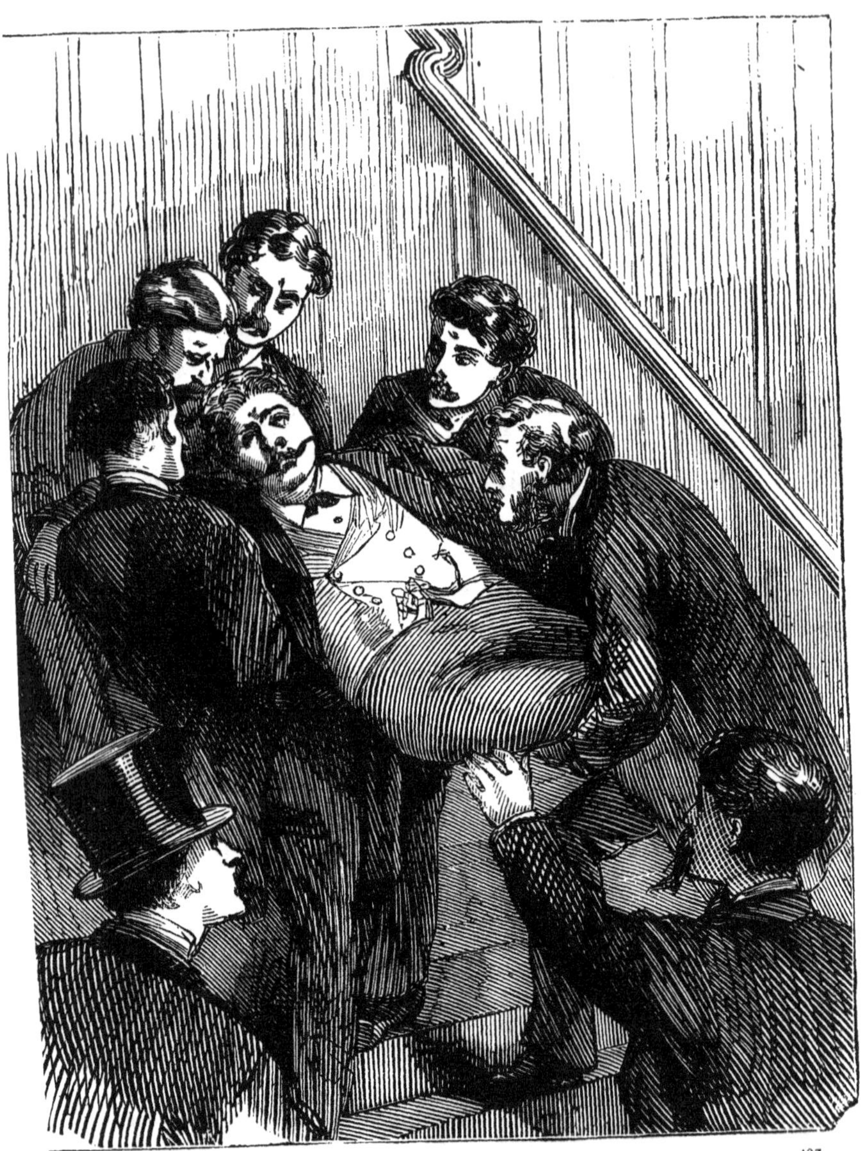

FISK CARRIED TO HIS ROOM.

G. Hooker, stock in the Narragansett Steamship Company of the par value of $100,000, for her sole and separate use forever.

3. I appoint my said wife and my friend Eben D. Jordan, of Boston, executors of this my last will and testament.

In witness whereof I have hereunto set my hand and seal this 6th day of January, 1872.

[L. S.] JAMES FISK, Jun.

Signed, sealed, published, and declared by the testator to be his last will and testament in the presence of us, who have hereto subscribed our names as witnesses, at his request, and in the presence of each other.

THOMAS G. SHERMAN,
No. 316 West Twenty-second Street, New York.

JAY GOULD,
No. 578 Fifth Avenue, New York.

F. WILLIS FISHER, M. D.,
Grand Central Hotel.

The total value of Colonel Fisk's property is not known, but it is believed that it will run considerably over a million of dollars. After a fresh copy of the will had been made it was taken into the bedroom of Colonel Fisk, who rapidly ran it over and signed it. He then began to complain of pain but the wounds did not bleed, and there were no signs of vomiting.

Fisk's Statement of the Assassination.

After the will had been signed, the Coroner came into the room with a jury, and having administered an oath to Fisk, took down his account of the manner in which he was shot by Stokes, as follows:

"This afternoon at about 4 o'clock I rode up to the Grand Central Hotel. I entered by the private entrance, and when I entered the first door I met the boy, of whom I inquired if Mrs. Morse was in. He told me that Mrs. Morse and her youngest daughter had gone out, but he thought the other daughter was in her grandmother's room. I asked him to go up and tell the daughter that I was there. I came through the other door, and was going up stairs, and had gone up about two steps, and on looking up I saw Edward S. Stokes at the head of the stairs. As soon as I saw him I noticed that he had something in his hand, and a second after I saw the flash, heard the report, and felt the ball enter my abdomen on the right side. A second after I heard another shot, and the bullet entered my left arm. When I received the first shot I staggered and ran toward the door, but noticing a crowd gathering in front, I ran back on the stairs again. I was then brought up stairs in the hotel. I saw nothing more of Stokes until he was brought before me by an officer for identification. I fully identified Edward S. Stokes as the person who shot me."

The Public Feeling.

The Colonel now began to complain of much pain and became very restless. The doctors gave him powerful anodynes, and he gradually sank into a gentle slumber. Meanwhile troops of his friends gathered around the door. Among those who visited Colonel Fisk during the evening were District Attorney Fellows and Captain Simons, David Dudley Field, counsel of the Erie Company; R. M. Simons, Managing Director of the Narragansett Steamship Company; Mr. White, Treasurer of the Erie Railway Company; W. H. Morgan, Homer H. Lane, Mr. Barr and Mr. Sisson, and others prominent for their connection, in one capacity or another, with Erie.

Policemen were stationed at the various staircases, and no person was allowed to ascend without a pass from the clerk or proprietor of the hotel, and at the door of the wounded man's room another sentinel refused admission to those whom Jay Gould did not care to see. Tweed himself, once all powerful, had to make his way to the bedside by the permission of the magnate of Erie.

The Scene in the Hotel.

The news of the Colonel having been shot spread like wildfire. All his friends at first discredited it. John Chamberlain, when he first heard of it, offered to bet $500 to $100 that it was untrue. Soon, however, the truth was realized. The Grand Central Hotel was jammed inside and outside. As the particulars of the case became known the excitement became intense. Colonel Fisk's good qualities were alone remembered. Men spoke of him with tears in their eyes, relating many acts of kindness and generosity, and denouncing in curses deep and loud the cowardly assassin, who had attempted to take his life.

The Night of Agony.

At eleven o'clock the physicians held a consultation. Dr. Carnochan was called in to assist It was decided that nothing more could be done for Mr. Fisk until Sunday morning, as he was doing at that time remarkably well, no attempt to extract the ball was made.

The night dragged wearily its slow hours along at the hotel, while the watchers in the room where Fisk was lying, disregarding the faint lightening of the approaching dawn, waited with intense anxiety in the short spaces that elapsed between each opinion given by the attending physicians about his condition. The circle of thoughtful faces looked at times strangely wan and haggard, as the features relaxed in involuntary forgetfulness, betrayed truly the nature of the thoughts that were driving one another through each brain. For, despite the common expectancy and the commoner hope that death would not at least come very speedily, a forboding, inexplicable but not less depressing seemed to have settled upon all. This could not have been

from any betrayal of feeling by the medical attendants, for their faces wore studiously cheerful looks, especially whenever the prostrate man showed any signs of consciousness of his surroundings.

At seven o'clock Sunday morning, it was announced that he was fast sinking, and that the danger of a sudden ending of his intense agony was very great. His pulse was at this time 130. Dr. Fisher went down stairs in a hurried manner and asked something of the night clerk; then went back again. He looked very anxious.

Mrs. Fisk.

Immediately after this, when the hand of the clock pointed a quarter after seven, a carriage driven very rapidly, the horses, wet and dappled with the foam that flew from their nostrils and congealed in the cold air, stopped short at the door. The coachman sprang from his perch, pulled open the door and helped out a lady in a dark traveling dress, who stepped wearily to the ground. She walked quickly into the portico. This was Mrs. Fisk. She had traveled nearly all night, and was almost exhausted from fatigue and anxiety.

She was accompanied by a traveling companion, Miss Harrot, and arrived at the hotel in company with Mr. Comer, Mr. Fisk's private secretary, who had been in constant and faithful attendance upon him from a short time after he was wounded. Mrs. Fisk was met at the head of the stairs by

Mrs. Morse, between these ladies a long and cordial friendship had existed. Upon repairing to the room of her husband, Mrs. Fisk gave vent to the most frantic exclamations of grief and endearment, which drew tears from the eyes of every one present. By this time the wounded man had become entirely unconscious, and the wails and grief of his wife were never heard by him. The room was occupied by a large number of the relatives and friends of the sufferer, among whom were Mrs. James Fisk, Jr.; Miss Harrot, Messrs. Moore and Sanderson, brothers-in-law of Mr. Fisk, and Messrs. Bolden, Pollard, Aspell, George Barden and Drs. Fisher and Triplet. Mrs. Fisk was at the head of the bed, with her arms around the neck of the dying man, uttering lamentations and crying as if her heart would break. "*Can nothing be done to save him?*" cried the grief-stricken lady, of Dr. Fisher. "Alas! I fear not" replied the physician. Gradually the pulse increased; the patient's breath grew shorter, and the breathing more labored. It was too evident that death was near. Around the bed were grouped the persons named above, who with sobs and cries, gave evidence of the grief that was filling their hearts over the approaching loss of a near and dear friend. At twenty minutes before eleven the patient's breath grew quite short, and at times nearly stopped. Occasionally it became louder, and the pale and tear-stained faces near the patient for the moment grew brighter. The hope, however, proved an illusory one; for at a quarter before eleven the soul of James Fisk, Jr., sped from its earthly tenement and he lay stiff and lifeless. The scene in the chamber was sad in the extreme. The widow of the great Erie magnate moaned and sobbed and called upon the attending physician to help him, who was of earth no more; but the cry was in vain. All pitied her and mingled their tears with hers. Thus was sympathy the only consolation she was able to obtain from those who—many of them—would gladly have laid down their lives to save that which had just been returned to Him who gave it. Her prayer at his death was, "*Oh, God, if you must take him, take his soul!*"

The Death Chamber.

The remains lay upon the bed in which Mr. Fisk was placed when first wounded. The sobbing mourners were finally induced to leave the room and the body was, for a time, watched over by the grief-stricken colored valet, who had for years attended Mr. Fisk. The room at this time was in a state of great confusion. Tumblers and vials and bandages were scattered about upon chairs, table, bureau and floor. On the back of the bed lay a palm-leaf fan, which had been used to cool the brow of the late sufferer. The head of the latter was bandaged with a napkin and the features wore their usual calm expression. The shirt was stained with the blood that had escaped from the wound, and the muscular arms were lying across the immense chest. At the head of the bed stood the colored valet, leaning his head upon his right hand, while with the other he caressed the form of his late master, occasionally placing it upon the bare arms, as if expecting that the flesh would yet become warm again and the soul of his late kind master once more return to the cold, clay form. Presently the undertaker arrived with a plain rosewood coffin, in which the body was temporarily placed for removal to the late residence of Mr. Fisk, in West Twenty-third street. A heavy velvet pall was thrown over the coffin, which was placed upon chairs in the front room, adjoining the ante-room in which the murdered man died. The features looked extremely natural. The lineaments were well preserved; the face was, of course, pale, but comparatively undiscolored, and the dead man looked as if enjoying a reposing sleep instead of one from which he would never awake upon earth. The doors of the rooms were then opened and permission given to those present to view the body. Instantly the assembly of friends formed in single file and commenced a short pilgrimage to the casket that contained all that remained of their late friend or associate. The scene was mournful in the extreme. Old men burst into tears as their gaze rested upon the dead man, and young men—strong, hale, and hearty——utterly broke down under the grief with which the painful sight inspired them. Even the clerks and messengers sobbed as if their hearts would break, and not a few were so carried away with grief that they were led out and taken to seats until they could become calm enough to leave the building.

Removal of the Body.

The body was prepared under directions of the Coroner for removal to Mr. Fisk's private rooms, in West Twenty-third street. At seven o'clock on Sunday evening, a *post mortem* examination was held by a committee of eminent physicians. The body and all the organs were found to be in a condition of perfect health. The heart weighed sixteen ounces, and the brain weighed fifty-eight ounces. It, therefore, appeared that if no accident had befallen him, Mr. Fisk would have lived to a green old age.

Public Excitement.

The report of the death flew on wings of light, and was in an incredibly short time known far and wide throughout the city.

The excitement at the Grand Central on Sunday morning continued unabated. The morning papers had made the news of the attempted assassination of Mr. Fisk more widespread, and the consequence was that thousands of people sought the hotel from a morbid curiosity to see every nook and corner of a place made memorable by the noted event. By three o'clock in the morning most of the friends of the injured man had taken their leave, and naught remained of the excitement of the night before but the anxious faces of the physicians and friends, who hovered at the bedside of the wounded sleeper. The gas in the room was turned down, so that a glimmering light made the scene more desolate than before. Servants and hall boys slid around upon their errands on tip-toe, and the silence was unbroken save by the heavy breathing of the sleeper in the sick room. Even Mr. Tweed had become weary of watching, and took leave of his stricken friend at one o'clock. Thus, one by one, the visitors departed and the room was left deserted save by the physicians in charge. Almost at daylight, however, the throng of friends and curiosity seekers again began to assemble in the corridors and lobby of the elegant hostelry, and the guests, descending from their rooms to breakfast, encountered many of those who had helped to crowd the hotel the evening before.

Thousands of people came to hear what further intelligence could be obtained of the condition of the sufferer. The Ninth regiment, of which Fisk was colonel, was largely represented. Indeed, it seemed as if the whole regiment had assembled. Officers and privates mingled together with sad countenances, eagerly discussing the details of the mournful event. Many anecdotes were related of the acts and humorous incidents of Mr. Fisk's military career. "It was only on the 12th of July last," said Adjutant Allen, "that Colonel Fisk remarked to the regiment at the armory, 'Well, boys, if there is not a large turncut to-day, I am pretty sure there will be at my funeral.' This remark was almost always repeated whenever there was a slim attendance at parade. At a meeting of the officers of the regiment last Tuesday evening Mr. Fisk gave eleven thousand dollars to the different companies. 'The boys will need new uniforms soon,' said he, 'and as there is owing to me some one thousand dollars, I will give it to them and add to it ten thousand dollars more.' This is but one of the many liberal acts toward the regiment," concluded the Adjutant, "which have given it the enviable position it now occupies in the National Guard."

Outside the hotel, there was also a clamorous crowd. Some tried to get in at the private door, but as orders had been issued to allow none to enter but the guests of the hotel, these efforts were, as a general thing, unsuccessful. The curiosity of these people, however, was partially satisfied by being allowed to peer through the door at the stairs upon which the victim stood when shot. Even on the opposite side of Broadway stood crowds of men, women and children, staring at the stately edifice as if expecting that the walls would become animate and tell all they knew about the bloody deed. As the hour of noon approached, the crowd, both inside and out, increased to such an extent that it became almost impossible to enter the hotel at all. The remarks made by this crowd of curiosity-seekers were many and varied; but scarcely one was heard in extenuation of the cowardly act.

The Feeling Throughout the Country.

The news of the assassination was flashed to every part of the country, and created a profound and startled impression among all classes. The excitement, comment, and general interest occasioned by the sudden slaying of a prominent man, in the full possession of health and wealth, and almost everything else rendering life desirable, became the theme of conversation in all parts of the land, and even in Europe, whence the news was cabled, the awful occurrence produced a marked stir. Not since the assassination of Abraham Lincoln has the death of any one man seemed to so excite public attention and comment in every quarter of the globe.

CHAPTER XV.

THE LAST OF FISK.

Obsequies—The Body Lying in State, in the Grand Opera House—The procession to the Depot—The Funeral at Brattleboro.

The Obsequies.

THE funeral ceremonies over the body of James Fisk, Jr., on Monday, attracted one of the largest crowds ever assembled together in New York. The extraordinary circumstances surrounding the tragedy, coupled with the notoriety of the principals, gave to the events an interest which otherwise would not attach itself to the obsequies of a private citizen. Many were, of course, present in the hope of gratifying a morbid curiosity so frequently manifested on such occasions. Despite the crowd and press of people, everything passed off quietly and with decorum.

When it became known that the murdered man's remains would lie in state at the Grand Opera House, the vestibule of the offices of the Erie Railroad Company were soon crowded with sight-seers representing every grade of society, anxious to get a glimpse of all that remained of a man whose history has been so remarkable. At his late residence a large concourse of people also gathered in consequence of an impression that the service would take place there, previous to the removal of the body to the Opera House, but on being informed by the police that such would not be the case, they quietly moved away, leaving the house deserted, save by a few knowing ones who hoped to catch a sight of the body as it was brought out, for in the hall of the house a temporary bier had been erected, and there the coffin, which was covered with beautiful flowers woven into beautiful emblems, was stationed till the time arrived for the removal of the body to the Opera House.

The street and every available spot in the vicinity of the house was packed with people. The interior of the great audience room and the passage ways were filled to their utmost capacities. The Directors of the Erie Company had held a special meeting, passed resolutions strongly expressive of sorrow over the calamity that had befallen their associate, James Fisk, Jr., paying a tribute to his personal qualities, and filled also with the deepest condolence for his widow and family. Among the resolutions was the following:

Resolved, That in token of respect, we will today follow his body from his late residence to the railway station, and a committee of this board will then accompany it to its last resting place in his native State.

The committee consisted of John Hilton, Henry Thompson, and Dr. Eldridge.

THE LAST TRIBUTE.

The officers of the Ninth regiment assembled in the hall soon after ten o'clock, attired in full uniform, wearing the accustomed crape on the left arm and the hilt of the sword. The command formed in Twenty-third Street, the regiment being the guard of honor. According to the original programme the mournful procession was to have started at 11 o'clock, but it was delayed some time. Long before that hour the wives of the Directors and principal officers began to arrive, as well as many other ladies, who had been able to procure admission, All were dressed in deep mourning, and many were in tears. Prominent among these were Miss Morse and her brother, the former weeping bitterly. Some surprise was expressed by many at the genuine sorrow which was so general, for it seemed to be from no desire for outward show, but simply a burst of genuine grief. The men of the Ninth, especially, evidently felt the deprivation very much. They spoke of the deceased with a tenderness that was touching.

Arrival of the Body.

At 11½ o'clock there was a sudden movement among the crowd in the Erie Building, and the body of Col. Fisk was borne to the bier prepared for its reception, by the following gentlemen belonging to the Ninth Regiment: Adj. Allen, Lieut. W. P. Montgomery, John H. Wood, Edward W. Bowland, George A. Hussey, Alonzo P. Bacon, and George W. Palfrey, who were a special committee to take charge of the body until it should arrive at the depot for transportation to Brattleboro. They also formed a guard of honor while the body was lying in state. As it was borne through the crowd there was a stillness as of death. The military had formed in line on both sides of the street, and stood with presented arms from the time the remains had left the house until it entered the hall of the Opera House. Every head in the crowd was uncovered, and although among those who were furthest off there was a pressing forward and a straining to catch a sight of the coffin, there was nothing unseemly or rude.

The catafalque was received at the top of the stairs by Col. Braine, and other officers of the Ninth, and placed in the centre of the vestibule, resting on a rich velvet pall, on which rested crowns, crosses and other devices, constructed of tube-roses and camelias, while beautiful lilies were scattered over the corpse, which was clothed in full regimentals, the cap and the sword resting on the body. The face, with the exception of its pallor, was unchanged, and no one unless knowing the circumstances would have believed that Fisk had died a violent death. The position of the head increased somewhat the always massive proportions of the lower jaw, but in other respects the face was that of a man asleep. The body was contained in a handsome rosewood casket, with gold-plated handles and a splendid plate bearing the inscription:

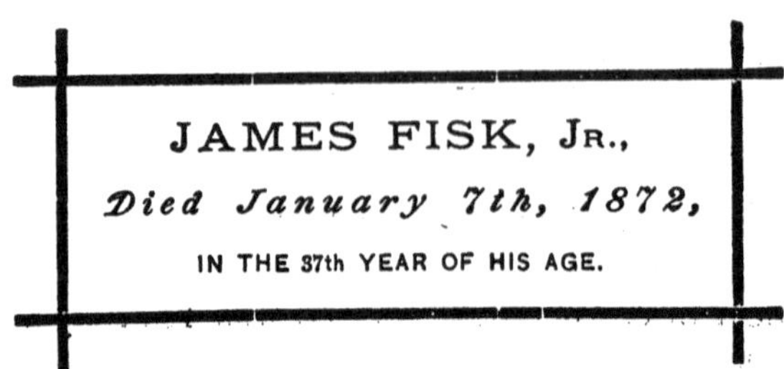

When the body had been arranged the undertaker took his place at the head of the bier. Lieut. Col. Braine and officers of the Ninth acting as a guard of honor.

The Lying in State.

The public were now admitted to view the body. Entering by the Twenty-second Street entrance, the spectators filed in a long line past the casket, and passing through the building, left by the door opening on Eighth avenue. Among the first to take the last look at the dead were several ladies professionally connected with the Grand Opera House. Their grief seemed almost uncontrollable. Many of those who followed in the continuous line were also in tears, and all were reverent. One man who, it was said, had been the Colonel's barber, reverently placed his hand on the dead man's brow, and with the other gently twisted the dead man's moustache. He, too, was plainly in deep grief. The "lying in state" continued till one o'clock, and at that hour the funeral services began in the presence of the Erie Directors, the officers of the Ninth Regiment and the personal friends of the deceased, some occupying seats around the coffin, while others stood in groups around the hall.

The Funeral Services.

The Episcopal burial service was read by Chaplain Flagg, of the Ninth Regiment. In the midst of the prayers, the wife, mother and sister were brought and seated near the catafalque. They were evidently in deep sorrow, and as their sobs and sighs broke forth the scene was a most affecting one. The chaplain concluded the services by announcing that the funeral services would be concluded on the following day, at Brattleboro. The relatives then advanced to take their last look of the body, the ladies bending over and kissing the lips of the deceased. The Ninth Regiment band, the Aschenbroden Verein, the officers of the Third Brigade, and the entire Ninth Regiment, then filed through the hall, taking a hasty look at the body, and departed by the eastern entrance. At this point the persons belonging to the Narragansett Steamship Company's steamers arrived, under the escort of a body of police, and with some difficulty made their way to the vestibule, and appeared to be deeply impressed with the sublime spectacle.

A few minutes before two o'clock the coffin was closed, draped with the American flag, and was then borne by the guard of honor to the hearse, the following gentlemen acting as pall-bearers:

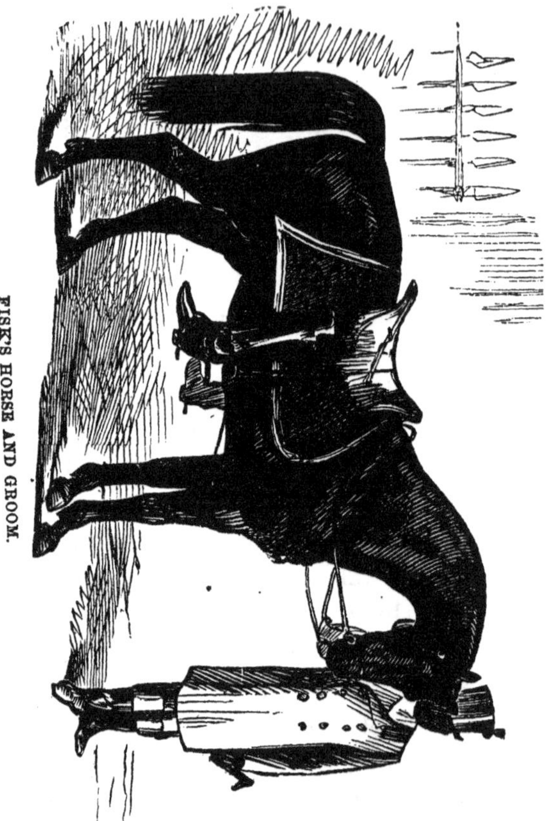

FISK'S HORSE AND GROOM.

Col. Emmons Clark, Seventh Regiment.
Col. Geo. D. Scott, Eighth Regiment.
Col. Wm. B. Allen, Fifty-fifth Regiment.
Col. Frank Story, Sixth Regiment.
Col. Josiah Porter, Twenty-second Regiment.
Lieut.-Col. A. P. Webster, First Regiment.

On reaching the hearse, which awaited it in Twenty-third street, the body was placed in its position, and the pall-bearers stood behind the hearse, the Erie Directors and the officers of the Ninth preceding it, while the officers of the Third Brigade followed. The Ninth Regiment was drawn up in line on the south side of Twenty-third street, the right resting on Eighth avenue. As the coffin was brought into the street, the band, assisted by the Aschenbrodel Verein, played a solemn dirge.

The Procession.

At two o'clock the procession started from the Grand Opera House. At this point of the proceedings the scene was a most impressive one. Every available spot from which the procession could be viewed was occupied, while the solemn stillness that prevailed added to its solemnity. Most of the stores in Eighth avenue were closed, and the blinds in the private houses in Twenty-third street were generally drawn, and small flags draped with crape floated from the telegraph and lamp poles. The following was the order of the procession:

First came a body of Police, one hundred strong, then the band of the Ninth Rigiment playing "The Dead March in Saul." After the band came a large number of persons in the employ of the Erie Railroad, wearing badges of crape on their left arms. Next followed the Veteran Corps of the regiment, Lieut. Col. Braine and Staff, and the other officers of the Ninth.

Then came the Ninth Regiment in full force, marching in triple line, and presenting a splendid appearance. Next followed the hearse containing the corpse, drawn by four black horses richly caparisoned. Following it was Col. Fisk's favorite charger, a splendid black horse, led by a tall, colored groom, and, in accordance with military precedent, a pair of spurred boots were inserted in the stirrups of the empty saddle, with the toes turned backward. The officers of the Third Brigade and another detachment of Erie officials followed, and finally came the carriages, extending nearly a quarter of a mile in line. In the first was Jay Gould, President of the Erie Railroad; then came Frederick A. Lane, Mortimer Smith and others, prominently connected with the great railroad. After these came the carriages of the private friends of the deceased.

The column moved through Twenty-third street and Fifth avenue to the New Haven depot, in Twenty-seventh street, where the remains were placed on board the cars for conveyance to Brattleboro. The whole route was thronged with spectators, who seemed deeply impressed by the spectacle.

Fifth avenue presented a striking appearance, the residents in that neighborhood filling all the windows, balconies and door steps. On the procession arriving at the corner of Madison avenue and Twenty-sixth street, the Ninth formed in two lines and the cortege passed between them. The remains were then placed in a private car, especially prepared for them, and the wife, mother and sister of the deceased were escorted to the car assigned them by Captain Fuller. The officers of the Ninth, the Erie Committee and the friends of the deceased, filled the remaining cars of the train, which was heavily draped, both inside and outside, with crape. It left shortly after amid breathless silence, and was watched with eager eyes till it was out of sight. The procession then returned, the carriages and the civilians going home, the Ninth Regiment marching to its armory, where it was quietly dismissed.

Thus were the mortal remains of one, who had, in a short and chequered life in the great metropolis, conquered and occupied a place of power and note in public affairs, carried back to the place of his birth, to be buried beneath the deep shadows of the Green Mountains, on whose slopes and through whose valleys he had been only a few years ago a sprightly, active, innocent country boy.

The Funeral at Brattleboro.

The funeral train from New York reached the station at Brattleboro at midnight, with its load of weary, sad and sorrowing passengers.

Most of the family mourners were taken to private residences in the village, but Mrs. Fisk and her friend, Miss Harrot, found a place at the Revere House. When the remains arrived the crowds eagerly watched every motion, paying, meanwhile, especial attention to the officers with their glittering uniforms. For a long time the crowds lingered about the Revere, looking into the windows of the room in which the coffin had been placed, and striving to obtain a glimpse of the dead man. During the night the remains were laid in state in a northwest room of the hotel, fronting on Main street, and were surrounded by a guard of honor, the night being divided into watches of two hours each, and the officers keeping vigils by turns. In the morning the room was open and free to the friends of the dead man until 11 o'clock, and at that hour the remains were removed to the Baptist church, where they were again laid in state and open to the public gaze.

For the reception of the dead, and the partial expression of the sorrow felt by the town, the church was neatly draped in mourning, and the organ decked with wreaths, and upon it, placed in white letters on a black ground, the words, "In the midst

BAPTIST CHURCH, BRATTLEBORO.

of life we are in death.". Over the coffin was thrown in graceful folds the flag of the Ninth New York Regiment. As at the hotel, so in the church, it was surrounded with a profusion of flowers, beautiful to look upon and filling the church with a sweet and subtle perfume. The appearance of the body as it lay in the magnificent casket, was that of one in sleep, rather than in death. All expression of pain had disappeared; there was calmness only, and that which seemed the calmness of action in repose, not activity destroyed. Toward the close of the morning the face became slightly discolored, but not sufficiently so to attract attention. Between 11 o'clock and half-past 12, when the coffin was closed, the church was constantly crowded with those who, from idle curiosity or out of true regard, came in and went out in long and uninterrupted file, and, as at the hotel, many hundreds must have come to look at the remains. Near the coffin stood different members of Col. Fisk's staff—Capt. E. M. Smith, Capt. Miller, Adjutant Allen, and Sergeant A. S. Fill. After 1 o'clock the bell of the Baptist church announced the hour of the funeral. The officers formed in procession and marched to the church, accompanied by the officers of the Narragansett Steamboat Company, most of the other immediate friends being carried to the church door in sleighs. The church was crowded. Even the corridors were filled with a struggling crowd, eager to catch a glimpse of what was being done, or hear a few words that were said in the audience room

The services opened with the motette, "Cast thy burden on the Lord," rendered by the quartet choir. Selections from the Scriptures were then read, and a simple and touching prayer offered by Rev. Mr. Jenkins, pastor of the Unitarian church, after which a second hymn was sung and remarks made by Rev. Chaplain E. O. Flagg. Mr. Flagg said that he did not come to utter vituperative malice or fulsome praise, but to pay a tribute to one whom he had known only a short time, and one whom he had found a friend. He referred to the position to which Col. Fisk had raised the Ninth Regiment, and alluded to the manner of his death. A sad and lamentable tragedy, he said, had been committed, in which the deceased bore a prominent part. Assassination is the meanest, lowest thing in the world. It calls for rectification and should be put down by legislation. He then spoke more directly of Col. Fisk, saying that he was no common man. A great thing, a noble thing and a true thing is not often appreciated in its time. Shakspeare was not fully appreciated during his life, nor had Col. Fisk been during his. Of his faults he said that he would not speak. He was a man of strong good qualities, and it was not to be wondered at that he also had strong faults. Of his generosity, which was not that which gives merely for show; of his independence and manly character, which were such that he was respected even by his enemies, and of his freedom from hypocrisy, which was entire, the chaplain spoke at length. He closed by urging each man

THE GRAVE AT BRATTLEBORO.

to remember his duty to his fellow man, to his country, and to his God.

After Mr. Flagg had concluded his remarks he read the Episcopal burial service. The wife, sister, and other near relatives then took final leave of the dead, and few in that large audience could look on so great grief without a feeling of sympathy. The coffin was closed and carried out, the friends followed, and the funeral procession slowly passed on to the cemetery on the hill, the final home of James Fisk, Jr. The order of the procession, if there can be said to have been any order, was: Officers of the Ninth Regiment and of the Narragansett Steamboat Company; hearse; pall bearers; followed by the friends in sleighs. The pall bearers were Richard Bradley, Francis Goodhue, D. S. Pratt, O. J Pratt, H. O. Willard and Charles F. Thompson, all citizens of Brattleboro, and old acquaintances of Col. Fisk. The services at the grave were very brief, only a few words being said before lowering the coffin into the earth. This was the saddest scene of all, the consignment of his body to the chill and snow-bound earth. While on a visit there, quite recently, Mr. Fisk bought a lot in the village cemetery, little thinking then, in the prime and flush of successful manhood, that he would be the first of his family to occupy it. But so it was.

The snow was deep upon the ground; the bleak north winds whistled and howled through the leafless branches of the trees and amid even more than a funeral solemnity, the body so lately hot with ambition and fierce with strife in this battle, called living, was lowered to its final resting-place, and the frozen clods of earth fell heavily upon his coffin lid. It was a sad, sad spectacle, and eyes that up to then had remained dry, now swam in tears.

CHAPTER XVI.

CHARACTERISTIC INCIDENTS.

How he Lived—His Generosity—His Theory of Life—Business Qualifications—His Liberality—Anecdotes—Money for Pleasure—Brattleboro Incidents—Old Hostler—Boys—Tumble-down Row.

How he Lived.

IF we may trust the assurances of those who knew him best, there probably never was a man who was more generally misunderstood by the public than James Fisk, Jr. He was a man who had a great abhorence of all hypocrisy, and whose theory of life was to show to the world his worst side, and to conceal very carefully all his good qualities from the public knowledge. He was ostentatious of his faults, and never could be persuaded to do anything in public, except on rare occasions, such as that of the Chicago fire, which would lead the public to believe him to be the generous and large-hearted man he really was. During the last four or five years of his life, in which it has been generally supposed that he lived in a style of unexampled luxury and spent enormous amounts upon his personal enjoyments, the truth was that except his four-in-hand and his box at the theatre, and one or two matters of that kind, which all the world knows about, he lived in a much more simple style than three-fourths of the persons who have his income. At the time of his death, and for a long time previous, he lived in a little two-story house of the very plainest kind—rather dilapidated—occupying only two rooms in it, and the only real luxury in which he indulged was the luxury of unusual cleanliness. He was probably one of the most scrupulously neat and clean persons that ever lived. His personal expenses were, at a liberal estimate, not one-fifth as large as the amount which he spent in providing for persons in whose affairs he took a kindly interest, who had seen misfortune in life, and whom he felt to be dependent on him for assistance. He gave away constantly enormous amounts in still more direct charities, concerning which he rarely spoke to any one, and it was only by accident that even his most intimate friends found out what he was doing. He supported for some years an entire family of blind persons, without ever saying a word about it to his nearest friends. He was particularly generous toward actors and actresses, who, whenever they suffered from misfortune, would always appeal to him.

An Illustration of Generosity.

The latest instance of characteristic liberality on the part of Mr. Fisk occurred a few days before his death, and was mentioned, it is believed for the first time, to-day. On Friday last a rough looking man applied to see Col. Fisk, at the Grand Opera House entrance in New York, and was asked his business by the porter. "My business," said he, "is with Col. Fisk alone." This message was communicated to the Master of Erie, who at once desired to see the man. When they were alone the rough man said, "Col. Fisk, I am a convict, released from Sing Sing only a short time since. My term of imprisonment was for five years, but I have been pardoned at the end of four and a half. I have not any money, and I want a pass to —— " The Colonel asked for proofs and received them—went to the cashier and said, "Give this man twenty dollars and a pass to ——." Then turning to the ex-convict he said, "Now, my man, next time you feel the need of stealing, come to me and I will help you to get an honest living."

His Theory of Life.

Col. Fisk's personal energy was one of his most remarkable characteristics. Brought up in a school in which success depended upon individual exertion and promptness in meeting emergencies, great and small, he carried his teachings through life. No occasion found him wanting, and, with his own hands, as well as with his directions, he was always prompt and efficient. All will remember that Sunday in Boston when he sent off supplies to our troops at the front, and a whole community watched with admiration. Later, when the disaster at Chicago first flashed upon us at the East across the wires, Col. Fisk was the first to organize relief and despatch supplies. He himself mounted a wagon and drove about the streets of New York City, collecting contributions for the suffering city. He worked early and late, and when he had made up his relief trains they went through to Chicago, over the steel rails of the Erie road, at a speed that was never before equalled for such a distance. It was a characteristic act of his to decorate the engine-drivers with gold medals on their return without accident.

Col. Fisk has furnished the material for many tales illustrative of the proverbial Yankee pluck and energy, and it is not strange that one so prominent in every affair requiring dash and brilliant management should find the number of his envious detractors even exceed that of his open admirers. No one is at a loss for an anecdote of "Jim Fisk," of one sort or another, and this fact alone demonstrates how thoroughly he has impressed his individuality upon the American people. He has fought his way to the end against enemies, at home and abroad, and the very cause of his death was the defeat of a blackmailer, who had forced him into court as the last means of extorting money. Had Col. Fisk been less free-handed this fate might never have befallen him. He was liberality itself, scattering his money as magnificently as he planned to make it, and he was a man whose memory will be that of a good friend and a charitable citizen. Over such failings as he had, few will refuse to draw the veil, acknowledging that he was open, frank, and far above meanness, and that his faults will not leave a sting after the grave closes upon their owner.

His Extraordinary Business Qualifications.

The *World* concedes that the business qualifications of Colonel Fisk were of the highest order. He possessed prodigious executive capacity, indomitable pluck and clearness of perception in forecasting results which was truly remarkable. In fertility of resource he was in no sense the equal of Jay Gould, and he seldom entered upon any really important enterprise without first taking the advice of that astute and wily deviser of the great campaigns which have marked the present Erie management; but in power to execute difficult undertakings he was altogether the superior of the latter. His daily round of duties embraced an amount of work which no man of less natural exuberance and elasticity of temper could possibly have carried through. From nine o'clock in the morning until four o'clock in the afternoon of each working day he was constantly employed, literally never having a spare moment. At times as many as forty or fifty persons would be found in the ante-rooms waiting to bring before him matters of every sort and description, and to each he gave prompt, ready attention, deciding instantly upon the case presented. Often he was importuned by applicants for charity; women thronged to his presence begging for "passes" over some of the many lines of travel under his control; frequently disabled soldiers applied for situations, pleading their services in the Union cause as a reason why they should be favorably considered. It is said that none of the latter, who were able to bring credentials, were ever turned away without an order directing that a place be found for them somewhere in the Erie service, and he seldom, if ever refused to "extend the courtesy of the road" to any person in actual need.

One notable feature of Colonel Fisk's business policy was the directness and celerity with which he got at the heart of every subject coming up for consideration. He abominated "red-tape," and required of every one having business with him to state it without circumlocution, and then, when his answer was given to depart without further words. He admitted no appeal from a decision once made upon the facts of the case. His good humor was unfailing, and in the presence of the gravest emergency he was as jolly and cheerful as when all the world was smiling fair. Under other circumstances and in some other sphere, with his energies properly directed, he might have accomplished services for mankind of almost incalculable value, for, in his capacity to look on the right side of life, and to utilize every resource in the prosecution of great enterprises, he had two at least of the qualifications essential to a successful leader.

Colonel Fisk's relations with his subordinates

FISK ADVISING BRATTLEBORO BOYS.

were of the closest and most sympathetic nature. He was prompt to recognize faithful service, and to resent any ingratitude or wrong to any one to whom he was attached. About a year ago he handed a check for $10,000 to a clerk, who having been charged with the management of a special interest, carried it through with an unexpected degree of success.

Liberality.

Commissioner Manierre on Sunday evening, said that the death of Colonel Fisk was a greater loss to the police than many supposed. On the previous Friday, Colonel Fisk called on the Treasurer of the Police Department and said that he understood that the police had not been paid as usual on the 1st of the month. On being informed that such was the case, he told him that he would call the next day and have the money ($250,000) ready for their use, if they required it, so that the men might be paid off as soon as possible.

Anecdote of the Colonel.

On Saturday morning a gentleman of dejected appearance and wearing seedy garments called at the Erie offices and asked for Colonel Fisk. He was shown up to the Colonel, when the visitor explained that he was a clergyman, having a daughter in St. Louis who was dying of consumption. He had no money, and wanted a pass to enable him to reach his daughter. Colonel Fisk received him kindly, and after talking with him, appointed a clerk to look into the matter. The clerk came back and reported his belief that the man was not a clergyman. Fisk looked at the man again, marked his woe-begone expression, and said to the clerk:

"Maybe he says he's a clergyman, thinking that will help him to get the pass. That may not be true; but I think his story is. He looks needy and honest, and I am going to give him a pass;" and the Colonel did.

The London Times on Fisk.

After the assassination of Fisk, the English papers commented very freely on his life and the character of his exploits. Referring to the "Black Friday" operation, the *London Times* says:

"Even his failure in the great conspiracy of September, 1869, rather attracted the crowd of money-worshippers, by its audacity of conception. The attempt to 'corner gold' in that terrible week was so near complete success that it appeared to the imagination of Wall street like the defeat of Hannibal or Napoleon—a victory of Fate over Genius. At least until quite recently, when the shock of the fall of Tammany had been felt by the allied power, Col. Fisk was as omnipotent as ever in his control of the corporation, as magnificent in his expenditure, as reckless in his pleasures, as favored by the populace, as implicitly obeyed by his creatures in the Legislature, and on the bench. Of late, however, he must have felt the edifice of his autocracy —for he had completely asserted his supremacy over his colleague, Gould—crumbling under his feet. The courts in which he sought refuge whenever he was threatened seemed to be no longer safe against the intrusions of justice, and it was doubtful whether the old policy of issuing fraudulent stock could be tried again with success. New York was waiting with curious expectancy to see what new move the crafty 'Admiral'—so they admiringly dubbed the conqueror of 'Commodore' Vanderbilt —would try. The assassin's bullet has cut short all such questionings, and left us in doubt whether James Fisk was, indeed, at last 'played out,' or whether his fertile mind was not prepared with an expedient adequate for the coming crisis."

"Where the Woodbine Twineth."

"What do you mean, colonel," said senator Cox to Fisk, "by the place where the woodbine twineth?" To which interrogatory Fisk responded: "You see, I was before that learned and dignified body, the Committee on Banking and Currency, and when Garfield asked me where the money got by Corbin went to, I could not make a vulgar reply and say 'up a spout,' but observing, while peddling through New England, that every spout of house or cottage had woodbine twining about it, I said, naturally enough, where the woodbine twineth."

In the Old Stable.

While making his last visit to Battleboro not long since, he went around among his old friends and acquaintances, many of whom he remembered in a very substantial way where he found them needy. One incident is related which presents a touching picture. When he was a peddler there was a man who acted as hostler for his father and himself. This man was still a hostler in the same stable, although for other parties. He had grown old, but still remained the same cheerful fellow that he had always been. Mr. Fisk did not forget him, and seating himself in the stable upon an inverted feed-tub, he conversed with the old hostler for a long time, asking many questions about those whom they had both known years ago, and relating incidents of his career as a peddler among the hills and dales of the Green Mountain State. On taking leave of the old hostler, he gave him something substantial as a token of his friendship.

It was on the occasion of this visit that he met and brought to his room several Battleboro boys who were beginning to be old enough to think of going out into the world. To them he gave some very good advice, pointing out the way to success, and not only that but taking them under his own charge and into his own employ, and giving them a start in the world. More than one dozen of the youths of his native village owe to him their start and present success.

THE OLD HOSTLER.

Fisk's Stables.

The building stands in Twenty-fourth street, and as the proprietor lived on Twenty-third street, the intervening distance was very short. In fact, Fisk's domestic establishment and business arrangements were very compact and convenient. On the corner of the Eighth avenue and Twenty-third street stood the Grand Opera House, the cost of which was $850,000, and two doors below was his own dwelling. This was one of a row of small houses, and here he had a plain suite of rooms, the rest of the building being occupied by a family who attended to the latter. There was no need of style here, for he seldom, if ever, saw his friends in this domicile. The Erie rooms at the Opera House were his place of reception. He had rented these rooms for $75,000 per year to the company, in addition to which he had the rents of the stores and the Opera House. The set of safes which he built here was a curiosity. Commencing at a stone foundation, they extended through three floors, and cost $60,000. Connected with the establishment was a first-class restaurant for the accommodation of clerks, and here he took the largest part of his meals. Four hundred feet down Twenty-third street was the stately mansion occupied by Helen Josephine Mansfield, and all the intervening property stood in Fisk's name. It was mortgaged, however, for nearly its cost, and the decline in property will effectually wipe out all the money thus invested. Directly in the rear of Helen Josephine's stood his stable, fronting on Twenty-fourth street, and a very large amount of the neighboring real estate was held by him in the manner above described.

He persistently pursued pleasure, and sought everywhere to purchase it by the most prodigal use of money. Two years before his death he owned and drove four fine horses, which ought certainly be sufficient to satisfy any private man living alone as Fisk was in New York. Prince Erie, however, was as extraordinary in this as in other investments; the number of his horses was soon increased to fifteen. He paid for his stable the handsome sum of $20,000, and then built an addition, which made the entire cost $30,000. This building has a front of twenty-five feet, and in depth extends 100 feet, thus covering the entire lot. The space for the first forty feet was occupied by carriages and other appurtenances of driving, and among these were a very large barouche sleigh and also a very large phaeton, which cost $1,500. This was intended for use in the Central Park; besides which there were four "drags" (as they are called), or smaller carriages of a similar style. It is surprising to think how he could find use for so many vehicles; and yet there must be added to the number a pair of costly Clarences—a sort of covered coach with a front entirely of plate glass, which enables the inmate to see all that passes in the street without exposure; to add to its beauty the glass front is handsomely curved. It is the most fashionable style of visiting carriage and is also one of the most expensive. Mr. Fisk had one of these which cost $2,000, but it was not sufficient

IN CENTRAL PARK

elegant, and therefore he ordered another last summer. This carriage in point of finish exhausted the taste and skill of the manufacturer. It was lined in part with gold cloth, and cost $3,500. In this carriage its owner rode to his death. On the fatal Saturday he rolled down Broadway in splendid style, halting at the Grand Hotel, and the driver soon returned to the stable to report the assassination of his master.

As Fisk frequently appeared in public with six horses, he had a set of blankets manufactured for this especial service. The price of this half dozen blankets was $650, or $108.33 apiece. They are elegantly embroidered and have their owner's monogram on the corner. It will be difficult to match them in point of elegance in this country. The harness was of corresponding beauty, and hung in a large closet with glass doors. This room was handsomely ceiled in imitation of black walnut, and was ornamented with appropriate pictures. Over head was a suite of rooms for the coachman, Frank Houseman, who is a very handsome colored man. He can drive six in hand with perfect ease, and is one of the best "whips" in the city. Fisk's ambition led him to engage this man at $100 per month, and four other colored men were employed at $60 per month to groom the horses. In this way $350 per month were paid for wages, and the entire cost of maintaining the establishment could not have been less than $10,000 per year. Houseman said that a ton of hay was fed weekly with a proportionate quantity of oats—but ground feed was not used. Immediately in the rear were the stalls, each of which bore the name of the occupant, in the following order: Jim, Elias, Colonel, Messenger, Blucher, Andy, Jubilee, Prince, Frank, &c. This entire establishment was closed out at auction a few weeks after the death of its owner. The sum realized from the sale was over $50,000.

Fisk's Canary Birds.

Among the effects of "Admiral" Fisk were two hundred and fifty canary birds. These birds constituted part of the outfit of the great steamers of the "Narragansett line." They were permitted to fly about on these boats and to entertain the passengers. The little songsters after the death of their owner were all, one day, brought to the block, and were knocked down to the highest bidder, by an unsentimental auctioneer. They were sold at prices ranging from five to twenty-six dollars; the highest sum was given for the bird known as "Colonel Jim," which used to fly about the *Plymouth Rock* and settle on ladies' heads, invariably selecting young and pretty passengers. It was purchased by a "drummer" from Chicago.

The famous music-box, surmounted by a fine model in gold and silver of the *Providence*, was sold for the sum of $1,600.

Pen Sketch.

Rev. Henry Ward Beecher thus characterizes James Fisk, Jr.

"And that supreme mountebank of fortune—the astounding event of this age: that a man with some smartness in business, but absolutely without moral sense, and as absolutely devoid of shame as the desert of Sahara is of grass—that this man, with one leap, should have vaulted to the very summit of power in New York, and for seven to ten years should have held the courts in his hands, and the Legislature and the most consummate invested interest of the land in his hands, and laughed at England and laughed at New York, and matched himself against the financial skill of the whole city, and outwitted the whole, and rode out to this hour in glaring and magnificent prosperity —shameless, vicious, criminal, abominable in his lusts, and flagrant in his violation of public decency—that this man should have been the supremest there; and yet in an instant, by the hand of a fellow culprit, God's providence struck him to the ground! And yet I say to every young man who has looked upon this glaring meteor, and seen his course of prosperity, and thought that perhaps integrity was not so necessary, 'Mark the end of the wicked man,' and turn back again to the ways of integrity."

30

Mrs. Fisk.

Though Fisk lived for the last seven years wholly in New York, his domestic headquarters were maintained in Boston. His wife has remained there, occasionally visiting New York, and once making a tour of Europe. The relations of the pair have been much discussed, and have provoked much sneering comment upon the sanctity of the marriage vows. Fisk's infidelity was too open to be glossed over, and it is hardly a violation of the maxim, *de mortuis nil nisi bonum*, to refer to his numerous and ostentatious *liasons*. Mrs. Fisk has lived quietly but luxuriously, enjoying the society of a few friends, of whom Eben Jordan, Fisk's former partner, and now his executor, is said to have been especially esteemed. She is a woman of somewhat massive charms, and never fails to command attention as she rides about. The inference would be rational, I think, that the two had agreed to "gang their ain gait," each unreproached by the other, and one would also naturally infer that their affection for each other could not be very strong. But one of our papers said, after the assassination, that there was hardly a more devoted couple in the land; that during their separation not a day passed in which they did not exchange letters. It is said that Mrs. Fisk is a woman of strong mind and great natural talents, and that she had rendered important assistance to her late husband in many of his enterprises. Fisk made frequent visits to Boston to attend to the business of the Narragansett Steamship Company, and his arrival at the office of that company, in the old State House, always drew a crowd of curious gazers upon the magnificence of his equipage and the splendor of his costume.

It is said his wife was his senior by several years; that she regarded him as under her charge. "With all his notorious sins against her, there had never been estrangement between them. She excused everything, and he held for her a sort of platonic affection. He wrote to her constantly, and visited her very often. She was his confidante always, and his adviser in many things. She was more like an elder sister than a wife to this mercurial being, who appears to have had the highest respect for her traits of character, and to have been passionately regarded by herself as an incorrigibly wayward member of the family who must be humored in almost any eccentricities."

Why Poor People Loved Col. Fisk.

Early one winter, while Capt. Killalee was in command of the Sixteenth Precinct, he met the late Col. James Fisk, Jr., at the entrance to the Grand Opera House. They were strangers to each other, but the Colonel recognized the Captain by his uniform. The following conversation took place:

Col. Fisk—I see by your cap that you are Captain of this precinct. Why don't you come and see me.

Capt. Killalee—Thank you, Colonel. I will some of these days.

Col. Fisk—If you'll step in now I'll get you to do something for me on the quiet.

Then together they mounted the broad stairs leading to Col. Fisk's private office. Once in the room with the door locked Col. Fisk handed the Captain a cigar and thus addressed him:

"Captain, I want to be charitable, and I don't want any one to know it. I want what I do in this way kept out of the newspapers. I know there are a large number of poor widows and helpless orphans in this ward, and no one ought to know their circumstances better than you. Whenever you come across any that are really needy send them to me, and each family can have either a ton of coal or a barrel of flour. Yes (oath), they can have both the coal and the flour too if they're very poor."

The Captain thanked him for his kind offer, and promised to attend to it. As he was taking his leave the Colonel called him back and said:

"And, Captain, if you hear of any poor people who want to go West and have no money, you can have a ticket for them at any time. Come yourself and get it."

Capt. Killalee, under this promise, sent over twenty poor widows to Col. Fisk, to each of whom he gave an order for coal or flour, and in many instances both. They deplore his dastardly murder as much as though they had lost a relative, and are loud in their cries for the assassin's blood.

The Lesson as Read.

After the death of Col. Fisk the newspapers of every class commented very freely on the "lesson of his life." Many kind and numerous unkind things were said of him; and of the former enough was proven to convince the world that James Fisk, Jr., was a representative man in immorality of a certain phase; while of the latter there was an authenticated supply sufficient to show conclusively that he was generous, kind, genial, and munificent in his treatment of the poor. "Charity covereth a multitude of sins." This, however, the majority of commentators on the life and character of Mr. Fisk do not seem to recollect. They have also forgotten, in holding up his faults and vices as the incentives and instigators of his cruel end, very properly, too, and for an example for others to profit by, to present Stokes, the assassin, as a man equally faulty and vicious. They have said "Behold Fisk!—had he been strictly virtuous, and unequivocally fair in all his dealings; had he avoided the woman whose steps lead down to hell—had he ignored silly ostentations and licentious display, he would now be living." They do not say that Stokes, had he kept to the right as the law directs, had *he* avoided questionable speculations, lewd female associations, "fast" habits, improper male companionship, and also quenched his thirst for financial gain at the legitimate fountain only, he would not now be standing in the shadow of the gallows, with the execrations, maledictions and contempt of the entire population of the United States resting upon his cowardly head. Of the two frightful examples, his is the most frightful. Whether he be hanged or spared the rope, he had better be dead, for he is lost to all usefulness in this life, and happiness will flee his presence forevermore.

Good Deeds.

Fisk, Jr., had many good qualities in his character, and kept large amounts of money constantly in circulation, which benefited a large number of deserving people. To professional persons he was ever kind and generous, rewarding them in a princely manner for the slightest service rendered. To musicians he was a benefactor, for besides giving to their organized society recently a large sum of money, he has maintained, at no little cost, the Ninth Regiment Band, numbering one hundred pieces. In the various business enterprises with which he was connected, he gave employment to a large number of worthy people, and all those who have been in his employ spoke well of him as being kind and considerate in his treatment. In fact, he may generally be considered as having been a "generous soul." Owing to the necessary haste with which his will was prepared, many old friends and employees were, doubtless, forgotten. The disposition of his property, however, was such as proves him to have been wholly unselfish; generous to his friends, and kind to all who were near and dear to him.

In Full View.

"No career in our time has been more intensely dramatic, than the one which closed in the death of James Fisk. His life was passed entirely in the public view. The whole world rang with the reports of his preposterous transgressions. No name of any American was better known at home or abroad. He rose at one bound to the summit of apparent success. He seemed for a time impregnable to the combined attack of honest creditors and dishonest foes. It appeared as if he were likely to defy and evade retribution, closing a youth of audacious fraud with an age of opulence and impunity—still further demoralizing and poisoning the public conscience by the spectacle of a hollow decorum assumed when the objects of villany were accomplished. It is true there were strong hopes indulged in these last few days that the law was to prove stronger than the cunning of the conspirators who had so long defied it. But we were not to see so commonplace a close to so mavellous a history. The crime and disorder he had thriven by, were to betray him. The fabric reared by fraud and violence, was to crumble by the touch of murder. The short and vivid life was to end in a tragedy which should form a fitting close to it, and point its meaning forever as a memory and a warning."

One of his bitterest pen-and-ink foes says:

"We know the worst of him. What there was good in him the world has had little chance to learn.

He was no hypocrite—if that is any praise. When he devoured the widow's substance, he differed from many of his associates in refraining from the pretence of long prayers. In the household circle where he was known before he became the James Fisk, Jr., of history, he will be sincerely mourned and wept. Perhaps it is as well that we should leave his story as it is known to the world—a warning and a lesson. There would be little to regret in the close of his career, if the public reprobation which was so freely lavished upon him could be turned upon the system that produced him and the slayer, but as vile transgressors he has left behind."

The Women of America.

The female world seems to be about equally divided in regard to Mr. Fisk's career. As a rule actresses, ballet-girls, and adventuresses on the one hand, and the higher order of truly Christian women on the other, seem disposed—the former class from professional sympathy, the latter from their true piety and liberality—to look upon the late speculator with emotions of kindness and pity; but the large, orthodox, reputable, domestic, home-loving middle class of females—in other words, the great majority of women—regard the departed with the same aversion in death as in life. But *all* women of whatever class or social position unite in condemning in toto the notorious woman who has been the cause of all this trouble.

Tumble-Down Row.

This somewhat dilapidated row of buildings in Brattleboro is connected with Mr. Fisk only so far as being owned by him at one time. Some time since he made this property over to his wife, and it was in her name at the time of his death.

Funeral Scenes.

The arrival of the mournful procession at the Brattleboro depot, where thousands of his townsmen had gathered to see the body and pay respect to his memory, marked an epoch in the quiet little town of his nativity. People came to the village from the country miles away, and a larger concourse gathered on this occasion than ever congregated there at one time before.

ANECDOTES ABOUT FISK.

A friend wrote from New York: Once, two years ago, I had occasion to spend an hour with him in the Erie office. The Colonel was being shaved as I entered, and his face was half covered with foaming lather. Just then some one came and told him that the gentlemen in the office had made up a purse of $34 to be presented to little Peter, Fisk's favorite little office-boy.

"All right," said the Colonel, smiling, and wiping the lather from his face, "call in Peter."

In a moment little Peter entered with a shy look, and seemingly half frightened.

"Well Peter," said the Colonel, as he held the envelope with the money in one hand and the towel in the other, "what did you mean, sir, by absenting yourself from the Erie Office the other day when both Mr. Gould and I were away, leaving the whole mass of business on Mr. Rucker's shoulders." Then he frowned fearfully, while Peter trembled from head to foot. "But, my boy" continued Fisk, "I will not blame you; there may be extenuating circumstances. Evil associates may have tempted you away. Here, Peter, take this, (handing him $34), and henceforth let your life be one of rectitude—quiet rectitude—Peter, and remember that evil communications are not always the best policy, and that honesty is worth two in the bush." As Peter went back to his place bedside the outside door everybody laughed and Fisk sat down to have the other side of his face shaved.

Peter and Daniel Drew.

Pretty quick in came a little dried up old gentleman, with keen gray eyes, surmounted by an overpowering Panama hat. The Erie Railway Office was then the old gentleman's daily rendezvous. Here he would sit for hours at a time and peer out from under his broadbrim at the wonderful movements of Col. Fisk. Cautious, because he could move but slowly, this venerable gentleman, who has made Wall street tremble, hitched up to the gold indicator, all the time keeping an eye on the quotations and the other on the Colonel. As a feeler, he ventured to ask:—

" How is Lake Shore this morning, Colonel?"

" Peter, said Fisk, with awful gravity, " communicate with the Great American Speculator and show him how they are dealing on the street!"

The old man chuckled, Gould had a smile while smoothing his jetty whiskers, and little Peter took hold of the running wire with Daniel Drew. It was the beginning and the ending—youth and experience—simplicity and shrewdness—Peter and Daniel!

Exuberance of Feeling.

Fisk always had an exuberance of feeling.

During my stay a journalist sent in his card.

"All right," said the Colonel—"let him come in;" then turning to the gentleman of the press, he said:

"Well, sir, what is the news?"

"But, Mr. Fisk, I came here to get the news—"

"Thunderation, you did, hey! Well, I wish you would only tell as much here as you go right off and tell in the newspapers. If I thought you would, I'd say, 'Here Peter, wind up the nickel reporter and let him talk.'"

"You seem very busy to-day," remarked the reporter, resorting to the drawing out process.

"Yes," said Fisk, smiling, "I'm trying to find out from all these papers where Gould gets money enough to pay his income tax. He never has any money—fact, sir! He even wanted to borrow of me to pay his income tax last September, and I lent him, and that's gone, too! This income business will be the ruination of Gould." Here the venerable Daniel Drew concealed a laugh, and Gould turned clear around, so that Fisk could only see the back of his head, while his eyes twinkled in enjoyment of the Colonel's fun.

Col. James Fisk's Retreat.

The following amusing account of Col. Fisk's flight was published in the newspapers two days after the riots: "When the doughty knight who guides the fortunes of the 9th regiment first took the command of that branch of the militia, he doubtless flattered himself that after the war just passed, he would count on a long series of bloodless victories, and such martial glory as is to be won on the "field of the cloth of gold." The 9th had labored on many a gory field, and he should enter into their labors. His vaulting ambition showed him a long series of campaigns at watering places and city fetes, and celebrations such as few military heroes since Xerxes had ever planned and carried out. Great, then, was the dismay of this resplendent carpet knight when it became known that there was danger in the air; that his fellow patriots of the Tammany persuasion were so longing for an opportunity to test his military qualities, that they had determined to draw him out in this direction, by offering their bodies as food for his powder.

The hero of so many railroad battles and sieges was seized with an attack of perspiration when he heard that his valorous purpose of guarding the Twenty-third street ferry from the river thieves was overruled, and that he must face the Mackerelville spectors. He says in his Long Branch manifesto, the prompt insurance of which showed a wholesome fear of unpleasant remarks as the result of his flight: "I received an order from the Governor to stop all Orangemen from crossing the ferry from Jersey City. I came back to the Opera House and heard of the trouble. I put on my sword and coat and tried to get to the regiment. The fighting had commenced. I told Cols. Scott and Clark that the only way to save *us* was to pitch into them. I made my way to the regiment to give the order to fire. Braine had already given the order." Why is it that a man so given to offering sworn testimony cannot come nearer to the truth than the above statement? No order to fire was given until he had been at least five minutes in his shirt sleeves at the head of his regiment at Twenty-fifth street. The writer and several other eye witnesses can testify to this.

But to return to the perspiration. Reeking at every pore, the valiant knight dashed down his coat and sword, and then, when he started for the street, was so demoralized that he forgot to take his outer garment, and the weapon that he had sworn to keep ever ready for use against the enemies of the Republic. One report has him driving in a carriage to his regiment, just as some novelists cause their heroes and heroines to "call a carriage" in every emergency. Another says, "They all agree that he ran up the avenue from the direction of the Opera House until he reached his regiment, when he borrowed a sword and took command." Here, then, at last, stands the great captain, sword in hand, with one garment more upon him than he wore in his first field day at Long Branch, to wit, his pantaloons. "He was flourishing his sabre," says one; and again, "The mob appeared to be surrounding Col. Fisk, and he was seen to raise his sabre." No wonder this portentious behavior precipitated a crisis, and was a signal for an indiscriminate fusilade by three regiments. In the Long Branch manifesto the admirable admiral covers this point thus: "The crowd came for me." He was, he felt, the goal of all their wishes. It is always so, and he knew it and expected it. Crowds always "go for" *him*. "A rush was made. Col. Fisk was soon after picked up out of the gutter, with his ankle dislocated."

He forgets about the coat when he reaches Long Branch, and says, "When I got up my coat was all torn off, and I found that I was wounded." Ah, honest Jack Falstaff, an' thy person be no worse slashed than thy doublet' thou'rt but a lying varlet after all. Thy coat, forsooth! all torn off! when it lay snugly enough all through the fray upon some couch in the Grand Erie Opera House. Our warrior says: "I limped into the house [after the enemy had fled]. I there got a big overcoat." All his further proceedings were big. After blacking his blonde moustache, and otherwise disguising himself [some says by smearing his whole face with blacking], he drove to the Hoffman House, "followed by the mob." He must have changed his mind after starting for the Hoffman House, as he never reached there. He was afraid they would make a bonfire of the house in his honor. "I telegraphed for an engine to meet me at Sandy Hook. I hired a tug and arrived here at ten o'clock. I had to be carried to my room." This he would have the public to understand capped the climax of the events of the day. As such the publicans in his pay doubtless accepted it.

Here, then, ended this ever memorable retreat, equalled only by that of Xenophon with his small army, or McClellan with his large one. What might have happened to the city if the Commodore had not taken to his ship it is hard to say.

ecutive Committee." The motion was immediately seconded, and, without discussion, adopted by a unanimous vote. A motion to elect a new President followed, and Gen. John A. Dix receiving the entire nine ballots, was declared elected, and was escorted to the President's chair by Vice President Archer. Up to this time Gould's police officials had remained in the room, but at the suggestion of Mr. Barlow, that their further attendance could be dispensed with, they left, although Mr. Shearman Gould's lawyer, secured the privilege of having his stenographer remain.

No useless speech-making followed the election of Gen. Dix as President, but the new Board proceeded immediately to the transaction of necessary business, as men impressed with the responsibility they had voluntarily assumed. It was voted that Mr. Shearman, the newly elected Treasurer, be authorized to pay out of the funds of the company any maturing debts which are certified by the Vice President.

It was necessary to serve written notices of the action of the Board on Jay Gould, and also on the dismissed attorneys. President Dix wrote two letters for this purpose, and placed that for the Ex-president in the hands of Gen. Sickels with instructions to serve it on Gould. It was as follows:

"SIR:—At a regular meeting of the Board of Directors of the Erie Railway Company, held this day, a full quorum of the Board being present, you were unanimously removed from the office of President of this Board, and as President of this Company, and as a member of the Executive Committee, and I was

BIOGRAPHICAL SKETCH

OF

EDWARD S. STOKES.

CHAPTER XVII.

EDWARD. S. STOKES.

Biographical Sketch of the assassin—Who he was—How he lived—His quarrel—His crime—In prison.

Edward S. Stokes was born in Philadelphia, in the year 1841, and is now in his thirty-first year. His parents were people in very comfortable circumstances, and moved in the best society in the Quaker City. When quite a young lad he came to this city with his family, and many of our oldest citizens will remember the firm of Stokes & Budlong, the principal member of the firm being the father of Edward S. Stokes, who has for the last twelve months been the theme of newspaper articles from Maine to the Rio Grande. Stokes was always in early life fond of athletic sports, and until lately was considered a gymnast by those who knew him best. He was educated at the High School in Philadelphia, and received a first-class English and Latin education. He was quick to learn and very proficient in his studies. He was with his father's firm in the provision business in Chambers street, in this city, at an early age, and manifested great energy and business tact. He had one great fault, however. His blood was hot, and being of a nervous, sanguine temperament, he was liable at any moment to break out when he deemed himself imposed upon or outraged. He has always been sensitive to an insult and quick to resent an injury. Stokes is five feet nine inches high, and weighs about one hundred and forty pounds. He is slightly built, but is very wiry and active on his feet. In conversation he talks quickly and to the point, and hurries his affairs through as rapidly as possible. Stokes is a man of fine personal appearance, of a dark complexion, with piercing black eyes and regular features. His hair, which was jet black a couple of years ago, is now partly gray, and were it not for his active movements he would pass for a man of forty-five years. Mr. Stokes married a lady of good family some ten years ago, and has by her one child, a very beautiful girl of nine years of age. In June of last year, Mrs. Stokes, who was in bad health, visited Europe to seek some benefit from the mineral springs of Central Germany, and when last heard from, as late as December 3d, was in Paris. The family while in New York had an elegant suit of apartments at the Worth House, corner of Fifth avenue and Twenty-sixth street. These apartments were furnished with every article of luxury and refinement that taste could devise or that money could buy. Nearly a year and a half ago Mr. Stokes became acquainted with Mr. Fisk, and through the introduction of the latter he made the acquaintance of Helen Josephine Mansfield. An intimacy sprung up between the two, which has resulted in the shooting of James Fisk. This fatal intimacy was the cause of serious trouble between Edward Stokes and his wife, and although there is a great deal of affection subsisting between the couple, yet human nature is weak, and such wandering from the straight course is certain to bring serious trouble. It is hard to tell whether there be any real feeling of affection on the part of Helen Mansfield towards Edward S. Stokes. Stokes has always asserted that Fisk robbed him of a fortune of $200,000, accumulated in the oil refinery business, which was the joint property of Edward Stokes and his mother. Stokes expended in lawyers' fees during the last twelve months nearly thirty-eight thousand dollars, and this contest beggared him and rendered him desperate.

The Styles family of Philadelphia, to which Mr. Stokes, through his mother's side, belongs, is one of the oldest and most intensely respectable families in the Quaker City. By blood and by marriage Mr. Stokes is also connected with several of the most influential families and firms in New York city.

His father-in-law, John W. Southwick, is a millionaire, a retired furniture dealer, residing on Fifth avenue. Stokes while at school had developed quite a taste for literature, he was an admirer of the works of Addison, Steele Goldsmith, and Irving, but utterly failed to appreciate Shelly and Byron. He had spent considerable time in foreign travel, and was well known in Europe. He resided at times in London, Paris, Vienna, and the other large capitals. In Paris he was very popular with the American colony, and in London was received with more favor than is accorded to the average American. His adventures in Vienna were many and romantic, and he is the hero of several continental episodes. It is claimed by his friends, that he was a rich man prior to his introduction to Fisk, and that it was the latter who solicited his acquaintance; that Mr. Fisk from the first used Stokes as his tool, and determined to "bleed" him.

Edward S. Stokes should have been a prosperous and useful man. His family was, in both paternal and maternal branches, good, and he lost nothing of this position by marriage.

Miss Southwick was the daughter of very wealthy and respectable parents. In her school days she became deeply attached to a youth who was in every way her equal, excepting in worldly wealth and prospects. He was a poor clerk. His business talents were not great, and he gave little if any promise of advancing his interests to a high standard. Nevertheless, Miss Southwick loved and would have married him. Her father, however, was a shrewd business legislator, and did not approve of his daughter wedding a man whose chief qualification for taking the responsibilities of married life upon his shoulders was poverty. The father opposed the match with all his might. He urged nothing against the young man but poverty and the incapacity to overcome it. He told his daughter she must choose a man of means, or at least one who had facilities and talents for acquiring them.

Finding argument of no avail he closed his doors

against the poor young lover, and finally the engagement was completely broken off by parental influence. Mr. Stokes was introduced to Miss Southwick by her father. The latter, it is stated, engineered the match altogether, and it was by his persuasion solely that the union was consummated. After awhile she discovered, as we are informed, that her husband was too fond of intrigues with other females, and that his conduct was such as to render her further association with him unhappy. She ultimately went back to the parental home to reside, declaring that she only married Stokes to please her father, that she never loved him, and that her first and only love still found a place in her heart.

Whether this story of the bringing of these two together is the whole truth or not, the fact remains that both Mr. and Mrs. Stokes were intelligent and respectable. In the face of all this, he deliberately threw away all his advantages, joined himself to a "strange woman," whose steps led him down to destruction. There was wealth, family, good name, everything worthy and noble to restrain him; there was passion —base lust—stronger than all else to lead him onward in the path of crime. His early training, his respectable associations, the honor of his name, the peace of his family, were sacrificed. The flesh was made to rule over the spirit; the human was dethroned, and the brute nature was enthroned. The gentleman became a beast. Then he was lost. He went after a wicked woman to lust after her. He espoused her cause, championed her quarrels, conspired with her in crime, partook of her shame. Down this terrible road he travelled boldly and rapidly. He spent his substance in wicked living, and when both he and his mistress, by their quarrels with Fisk, had cut off their own supplies, they conspired to rob the rejected suitor, who was likewise guilty of the grossest outrages upon society. They were defeated in every effort, and then resolved on vengeance.

From the court-room in Fifty-seventh street, near Third avenue, on the fatal day, Stokes came down town at two o'clock in Miss Mansfield's carriage in company with Hon. John McKeon and Assistant District Attorney Fellows, Miss Mansfield and her cousin-companion, Mrs. Williams, coming down to their Twenty-third street residence, in Mr. Fellows' coupe, parting with Stokes at the door of the court-room. The trio at once repaired to Delmonico's, corner of Chambers street and Broadway, for dinner, after the arduous morning's work, all with keen appetites but Stokes, a little, apparently, out of humor, though not absolutely petulant, over the severe handling Miss Mansfield and himself had received at the hands of Messrs. Beach and Spencer, the counsel for Col. Fisk. It was near three o'clock when the refreshments were set before the party. Being business men they did not linger long over the repast, and it was just concluded, when Hon. G. C. Barnard, Judge of the Supreme Court, entered the room, and saluting Messrs. McKeon and Fellows, entered into a conversation with the latter in a low tone, saying to him that the grand jury of the Oyer and Terminer had found an indict-

ARREST OF THE ASSASSIN.

ment against Stokes and Miss Mansfield for libel, and warrants for their arrest had been issued. Stokes was near enough to hear this, it is supposed, though he said nothing indicating the knowledge, but at once parted from his friends and entered a stage going up-town. He undoubtedly, when apprised of the finding of an indictment, concluded that the warrant would be served at once, too late Saturday afternoon for him to procure bail, and that he would be forced to pass the time till Monday at least in the Tombs.

Having once before been locked up by Fisk in Ludlow Street Jail, Stokes knew the sensation of unwelcome restraint, which is apt to prey on an independent spirit. He had no inclination to allow himself to be an unwilling guest at the Tombs. It is probable his first thought was to evade the arrest; hence he entered the stage. He changed his plan when separated from his companions; he had a chance for thought. Before four o'clock he was seen in a coupe at the Erie Railway building, corner of Twenty-third street and Eighth avenue. Here he doubtless learned that Col. Fisk was to be at the Grand Central Hotel, on Broadway, at four o'clock. Very soon after, Fisk's elegant carriage was driving down Broadway, and was passed below Fourteenth street by the coupe in which his pursuer sat. Stokes left the vehicle, and in a deliberate manner walked up the grand staircase to the corridor in the second story, which runs parallel to Broadway, its northern ends reaching to the head of the ladies' stairway, by which it is reached directly from the street. In the corridor Stokes walked up and down with the air of confidently waiting for one he knew was soon to come. Of a tall commanding figure, well formed, elegant in appearance and handsomely dressed, looking entirely the gentleman of the world, and one entirely understanding himself and his business, he was the object of admiring glances from the ladies who sat and walked in the corridor and adjoining parlors. He threw no admiring glances back. He was evidently mentally occupied. As his walk brought him to the head of the stairs, he looked keenly down it at each turn of his solitary promenade.

The ladies' stairway is divided into three sections. You enter the door from the street, ascend seven steps and reach a landing; then turning to the left up again to a second landing; turn again in the same direction and ascend again. One at the head of the stairway could watch the opening of the outer door and hear conversation within it, but the view was obstructed by the turnings. Inside the outer door stood a servant, John Redmond, a young Irishmen of pleasant address, who had a sharp eye on those who went in and out.

Col. Fisk was a punctual man. Only a punctual man could carry on so much business and so much pleasure as he. Stokes in his hurried call at the Erie building had learned that at four o'clock his foe proposed to be at the Grand Central Hotel, the home of his friends—the Moss family. Stokes knew Fisk's habits well, and was sure he would be promptly at the indicated spot. As the clock in the Grand Central marked four o'clock, Col. Fisk's magnificent team drove up in front of the ladies' entrance. Not waiting for the attentions of his servant, Col. Fisk threw open the coach door and bounded lightly to the walk. He was dressed with his usual care. His mustache carefully stiffened and light hair brushed back smoothly from the straight central parting which divided his well-formed head into two equal hemispheres, told by their perfect smoothness of recent care. His diamond flashed brightly among the dazzling whiteness of his shirt-frills. He walked lightly across the pavement, carrying his head erect on his short neck with the air of a conqueror. Had he heard of the advantage his counsel had won for him in the legal examinations before Justice Bixby? Or had he, too, been informed that a warrant was out for the arrest of his successful rival in the affections of Josie Mansfield? From one cause or another, or the combination of many, there was conscious victory in the step of Col. James Fisk, Jr., as he strode from his coach to the door surmounted by the gilded words, "Ladies' Entrance."

As he passed within the portal he asked Redmond, a servant, if Mrs. Moss was in. Redmond replied that she was not, but that he believed her daughter was in her grandmother's room. Fisk then said, "Tell her I am here," but he started up the stairs before the porter. Reaching the first landing, Fisk glanced upward, and there saw standing on the second landing the imperturbable, well-dressed man, whom he instantly recognized as Edward S. Stokes. This man had his right arm resting on the newel at the turn of the balustrade, and Fisk noticed that there was something in the right hand. Before the victim could see that this something was a pistol, without a word having been uttered by either of the men, Stokes, seeming to take deliberate aim, fired.

After firing the second shot, Stokes paused for a single instant, as if to look upon his work; then turned, went up the stairs, and walked leisurely away. Reaching the door of the ladies' parlor, a few paces distant from the head of the stairs, he stepped inside, and threw his still smoking and blackened Derringer pistol upon the sofa. He instantly stepped back into the corridor, and walking more hurriedly, passed to and down the grand stairway, which leads up from the main hall and office of the hotel. Just as he gained the hall, and was opposite the office, headed to the rear entrance, as if seeking to escape into Mercer street, the alarm was raised that a man had been shot up stairs. Hearing this Stokes started upon a run, and Mr. Powers, the proprietor of the hotel, who was behind the desk of the office, cried out, "Stop that man." Just as he had reached the entrance to the barber-shop of the house, and when he was only a few steps distant from the door opening into Mercer street, Stokes slipped and fell. Before he could regain his feet he was seized by some of the men attached to the hotel, who were in pursuit of him, and was carefully guarded by his captors until the arrival of the police. He was then taken by a police guard and conducted to the city jail, where he was securely locked in a cell to await the result of his deadly assault, and the decision of the courts relative thereto.

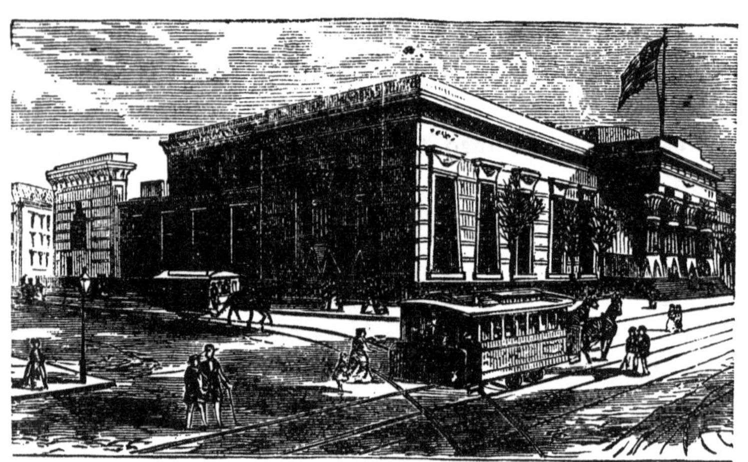

THE TOMBS.

A Deliberate Murder.

The killing of JAMES FISK, JR., bears all the characteristics of a deliberate murder. The assassin followed him for the purpose of killing him. He lay in wait at the head of the stairs in the Grand Central Hotel to slay his victim as he came up. He took aim at him, resting his pistol upon the balustrade of the stairway. He gave him no warning, and allowed him no chance to defend himself. As the facts now appear, it was a cowardly murder, and nothing else.

Col. FISK was regarded by many with detestation; by many with admiration; by all with interest. He was a man of prodigious vitality. His energy, his audacity, his love of display, his wit, his adventures, his ready generosity, his freedom from religious or mortal scruples, all combined to make him a conspicuous figure. Among the staid, the religious, and the conventional classes he was habitually condemned; with a great part of the population he was a kind of favorite; with his employees and dependants he was a hero. His funeral was followed by throngs of sincere mourners, and even those who were wont to blame his life were sorry for his sudden and bloody death.

In respect of moral and religious principles these two men were about upon the same level, while in respect of natural goodness of heart FISK seems to have been much the superior. The one was born to adventure and recklessness, with scanty advantages of early training, and with ideas gathered by chance as he was tossed about in the world; the other is the son of wealthy and most respectable parents, and was educated amid all the good influences both of precept and example which belong to the most careful moral and religious culture.

There are doubtless those who will look upon this tragedy, beginning in a dispute for the possession of an abandoned woman and ending in murder, with a sense of spiritual superiority, as the Pharisee of old thanked God that he was not like the sinners he saw around him. What an insane delusion! FISK and STOKES were not different from other men. Their natures, their passions, their desires were the same as belong to all the rest; their acts were such as other men might commit. The catastrophe which has overtaken them is but one more illustration of the ancient truth that there is no safety except in a firm and unpresuming adherence to the Divine Law which the Father of all has given for the government of His creatures.

CHAPTER XVIII.

WHAT FOLLOWED.

The fall of the "Erie ring"—The rescue of "Erie"—Gould driven from the management—Lively scene in the Grand Opera House—General Dix president—Gould "served"—The bivouac—The surrender—The end.

THE death of James Fisk encouraged the hope, that the affairs of the Erie Railway Company would be speedily wrested from the control of the "Erie Ring." The overthrow of the Tammany Ring had so thoroughly demoralized the chief manipulators in legislative, municipal and Erie affairs, that renewed efforts were immediately put forth to rescue the management of Erie. Gen. Daniel E. Sickles, United States minister to Spain, had been employed by the foreign stockholders to represent them in their case against the Erie directors. He procured a leave of absence from the President of the United States, and came to this country in December, 1871.

Immediately on his return Gen. Sickles quietly but actively began operations. His first movements were directed against the legal and legislative strongholds of Erie, and these he found very formidable indeed. Gould literally owned the Supreme Court, whose judges were his willing and subtle tools. Able New York lawyers had prostituted their talents to his service, and by every quibble and subterfuge which they could invent, and by every base conspiracy with the hired judges, which they could contrive, aided him to keep his great power and intimidate his associates in the directory as well as the stockholders. His office was filled with spies and special sheriffs, and the directors who where not in his confidence were the objects of their constant surveillance. These Directors were afraid not merely for their liberty and property, but for their lives. Gould's hold on the Legislature, in spite of the success of reform, proved to be very strong, and Gen. Sickles found himself greatly embarrassed here. The movements against the legal and legislative strongholds did not, therefore, promise brilliant or immediate success, when the idea was suggested, that the undermining of the Ring was a quicker though more dangerous method of gaining possession of the Company.

The person who suggested this scheme was a young man, formerly a journalist, whose intimacy with Gould and Fisk, and long service under their Ring, had given him an evil reputation, less flattering perhaps than he deserved. He was suspected of being a spy of Gould, a dummy of the Ring, and was generally understood to be the mysterious English stockholder who figured in various suits and financial schemes. But no matter what he may have been, he has redeemed much of his lost reputation by the thorough aid and loyal assistance which he gave Gen. Sickles in redeeming the road from the highwaymen who so long had possession of it.

Though Jay Gould was President of the Company, a majority of the members of the Board of Directors were not satisfied with his administration. Gen. Sickles secretly ascertained the sentiments of each member of the Board, and put himself in communication with those who were unfavorable to Gould. A combination was formed in which eleven out of the seventeen Directors joined.

Gould was at Albany, laboring by such arts as are common to State Capitals to obtain favorable legislation and also to prevent adverse action for his Company. Advantage was taken of this absence and a call for a meeting of the Erie Directors was issued by the Vice President of the Road. The meeting was held in the offices of the Company in the Grand Opera House on the 11th of March, 1872.

The purpose of the conspirators was to compel several of the Directors to resign, to choose their own men to fill the vacancies caused by their resignations, and finally to remove Gould from the office of President, and elect Gen. John A. Dix in his stead.

O. H. P. Archer was Vice President of the Company, and was among those opposed to Gould. The charter of the Company provides that in the absence of the President the Vice President shall perform his duties. By virtue of this authority, therefore, the President being absent, Vice President Archer issued a call for a meeting by directing the Secretary to send out the usual notices to the members of the Board. The order of the Vice President to the Secretary was as follows:

"Having been requested by several of the Directors to call a meeting the Board, in the absence of the

President it becomes my duty to request and instruct you to that effect. You will therefore immediately send proper notices to the several Directors, requesting them to attend a meeting to be held on Monday next, the 11th inst., at 12 M., at the office of the Company."

The appearance of this notice was the first alarm signal in the Erie offices. Gould returned immediately from Albany, where he had been for several days past negotiating with the members of the Assembly for needful legislation. Early in the morning of the day appointed for the meeting of the Board, he, with a few faithful adherents, was in the President's room in earnest consultation. The attaches, the hangers on, spies and secret agents in the employ of the Ring had been summoned to the Grand Opera House and were stationed at the doors, in the passage ways and in the apartments, under strict orders to exclude from the building all persons not members of the Company, or in its employ, and to watch all who came in, and to report instantly all matters of importance to the President.

When the "regulator" marked 12 o'clock, the directors were in their room; Gould, though in an adjoining room, did not attend the meeting; Vice President Archer promptly called the Board to order, and presided over the meeting. As soon as the Board had convened, an "injunction," issued by Judge Ingraham was served on one of the directors, forbidding him to act in that capacity. The whole number of directors present was required to constitute a quorum, and of course, therefore, if one were removed by an order of the court, there would be no quorum and consequently no business could be transacted. The injunction was addressed to Mr. F. A. Lane; this gentleman had been long enough intimately connected with Fisk, Gould, Tweed and other New York characters to know that writs issued by corrupt judges might be safely disregarded, now that the people had been aroused against the thieves and their tools. He knew that "injunctions" from city courts were bought for a price, and were unworthy of respect, he, therefore, ignored the order of the corrupt judge and proceeded to discharge his duties as a director.

There was no time wasted in reading the minutes. The first business was the passage of a resolution suspending all the attorneys and counsellors employed by the company and forbidding them to act in its name. Thus at one stroke one very dangerous enemy was disposed of. The Board then proceeded to fill vacancies. In place of James Fisk, Jr., deceased, Gen. John A. Dix, was chosen a member of the Board. Gen. George B. McClellan and Hon. S. L. M. Barlow were elected to fill vacancies caused by resignations. Several of the gentlemen who had joined in the conspiracy against Gould also resigned, and their successors were immediately chosen. In this way almost an entire new Board was constructed within an hour. There was a new treasurer, secretary, and counsellor, and then finally came the boldest stroke of all:

Mr. Barlow offered a resolution that Jay Gould, the President of the road, "be and he is hereby removed from his office as President of the Erie Railway, and from his position as director and member of the Executive Committee." The motion was immediately seconded, and, without discussion, adopted by a unanimous vote. A motion to elect a new President followed, and Gen. John A. Dix receiving the entire nine ballots, was declared elected, and was escorted to the President's chair by Vice President Archer. Up to this time Gould's police officials had remained in the room, but at the suggestion of Mr. Barlow, that their further attendance could be dispensed with, they left, although Mr. Shearman Gould's lawyer, secured the privilege of having his stenographer remain.

No useless speech-making followed the election of Gen. Dix as President, but the new Board proceeded immediately to the transaction of necessary business, as men impressed with the responsibility they had voluntarily assumed. It was voted that Mr. Shearman, the newly elected Treasurer, be authorized to pay out of the funds of the company any maturing debts which are certified by the Vice President.

It was necessary to serve written notices of the action of the Board on Jay Gould, and also on the dismissed attorneys. President Dix wrote two letters for this purpose, and placed that for the Ex-president in the hands of Gen. Sickels with instructions to serve it on Gould. It was as follows:

"SIR:—At a regular meeting of the Board of Directors of the Erie Railway Company, held this day, a full quorum of the Board being present, you were unanimously removed from the office of President of this Board, and as President of this Company, and as a member of the Executive Committee, and I was unanimously elected as such President in your place, and I now notify you of these facts by order of the Board of Directors, and demand that you shall surrender to me all papers and documents in your possession heretofore as such President, and that you further cease to interfere with the due performance of my duty as such President of the Erie Railway Company."

Gould had from the first resolved to resist any effort that would be made to displace or dispossess him. He had called in the services of a large police force commanded by Captain Petty, who was ordered to take instructions only from Jay Gould. All day these "presevers of the peace" had been concealed in the private rooms of the Grand Opera House, but now as the crisis approached they were marshalled in the great hall and took possession of the Erie offices.

Shortly after the posting of the policemen, the Board of Directors having concluded their private business, adjourned, and headed by Gens. Dix and Sickles, walked into the room of Vice President Archer, which adjoined that of the late President, Jay Gould. Here it was observed that the sliding-doors which separated the rooms of the President and the Vice President were closed. Gen. Sickels having in his hand a written order from President Dix, ordering Jay Gould to relinquish all the property of the Erie Railway Company, desired Captain Petty to serve it upon Gould, but Petty declined to do so, alleging in effect that it was not his business, as he was simply there to preserve the peace. Gen. Sickles then said that he would serve it, and requested Capt. Petty to go with him and protect him by his presence. This, Capt. Petty also declined to do, but stated that he would send one of his men. Gen. Sickles declined this offer, and demanded that Capt. Petty should go with him and protect him. Petty still refused to go, and Gen. Sickles said he would call upon the United States to protect him, and would serve President Dix's order himself. Upon proceeding to open the doors dividing the offices, it was discovered that they were held on the other side by a number of persons, and could not be opened. Frederick A. Lane, counsel to the old Board of Directors, and now an ex-director, sprang to one of the sliding doors, and a stout, burly individual named John E. Kennedy to the other, for the purpose of forcing them open. Mr. Lane's strength was not equal to the occasion, who gave way to a Tribune reporter, who also tugged in vain. Without instruments of some kind it would be impossible to obtain access to Gould. An ice-pick was obtained and the doors slightly forced apart, when it was discovered that a number of policemen held the doors against the Erie Reformers and in the interests of Jay Gould. A wrench was then procured and wedged in between the doors, gradually forcing them asunder, until they parted with a loud noise and allowed T. G. Shearman, Gould's counsel, to spring like a rat into the midst of Sickles' friends, who caught him and held him for a second, and then let him go. The doors in the meantime had been closed again, and the besiegers continued to work with their wrench until they were again forced open, when there was an instantaneous and unanimous cry of "There goes Gould; there goes Gould!" as the late President of Erie was seen springing successively through the doors of the suite of luxuriously appointed offices, followed hotly by the besiegers, until he secured a temporary safety in the office of the Counsellor of the Erie Railway, at the further end of the hall. A short consultation was held, and another effort was made to get into the apartment where Gould had secreted himself, but without effect. It was then determined to effect an entrance through the transom of another door situated at the head of the stairs, on the Twenty-third street entrance, and Gen. Sickles called for a ladder, in order that he might mount it and get on the other side of the door, but just as the ladder was brought and he was about to ascend, Capt. Petty appeared and prohibited its use on the ground that it was a breach of the peace. Again baulked, Gen. Sickles went back to the door of Gould's hiding place first mentioned, followed by the police, but leaving a man with the order to secure an entrance when unobserved and serve it on Gould. Meanwhile Gen. Sickles maintained a loud conversation with Capt. Petty, his remarks not being entirely relished by that officer. This had the effect of distracting attention from Sickles' deputy, and when the door at which he was stationed was opened he sprang in, and after surveying the interior unobserved for ten minutes, cooly served the order on Gould, who was quite bitter and very much surprised at the proceeding.

After recovering his equanimity, Gould explained

that it was not so much the service of the writ he feared as personal violence. After the service the deputy appeared through the door at which Gen. Sickles and Capt. Petty were still disputing, and joyfully announced "he's served," "he's served." The cry was taken up and echoed from one end of the rooms to the other, while the deputy signed an affidavit of his service of the order. Notwithstanding the service, Gould still continued to keep possession of the President's rooms, and held them during the night.

Vice President Archer and his associates remained on duty all night. Finding the building swarming with police and gangs of city roughs, who might at any moment assault the reform party and drive the new directors from the offices, Archer secretly dispatched agents to the Erie officers in Jersey City and brought over several hundred of the employees, who were sworn in as deputy sheriffs, and stationed in and about the building. This was a very fortunate and necessary precaution; several times during the night efforts were made to rob the safes of the company, but these were successfully resisted by the forces under the Vice President.

After these midnight attacks on the safes, the rude gang of more than one hundred and fifty "roughs" from the worst purlieus of the West Side retired to the rooms still held by the Gould faction, laid down, and so awaited the next demand for their services. During the evening they had been liberally supplied with tobacco, cigars, and liquor, and under the combined influences of these potent narcotics they were in a state of semi-stupefaction, and slept. At 2 o'clock the Vice President, with his friends, held all the main offices on the Eighth avenue front, the corridors and smaller offices alone being retained by Gould and his men. Here lay sleeping, this motley crew of wicked men—some on the floor, some on the desks and tables, and others on the broad window sills; some snoring sonorously, and others rolling from side to side in a half-conscious condition, now and then venting an expletive on their companions. They were all ruffians of a type seldom seen on the street in honest daylight—a mass of scarred and battered humanity, with scarce an atom of the leaven of manhood in the whole lump. They had been called from alleys and cellars, from vile saloons, thieves' dens, and the resorts of the poorest prostitutes, and exhaled the odor of the gutter. All but a few were puny physical specimens, for they seemed to have neither strength, nor size, nor courage, and, save the wounds got in their base struggles with each other, there were no evidences of their ever having fought. Their appearance asleep, like their blasphemy awake, was purely bestial. They were of the class who dare not even follow until some leader has stricken down the victim and laid him at the mercy of their kicks. This was the throng whom, armed with pistol, knife, and club, Jay Gould had called to his assistance, and they were termed with apt alliteration, "Gould's guardian angels." "Tommy" Lynch was their leader, and while the little bullies lay down in their fustian on velvet and brussels, the bigger bully lounged about Jay Gould's headquarters in the counsellor's room awaiting the signal for his murderous services. The same leader and the same followers had been in the service of Erie before, and their former successes had inspired them with a confidence which induced them to deride the police and laugh in Superintendent Kelso's face when expulsion was hinted at. Beside this, they were hired bravos, and they knew that for holding themselves ready for bloodshed they were to have $25 per man, while their leader was to reap a fortune in the $500 promised him. It was the rate fixed when their services were first bought in Erie's interest.

In the offices on the Eighth avenue front, held by the new management, there were twenty-five men brought from the Erie passenger depot, men of tried courage, who knew their antagonists of old, and did not fear the conflict which they expected. At 4 o'clock A. M. the quietude of the "roughs" who surrounded and guarded Gould lulled these defenders of the management into a feeling of security, and they grew lax in their duty. It was only reasonable to suppose that this would be taken advantage of by the assailants, and, while the defenders slept, a storm was brewing outside. Jay Gould had determined for some reason, probably the desire to repossess himself of important papers he had left behind him in his hasty flight, to seize the President's room, and, to effect this, Lynch awoke his crowd, and massed them in the General Superintendent's room, from which there is a door leading into the President's room.

At five o'clock the men in the Vice President's room heard a crash, the police ran from the President's office, and before a defence could be made the throng had broken down the door and rushed in. A moment later the folding doors were closed and fastened, and, though the roughs had secured possession of Jay Gould's office, they were cut off from the rest of the main offices. This success induced an attempt to take the rest of the building. Knives were thrust between the folding doors to cut the cords which lashed the handles together, but the keen edges were kept away until the cords were protected by pieces of bent tin.

Early in the morning of the following day Gould issued orders to all employees, informing them that he was still President of the Erie Company and must be obeyed as such. Later in the day, however, his counsel sent for Gen. Sickles and invited him to a private conference. Sickles accepted the invitation, and, after a conference lasting over two hours, obtained from Gould a full and complete surrender. He then led his captives from the President's to the Directors' room, where the new Board was in session. In accordance with the conditions of the surrender, Gould, still assuming to be President of the Company, called to order the old Board of Directors, and tendered to them his resignation as President. This was at once accepted, and, to make doubly sure the action of Monday, Gen. Dix was re-elected President, and the proceedings of the previous meeting were duplicated, in the resignation of directors and the re-election of their successors. This was done partly as a concession to the dignity of the late President, and partly to remove any doubt as to the legality of the new Board. Mr. Gould, after resigning, escorted Gen. Dix to the Chairman's seat in a graceful and good-humored manner. Messrs. Eldridge, Sherwood, and Drake, also took their places at the new Board as directors, thus making a full Board of seventeen members. In order to secure to the new management full public confidence, Gould subsequently resigned from the Board and is, therefore, no longer concerned in the affairs of the corporation.

Thus was the management of the Erie Railway Company rescued from the grasp and control of the "Erie Ring," that had held it for years, and plundered it of millions, with an audacious boldness, that, but for its high-handed crime, would have challenged the admiration of the world.

www.ingramcontent.com/pod-product-compliance
Lightning Source LLC
LaVergne TN
LVHW021317110826
845150LV00003B/598

* 9 7 8 1 4 2 5 5 5 7 4 9 2 *